Windows® XP For Everyone

Windows® XP For Everyone

Jaime A. Restrepo

To order additional copies of this book, contact:
Xlibris Corporation
1-888-795-4274
www.Xlibris.com
Orders@Xlibris.com

35595

For my mother

Acknowledgements

I want to thank Mr. William F. Buckley publisher-at-large of the National Review magazine because without his very generous help this project would not have materialized and to Jason Steorts editor of the National Review magazine for going over the manuscript, and to Linda Bridges assistant to Mr. Buckley for her sound advise. Many thanks also to Laura Grey for helping me with the wording for the book cover.

My daughter Sara Andrea and her mother Sara also deserve mentioning for putting up with me while I wrote this computer manual.

I also want to give special thanks to the Jimenez Family (Alberto, Adiela, Michelle, Marilyn and Tyson) for their support.

Intro by William F. Buckley Jr:

I met Jaime Restrepo while he was working at a CompUsa store in Norwalk, Connecticut.

Shortly thereafter I asked him to tutor me in the complex world of Microsoft Windows.

One day while having trouble with a program I had come to love (called Magellan), he offered to help even after the people who had written the program could not.

After he found a solution I asked him to join the National Review payroll as a personal computer consultant.

Jaime has also done consulting work for companies as diverse as GE Management and the Perrier Group of America.

Now eleven years later I am still learning the art of Windows from him, and it is a pleasure to introduce him to you.

He has already produced four computer books in his native Spanish, but thank God he has decided to produce one in English for the rest of us.

Jaime's approach to the new version of Windows is very simple; Microsoft Windows XP is for everyone, not just the dummies or the learners.

I am sure you will find this book handy, as I have.—WFB

Dear reader;

First of all I want to thank you for buying this book.

Now, about me I can tell you that I began my career in the computer world selling copies of Windows 3.1, at a software store called Egghead Software. Back in those days Windows was really a combination of two operating systems (Windows and DOS), but the idea struck a cord, until today where we are in the midst of a real computer revolution with Windows XP, which hopefully will empower all of our lives.

My idea for this book was my first hand knowledge that most people, from the grandmother to the music teacher to the business owner, need to know or have chosen to know about the Windows XP operating system

In short Windows XP is not just for the rich or the poor or the learned, but rather Windows XP is for everyone.

Cordially,
Jaime A. Restrepo

PS: You can benefit from most of the instructions in this book, such as how to Copy/Cut and Paste, regardless of the version of Windows you own.

The writing of this book has been a long, but very worthwhile journey, and I hope you enjoy it, and if you don't please drop me an e-mail with your suggestions on how it can be improved at: *JRestrepo@Aol.com*.

I will also, in the coming months, setup a web site to provide some additional information about Windows XP and the incoming Vista version, at this URL address; http://www.windowsxpforeveryone.com/, and if you happen to live in the New York metropolitan area, and would like to discuss one on one computer consulting, or even training of groups of people in your company, then please send me an e-mail to the e-mail address shown above.

Table of Contents

Part I
Getting to know Microsoft Windows XP

Part III
Working with Programs Files/Folders in Windows

Part IV
Guide to your everyday computer work in Windows

Part V
The Internet & the Electronic mail or e-mail

Part VI
Using Hardware Devices in Windows XP

Part VII
Windows Technical Stuff

Introduction to the World of IBM-Compatible Personal Computers

The personal computer explained

At the beginning of the computer era, the only computers available were so big that they were housed in whole rooms and controlled from TV-like terminals called CRTs. These computers were called mainframes.

This all changed around 1984 with the introduction of the IBM personal computer, or PC. The PC was a computer compact enough to be used almost anywhere, allowing individual users to have at home a machine with processing power similar to that of the earlier mainframes.

Because the IBM computer corporation started this personal-computer revolution, you often hear the term "IBM compatible" used to describe personal computers that follow standards set by the first IBM PC.

In this book I will refer to your computer as your "Personal computer", "Your system" or as "Your PC", but please know they are the same thing.

The graphic above shows a complete IBM-compatible PC system. Similar PCs can be bought from any number of vendors, such as Dell or Hewlett Packard.

Additionally most of the components that you connect to a PC are interchangeable (such as the mouse, the keyboard or the monitor); for instance you can buy a Gateway monitor for your Dell PC, or vice versa.

The main components of a personal computer

A PC is composed of many different parts whose names you might have heard before: for example, the hard drive, which allows you to store your work for as long as you want.

In this chapter you will learn more about some of the most vital components of a PC.

These are the two main groups of components found on a personal computer:

- Hardware: A hardware component is something you can touch with your hands—for example, the keyboard or the mouse.
- Software: A software component is a virtual component that roams inside your PC, making it understand your commands—for example, the Microsoft word processor Word for Windows.

The main hardware components you should learn to recognize are:

- The computer chassis or CPU
- The Monitor
- The Keyboard
- The Mouse

The main software components are the operating system (for example, Windows XP Home Edition) and the application software or computer programs (such as the WordPerfect 11 word processor).

Although the basic idea of the PC hasn't changed much over the years, PCs have gotten much faster, and their storage capacity is hundreds of times that of the earlier machines. There have also been other, subtler changes. For example, at the beginning of the PC era, the preferred way to share data was to use removable floppy disks. Now, however, many computer manufacturers have stopped offering a floppy-disk drive, and instead use Flash drives to share data.

Now at this point I will like to explain why it is important for you to become a little familiar with the different parts that comprise your PC. For example you've been working at a company for a number of days, and on the second day the computer you've been using fails. If the company you work for is fairly small, say only 4 people, and you call the store from where they bought the computer, and they advise you to just bring the CPU, but because you don't know which one is the CPU, you have to bring all the parts into the store, instead of just bringing the main case itself.

The computer case or CPU

The computer case is the enclosure or chassis where the main parts of a PC reside, and to which you connect the peripheral components that allow you to use the computer, like the keyboard and the mouse. The computer case is also where the CPU or central processing unit (which is the chip that gives the personal computer its ability to solve problems) resides, snapped or soldered onto a board called the motherboard.

On a computer motherboard there are also many other parts, some attached by cables, others just snapped in to internal expansion slots. These parts might include, for example, a wireless network card, which allows you to connect to a wireless network.

The next graphic shows the CPU of a Dell personal computer model Dimension E310 (photo courtesy of Dell Inc) in a tower configuration; the main advantage of a PC with this profile is that you can put it on the floor instead of on your desk.

Generally speaking, this type of computer, when used at home, is also referred to as a desktop computer. It is primarily meant to perform work for individuals. By contrast, computers that store large amounts of information for companies and accept logins from users on a computer network are called server computers.

Tip

Another purpose of this chapter is to demystify computers a little bit, by showing you that a personal computer is just a group of parts put together, and that it needs **YOU** to be complete.

The monitor

The computer monitor is very similar to a TV monitor, and its main purpose is to present you with the information you need to interface with your computer. Generally speaking, a computer monitor offers you better picture detail than a regular TV monitor. That is why a DVD might look better when viewed on a computer screen than when viewed on a regular TV.

Computer monitors are sold in two main types:

- Standard TV-type monitors with a bulky CRT tube (still the most common type).
- Thin LCD-type monitors, which are no thicker than a few stacks of cards. The main advantage of this type of computer screen is that its thin profile allows you to put both the PC and the monitor on a crowded desk.

The LCD-type of monitor used to cost more than a thousand dollars for a 17" one, but now you can get a 19" for fewer than 400 dollars.

This is a photo of a thin LCD panel monitor—in this case, a Samsung LCD-type monitor model 173P-Silver. (Photo courtesy of Samsung) Notice the small footprint of this LCD monitor, which makes it ideal to put in places where you don't have the space for a large CRT type monitor.

Another very important difference among computer screens is something called the dot pitch. The dot pitch refers to the distance between the tiny dots that compose the image on a computer screen. When the dots are farther apart, they become noticeable and make the image look grainy—so the smaller the dot pitch, the more realistic and detailed the picture. If you are in the market for a monitor, as a general rule ask for one with a dot pitch of .25mm or smaller.

The keyboard

The keyboard allows you to communicate with the PC. Suppose, for example, you want to type a letter to one of your business associates. After opening a word-processing program, you use the keyboard to type the letter, and also to type its name when saving it as a computer file.

Typical computer keyboards have four basic sets of keys:

- Typing keys: These are the letter keys, and are similar to the ones found on old typewriters.
- Numeric keypad: This is a set of numeric keys that can function as a calculator.
- Function keys: The function keys (from F1 to F12) are arranged in a row across the top of the keyboard, and can be assigned specific commands by the application you are currently using or by the operating system.
- Control keys: These provide cursor and screen control, allowing you to jump to different places on a page by simply pressing a key.

The next graphic depicts a keyboard for a personal computer.

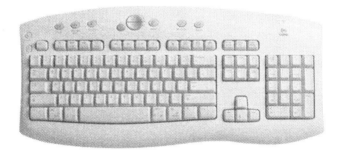

This Logitech Cordless Access Keyboard (Photo courtesy of Logitech), allows you to use it a little farther away from the PC.

Please note that the use of different graphics, depicting hardware devices from different vendors in this chapter, should not constitute an endorsement of the excellent products a particular vendor offers, but rather to illustrate the many different choices available to you as a computer user.

Here is a more detailed description of some of the specialized keys on a desktop PC keyboard, and their purpose:

- The programmable function keys, located on the top of the keyboard and numbered from F1 to F12: When you press them, the computer receives an order to present you with a menu or to perform a specific function.
- The Insert key allows you to replace existing text with the new text you type. To use it, press it and then click on the beginning of the word you want to replace. Now, when you type, the new text overrides the old text. To stop inserting text, press the key again.
- The Delete key allows you to delete files and folders while working on programs (such as Windows Explorer), and to delete text or graphics while using programs that can receive input from you.
- The Home, End, Page Up, and Page Down keys allow you to make large jumps in most programs. If you are working on a long Word document and you press Page Down, the screen will show you the next page on your document.
- The four Arrow keys allow you to move the cursor to a desirable location within a word-processing document or on any other program that accepts text, without changing the text of the document you are working on.
- The numeric keypad (on the right hand of the keyboard) mimics a 10-digit calculator. These keys are very useful to enter data into a program called a spreadsheet. To enable the numeric keypad, press the Num Lock key.
- The Esc key allows you literally to escape what you are doing at the moment; you could use it, for example, to close most open dialog box windows.
- The Ctrl key (press and hold it), when used in combination with other keys allows you to perform functions like, copying and pasting a selection.
- The Alt key (press and hold it), when used in combination with other keys, it too allows you to perform functions such as saving, opening files and rebooting the computer (CTRL + ALT + DEL, in Windows 98), for example.

The keyboard found on laptop computers (due to space constraints) is slightly different than a desktop one, although using the Function key or FN key, you can still achieve a good level of functionally. For instance you can use the Numeric Keypad feature, this way: press the FN key and then the NumLk key (toggle it on and off), now look at your laptop keyboard and read the numbers that share space with the regular keys on the keyboard. For instance on my laptop's keyboard, when I press the FN + NumLk key, and the letter K, I get the number 2 on my page.

 There is an excellent web site, at this URL: http://www. typing-lessons.org/, where you can take some free online instruction on the use of the computer keyboard.

The mouse

The computer mouse, an electronic device that fits in your hand and has two or three buttons, is among the most important component found on a personal computer. Today, almost every computer is equipped with a mouse.

Using a mouse, you can complete most of the command functions needed to use a PC, such as printing a document or opening a file.

Some mice also have a wheel in the middle. This wheel is useful for navigating the web or to move between pages in a word-processing document.

The next graphic represents a typical mouse for use with a PC.

The Microsoft Corporation (Photo courtesy of Microsoft) manufactures the mouse shown on this graphic; there are many other brands of mice on the market.

These are some of the functions you can accomplish using the mouse:

- open and close programs
- move windows
- copy files
- work with menus

Computer mice are sold according to the type of connector available in two main types: PS2 (round connector) and the USB port. If your computer doesn't have a PS2 port you have to use a USB mouse. But if you system has both a PS2 port and a USB one, then you can use either type of Mouse.

 In Chapter 2, you will learn how to use the mouse—for example, to close and open windows, and how many clicks are needed to accomplish these tasks in Windows.

The different types of memory storage

The main idea of using a computer is to create some type of document, such as a letter or a résumé for a job. Once you're done creating such a document, you have the choice to discard it or to save it.

There are two main types of storage found on PCs, that the computer uses to hold the computer work you do:

- temporary-storage memory
- permanent-storage memory

Temporary memory storage (for example, the memory bank in the next graphic) or Ram, is used by your programs to store your work, while the computer is on. When the computer is powered off, this information is erased from this chip, and only the information you've saved to a permanent storage device is kept.

This is a 128MB stick of memory, type PC133 SODIMM 133MHz. The PNY technologies company manufactures this stick of memory.

Generally speaking Ram is the type of memory that will make the most difference when you need to open many different programs to complete your work. For instance if you have a fairly good system, with 256 megabytes of Ram, and it seems sluggish at times (when you have a few windows open at the same time), and if everything else is working fine (also taking into account that your hard drive is not filled up to capacity with files), buying more Ram will definably speed the way your programs open as well as help your computer complete other tasks faster.

 In Chapter 9, you will learn step by step how to save your work to a permanent-storage memory unit (such as the hard drive), so that it is not lost when you power off your computer.

There are two types of devices widely used in PCs to store data permanently:

- The hard drive, which is the most widely used device to store data on a PC.
- Flash memory units, which are electronic devices with no moving parts, and are used to transfer data among computer systems and also to keep photos on devices like digital cameras.

Both of these types of memory allow you retrieve information after long periods of time—even after the computer and/or camera have been turned off for years.

The next two photos depict two of the most widely used devices that you can use to save your computer work permanently.

This is a hard drive of 40GB, manufactured by a company called Seagate.

This is a Flash Drive, model JumpDrive Pro 2.0, manufactured by Lexar Media.

To get a sense of how much information a gigabyte or GB can hold, think about it this way:

- A 20-page word-processing letter takes about 325 kilobytes of memory. One megabyte, then, will allow you to save four 20-page letters; and a 40 GB hard drive—which holds 40,000 megabytes—will allow you to save 160,000 letters.
- If you wanted to save an hour of MP2 video and had a computer with a video capture card, it would take about 400 or 500 megabytes of memory. So a computer with a 40 GB drive will allow you to save about 100 hours of video shows.

The main advantage of Flash memory, over the hard drive, is that it has no moving parts, so accessing the work you've saved there will be fast, and its main drawback is that because of its portability if you save important work ONLY to a flash memory unit, and you misplace it, then you will have no choice but to do it again.

What is an operating system?

An operating system is like a traffic cop inside the computer, and it performs basic tasks such as recognizing input from the keyboard, sending output to the display screen, keeping track of the work you create and save using your computer, in addition to controlling peripheral devices, such as printers. Without an operating system, nothing would happen inside the personal computer; with it, order and productivity are possible.

The most widely used operating system in the world is Windows, produced by the Microsoft Corporation. Windows 95—named after the year of its release, 1995—was the first important version of this family of operating systems.

Now, most computers sold today will include one of the different editions of the new Vista operating system, or even Windows XP (which Microsoft will support until 2012). In fact you can take advantage of most of the instructions in this book, even if you still use Windows 98.

Follow these steps to find out which edition of Windows your computer uses:

1. From the Desktop, right click your mouse on the My Computer icon.

2. Now click on the Properties label.
3. On the General Tab, you can clearly see the operating system your computer is using.

The graphic above, for example, is from the System Properties window of the Hewlett Packard Pavillion computer I bought at CompUsa to write this book. Under the System label, it displays the complete information about the version of the Windows operating system this computer has, and at what level (as you can see, on this screenshot, my computer is up to service pack 2).

Which computer should you buy?

Buying a personal computer or PC used to be very difficult, mainly because there were many different computer companies and prices ranged from thousands of dollars for low-end computers to many thousands of dollars for high-end ones.

If you are in the market for a computer now, you can get a complete PC system, including a printer, for less than a thousand dollars.

My recommendation is to shop around. You should also ask your family and friends what experiences they had buying computers locally or online or read the reviews of the different computer companies offerings, such as the one offered by PC Magazine, which URL or web address is: http://www.pcmag.com

Bear in mind that PCs come in many different configurations and with different memory capabilities, but the most obvious difference is whether the computer is a desktop or a laptop.

- The desktop computer is used primarily to perform work for individuals rather than to act as a server. This type of computer comes in two profiles:

  o   Tower configurations are ideal to be placed on the floor, away from your desk.
  o   Flat configurations are designed to sit on your desk and have the monitor placed atop of them.

- The laptop computer is a computer in which all the components have been packed into the size of an oversize notepad.

You might also have heard of a computer called a server, which is, in most cases, a high-end computer used by companies to host information that can be accessed by many different users.

If your needs aren't that great (for example, you are not a graphic designer) and you want a computer only for browsing the Web and typing some letters, your needs will be met by almost any new computer you buy.

One of the most important considerations, if you are a new computer user, is the type of service warranty a company offers you. Some computer companies offer you up to a year in parts and labor. In some cases you might want to use a specific type of credit card, that covers you for an additional time once the original warranty lapses.

The next picture shows a complete PC system made by Dell with a thin LCD-type monitor, which is an excellent choice for almost any kind of situation.

The computer in this graphic is a GX620 Ultra Small Form Factor PC. (Photo Courtesy of Dell Inc.), and it retails for about 800 dollars.

If you travel frequently, you should consider buying a laptop, as it will allow you to do your work while away and also to stay in touch with your office. The laptops available today come in many different styles and prices. They used to be much more expensive than desktop models, but today the price gap for a desktop and a laptop of comparable power is only a few hundred dollars.

The laptop in this graphic is a ThinkPad X Series Tablet Notebook made by Lenovo that features a screen that you can write on (Photo Courtesy of Lenovo Inc.), is also an excellent choice as it will allow you to write on the laptop screen, in the same fashion as using a legal pad, but with the advantage of being able to combine your writing with your computer work, to later print it or send it by e-mail.

If you are inclined to buy a laptop, I recommend buying one with a good screen. Remember, you can almost always add memory to your laptop or change its hard drive later, but you will not be able to change the size of the screen.

 Generally speaking it is better to buy a computer in the high-end range of what you can afford; and it is hard to go wrong if you spend at least $1200 on a complete system.

Another good addition to a personal computer system is a printer. Printers also come in many different varieties and prices.

The two main types of printers are:

- inkjet printers; which almost in every case are able to print black text as well as color photos.
- laser printers; which are offered in monochrome (black text) and in color models.

Inkjet printers use liquid ink delivered to the paper by various means; these printers are ideal for the home.

This is an inkjet printer made by Epson; model Stylus C68 (Photo courtesy of Epson.). This printer retails for about $60.

This is a Dell monochrome Laser Printer; model 1710 series (Photo courtesy of Dell Inc). This printer retails for about $199.99.

Laser printers use a type of ink called toner, which consists of small bits of dyed plastic that are fused to the page. Laser printers used to be very expensive, but today you can get one for under $300, albeit one that prints only in black ink. Color laser printers are becoming more affordable, however.

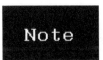

Note Find out the price of the ink, or the toner, for the printer you are thinking of buying. You might be surprised to discover that the ink for your $39 printer costs $30 or more per cartridge.

Where to put your computer

Because we use computers to perform a whole lot of our work and learning activities, it is very important to select a good location for your computer equipment.

In the above drawing you can see clearly that this computer desk has a tray for the keyboard and the mouse. This allows you to maintain your elbows at a 90-degree angle, which **might** prevent some health problems.

Please keep these recommendations in mind when choosing a location for your computer:

- The work area should be well lighted; this is to say that the monitor should not be the primary source of light in the room.
- Natural light from outside should not shine directly on the monitor, as it will create glare.
- Do not place a computer near a space heater or a place where the vents on the back of the CPU are too close to a wall.

My final recommendation is to always connect your computer equipment to a high-quality grounded surge suppressor that is able to protect it from fluctuations on the power grid, and never directly to a wall power outlet.

For instance you can use a good surge suppressor such as this Belkin SurgeMaster for HomePlug Networks (Photo courtesy of Belkin Corporation).

Part I
Getting to know Microsoft Windows XP

Chapter 1

Microsoft Windows XP Basics

Introduction to the Microsoft Windows XP operating system

On October 25, 2001, Microsoft Corporation released Windows XP to the world. This operating system offers many significant improvements over previous editions of Windows, such as the Windows Me version.

Fortunately for users of previous releases of Window the majority of these improvement are behind the scenes, like the more robust NTFS file system that offers better protection for the work you do on your computer.

Windows XP is available in five main editions:

- *Windows XP Home Edition*
  This version meets all the needs of the average home user, and it can also be upgraded later to the Professional Edition.
- *Windows XP Professional Edition*
  This version is geared to the office user who needs to work in a Local Area Network (LAN) environment, and is also suitable for some home power users.
- *Windows XP Tablet PC Edition*
  This is the operating system used on newest tablet PCs. It allows you to use a digital pen to write directly on the screen and control your computer just as you would with a mouse. You can also use the Tablet PC Input Panel to enter text into any application with your own handwriting.
- *Windows XP Media Center Edition*
  This is a version of Windows XP that is pre-installed on some new computers and lets you experience video, audio, photographs, and TV through a convenient user interface. In addition, if your computer has the necessary hardware, the new remote control for Windows XP will allow you to see and listen to all the videos or music in your computer from anywhere in the room where your computer is located.
- *Windows XP Professional x64 Edition*
  This is a version of Windows XP currently being developed for use on some high-end computers, like those equipped with the AMD Opteron™ 275 2.2 GHz 64-bit processor.

You can also upgrade an older computer to this operating system as long as it meets the hardware requirements set by Microsoft. To do this, simply buy and install a Windows XP upgrade.

To start/power-on a computer with any version of the Windows operating system, just press the power button, and the computer will follow a process called the "Boot" sequence, to check that all its hardware and software are working properly.

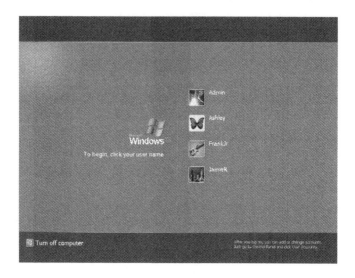

This is a typical opening screen you will see on a computer (with Windows XP) used by more than one person, or in one where the main user account is protected by a password. To gain access to the computer a user must click onto the name of his/her user account, and then provide the password (if the account is protected with one), otherwise the computer won't allow you to gain access to the Windows Desktop.

Please bear in mind that you will not see this welcome screen if the computer has only one user account (such as "Albert01"), which is not protected by a password. In that case, the computer will go directly to the Windows XP Desktop.

Additionally if, at the time you did the initial setup of the computer, you created a few user accounts (for instance John1, Mary1, Mom and Dad), then it is very important to follow the instructions outlined in chapter 5 (Working with Windows XP Local User Accounts) of this book to; 1—Reduce the permission privileges from *Administrator* to *Limited* for any accounts used by children, and 2—Create a password for each account. If you fail to take these steps any person (for instance Mary1, a 8 year old child) will be able to click on her Mary1 user name (shown on the Windows XP opening screen) and **if** you haven't applied step **one** (to reduce the permission privileges) to her account, gain access to the *Dad* files. This is true because, even if your own account is protected with a password, your work might not be protected from other users that have *Administrator* rights to the computer, unless you've taken extra steps to protect your files or folders.

Using the computer mouse in Windows

The Windows operating system is based on what the computer world refers to as a GUI, or graphical user interface. To take advantage of this graphical interface, you need to use a mouse, which is an electronic device that allows you to interact with the computer.

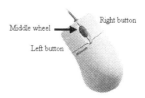

This graphic shows the most vital parts on a computer mouse (in this case, one manufactured by Microsoft):

- The left button is used to launch computer programs or to make selections. Throughout this book, when you read the instruction "click," that means you should press the left mouse button once. When you read the instruction to "double click," press it twice (without pausing).
- The right button is used to open pull-down menus, such as the Properties menu on the My Computer icon. When you read the instruction "right click," press the right mouse button once.
- The middle wheel, present on most computer mice sold today, can be used—instead of the right scroll bar on the window you are working on—to advance on a document (roll it towards you) or to return to the previous page (roll it away from you). Is your choice. Some programs even let you use the mouse wheel as a third mouse button.

A pointer with the shape of an arrow, which moves every time you move the mouse, represents the mouse position on your computer monitor. If you move the mouse up, the pointer moves higher on the screen. If you move the mouse down, the pointer moves lower on the screen.

The mouse pointer

As you saw on the previous page the mouse pointer pinpoints the exact location on the computer screen where your click will have an effect.

The mouse pointer changes shape when you move it around the screen. For example, if you move the mouse pointer,

- over the Desktop, the Start menu, or the menu of any program, it retains the form of an arrow;

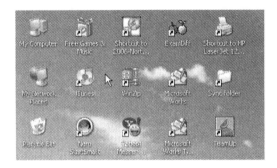

- over the working area of a word-processing document, it takes the form of an I (called the Text selection tool);

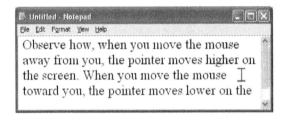

- over a link on a web page, it takes the form of a little hand;

If you press the left mouse button, while the mouse pointer is over a place on the Desktop with no icons, nothing will happen. But if you press the right mouse button on a place on your Desktop with no icons, a menu will offer you a list of choices—for example, *Arrange Icons By*.

Finding the mouse pointer on the screen

To use the mouse you must first locate its pointer on your computer screen. To do this, track the position of the pointer on your computer screen while you move the mouse, up, down or sideways.

The following graphic shows the desktop on a computer running Windows XP.

On your own computer, try moving the mouse around **while keeping your fingers off the two mouse buttons**. Observe how, when you move the mouse away from you, the pointer moves higher on the screen. When you move the mouse toward you, the pointer moves lower on the screen.

Double left clicking on an icon, on the Desktop, opens a program or a file. If you, after placing the mouse pointer over an icon, single Click on the right mouse button, then a menu of options will open. If you open a menu by mistake, then press the ESC key, to close it.

Note

The mouse pointer will change to an hourglass if the computer is busy. The computer will not be available for use until the hourglass again becomes a pointer.

How to increase the visibility of the mouse pointer

If you have trouble following the position of the mouse pointer, while you move the mouse, then you can change its profile so that it leaves trails when you move it across the computer screen.

To make this change, open the Control Panel as follows:

1. To begin click on the Start button, located on the lower-left part of the screen, then select *Run.*
2. In the dialog box that opens, type **Control** and then click on OK, to open the Control Panel.
3. Now look for the mouse icon, and (when you find it) double click on it to open the program that will let you change the mouse settings. If the mouse icon is not visible, click on Switch to Classic View in the upper left part of this window.
4. When the Mouse Properties window opens, click on *Pointer Options.*

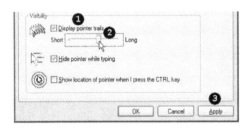

These are the steps to enable trails, on the mouse pointer, in order to increase its visibility:

1. On the Visibility part of this window, click on "Display pointer trails" if it is not already selected.
2. Now put the mouse pointer over the slider, then press and hold the left mouse button. While still holding the button, move the slider to the left to decrease the mouse-trail effect or to the right to increase it. Notice, while you have the Mouse Properties dialog box open, that there are other changes you can make here, such as changing the speed at which the pointer moves on the computer screen.
3. Finally click on Apply to save your changes, then click on OK to close it.

Later on—to undo this change—follow steps 1 to 4 (to return to the Mouse Properties window), and click on "Display pointer trails", to uncheck it.

Using the middle wheel on your mouse

The middle wheel, present on most mice today, allows you to scroll pages in some programs (such as word processors or even web browsers) without the need to use the keyboard or the scroll bars (on the side of a window).

Keep in mind that any action, as you will see later in this book, you do in Windows while using the keyboard or the mouse, applies to the foremost window on the computer screen called the "Active window".

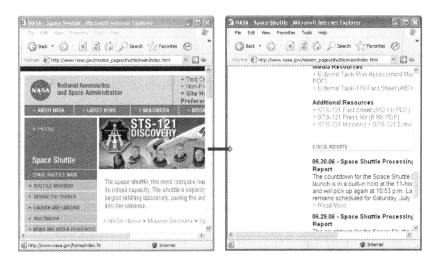

To test using the middle wheel of your mouse, open the Internet Explorer browser by double clicking on the Internet Explorer icon, located on the Windows Desktop. When your web browser opens, type; *http://www.nasa.gov/mission_pages/shuttle/main/index.html* in the address bar or open a word processing document that you know is several pages long.

Now click on "SPACE SUTLE MAIN", then place your index finger on the middle wheel and move it this way; towards you to scroll the pages down or away from you to scroll the pages up. This way is very convenient to move between pages, because previously you had to find and use the scroll bars of the program window you were using.

Note

The middle wheel can also be used in some programs as a third mouse button, and this is done by pressing hard on it until you hear it click, which will activate auto scrolling, if a program supports it.

The Windows XP Desktop

This is the virtual desk of a PC running a Windows operating system. From here you can open programs and files and manage your computer's resources.

The next graphic shows the Desktop of one of the computers I used to write this book (an HP Pavilion I bought at CompUSA), that came pre-installed with the Windows XP media center edition of the Microsoft Windows XP operating system.

If the Windows Desktop is not visible, then you can see it by: a) minimizing the programs you've opened, or b) by clicking on the "Show Desktop" icon on the Quick Launch Toolbar (see page 71.)

In Windows XP you can customize how many icons are displayed on your Desktop. You can also add new icons here that will act as shortcuts to files or programs found on your hard drive or on removable drives (such as a USB one). In Chapters 6 and 9, we will discuss how to do this.

Note

If your computer has a previous version of the Windows operating system, such as Windows 98, your desktop will look very similar to the Windows XP one.

How to customize the Windows XP Desktop

If your computer doesn't display the My Computer icon or the Internet Explorer icon on its Desktop after you turn it on, then you can add them with just a few clicks of the mouse. Likewise, if these icons are visible on your Desktop and you prefer not to see them, you can use the reverse process to hide them.

To begin adding or removing one of these Windows XP system icons, right click on any area of the Desktop that is free of icons. A menu will open. Now click on Properties, to open the Display Properties dialog box.

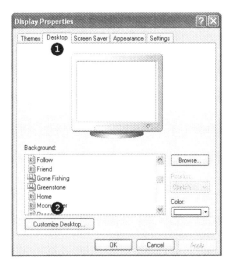

These are the steps to open the Desktop items Dialog box:

1. To begin click on the *Desktop* tab.
2. Now click on the *Customize Desktop* button, in order to begin adding these programs icons to the Desktop or removing them from it.

Bear in mind that if your personal computer has a previous version of the Microsoft Windows operating system (such as Windows 98 or 2000), you will always see these icons displayed on your Windows desktop, without taking these extra steps, but you won't also be able to hide them at will.

Remember that if you open a dialog box by mistake, you can close it by just pressing the Esc key, located on the top-left corner of your computer keyboard.

In a new Windows XP computer (as you can see on the next screenshot, of the *Desktop Items* dialog box window), or one in which the operating system has been reinstalled, these programs might not have a check mark next to them. If they aren't selected, then their icons won't be displayed on the Windows Desktop. The Recycle Bin is the only exception to this rule, because its icon will always be visible on the Windows Desktop.

Now, to display the missing icons on the Windows Desktop, just click inside the square box next to their names, or click on the names themselves to select to see their icons on the Windows Desktop.

For example, if you want to add the Internet Explorer Web browser icon to the Desktop, click on the words "Internet Explorer" to select this program. To remove an icon from the Desktop, simply uncheck it. To finish, click on OK to close the dialog box.

Bear in mind that the changes you make here only affect the user account used to login to the computer this time, which you will learn how to work with on chapter 5, and that this program icons are automatically added to a Windows XP Desktop if you chose to use the Windows Classic Start menu, which will be discussed later in this chapter.

Note   The advantage of adding these icons to the Windows Desktop is that you can launch the programs they represent without having to find them in the Start menu, by just double clicking over their icon.

How to change the screen resolution to ease eye strain

One of the easiest things you can do to ease eye strain, while using your Windows based PC, is to change the screen resolution. The lower the resolution, the easier it is to read the information on the computer screen (For instance 800 by 600 is easier to read than 1024 by 768.)

To change the screen resolution on any version of Microsoft Windows:

1. First right click on any part of the Desktop that is free of icons.
2. Now on the drop-down menu that opens, click on the *Properties* label (last item on this list) to open the Display Properties dialog box.
3. On the window that opens click on the Settings tab.

Now you can adjust the screen resolution as follows:

1. To begin place the mouse pointer over the slider guide located beneath the words "Screen Resolution." Press and hold the left mouse button. Now move the slider to the left while still holding the mouse button in order to decrease the screen resolution. To increase the resolution, move the slider to the right.
2. Finally click on Apply to confirm that you want to make this change. Now the screen will change to the new resolution, and a little dialog box will open asking you if you want to keep this new setting. Click on Yes to accept it or No to stay with the old settings. When you are finished and wish to close the dialog box, click on OK or on the X in the upper-right-hand corner of the screen.

Bear in mind that if the computer is using a generic video driver, such as a plain VGA, because it was not able to find the right device driver to match the type of video card (this is the one where you plug your computer monitor), then there might not be a choice to increase the resolution above 800 X 600. Using chapter 15 of this book, Working with hardware devices in Windows XP, you will learn how to correct this type of problem.

How to enable or disable screen savers

If you like the idea of flying stars or swimming fish on your screen while you are not using the computer, then you can enable the screen-saving function in Windows.

First, open the Display Properties dialog box the following way:

1. Right click on any part of the Desktop that is free of icons.
2. On the menu that opens, click on the Properties label to open the Display Properties dialog box, and then click on the Screen Saver tab.

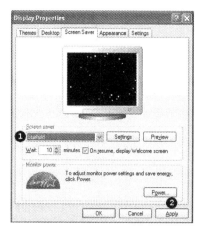

This is the way to enable or disable the screen-saving function, on the *Display Properties* dialog box window:

1. To begin click on the name shown (it might read None) under "Screen saver" to get a list of the available choices. Now click on the screen saver you want to use. You can click on Preview to see how your selection will look on the computer screen. If you decide not to use this screen saver, simply go back to the list and find another one. To disable the use of screen savers, click on *(None)*.
2. Finally click on Apply to accept this change, and then click on OK to close the dialog box.

Bear in mind that the idea to use screen savers came about because in the past, when you left a monitor on for a long time (displaying the same information), sometimes that information was etched onto the surface of the monitor, but this is no longer the case with the type of monitors used today.

The computer icons

A computer icon is a graphic linked to a program, a file or a folder. By clicking on the graphic, you can open the program, file, or folder in question. In Windows Icons are designed to be easily recognized. For example, the icons that are generated by Microsoft Excel for Windows have an X on the left corner.

For instance, on this screenshot (of the Desktop of a computer running Windows XP), notice (amongst these icons) the icon that represents The Mozilla Firefox Web browser (next to the arrow).

To find more information about a particular icon, place the mouse indicator over it and leave it there for a few seconds. In the graphic above, you can read the name of the program that created this file: "Type: Microsoft Excel Worksheet."

To rename a shortcut, for instance one named "Shortcut to Sync folder"; 1) Slowly click twice on its name (to select it), 2) Press the right arrow key (to un-select it). Now note the **blinking** cursor "| ". Press the Left arrow key to place the blinking cursor before the letter/word you want to delete, then press the Delete key, or after the one you want to add letters/words to, now type them. On this example I placed it after the "o", and tapped the Backspace key to remove the extra "Shortcut to". The new name is; "Sync folder". If the cursor is blinking to the right of the letter/word you want to remove, then press the Backspace key to remove them. To add a space, between words, press the Space bar. When you are done making changes, click once outside of the name. When renaming a file, using these steps, do not remove or change the three last letters (or file extension) of the name after the ".".

How to work with an icon in Windows

On a PC running Windows, you can work with its icons by clicking on them with the mouse. You can also work with icons using the keyboard, by pressing the Enter key once the icon is highlighted, but this can be more contentious to achieve.

To open files or programs with the mouse:

- If the icon is located on the Desktop, simply double click it. This will open the file, the folder or the program it represents.
- To open files or programs from the Start menu, just click on the relevant icon once.
- Right clicking on an icon allows you to see the many different ways of working with it.

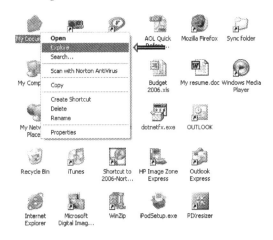

For example, if you right click on the My Documents icon, a drop-down menu appears and shows you a long list of actions that can be executed by clicking once on the related name. To open, say, the Windows Explorer, simply click on the Explore label.

To delete an icon, you don't need anymore, you can; select it, press the Delete key and then confirm this choice by pressing the Enter key, but bear in mind that if this is a shortcut to a program, that this action does not delete the program.

Please note, on this screen capture, that on the upper right hand corner there is a shortcut to a folder (Sync folder), which will open to show you its content when you double click on it.

You can even move an icon or a group of icons, on the Desktop, to suit your needs. But make sure you don't move them over to a folder (in yellow) whose shortcut is on the Desktop (if you do, by mistake, press and hold the *CTRL* key and then the *Z* one to undo the move), otherwise with a few exceptions (for instances you cannot move the My Computer icon to a folder on the desktop, and when you attempt to move those icons to a folder only a shortcut to these program will be created inside the folder you chose), they will be moved to the folder you drop them to.

To move several icons at the same time, press and hold the Ctrl key while clicking on each one of the icons you wish to move. If the icons are contiguous, you can also select them pressing the left mouse button to the left of one of the icons you need to select, and moving the mouse in a sweeping motion until all the icons you wish to move are selected (shaded). Once the icons you want to move are highlighted, lift your finger from the Ctrl key. Now click on one of the selected icons and, while holding down the left mouse button, drag the icons to a new location on the screen. When you are done moving them, lift your finger from the mouse button.

For example, move the Outlook 2003 icon to a new location on the Desktop:

1. First single click on the Outlook 2003 icon and hold down the left mouse button. If you don't have Outlook 2003, then try moving a different icon.
2. Keep holding down the button, and drag the icon to the desired location. When you are done moving the icon, lift your finger from the button.

Check the following setting if the icon you've tried to move reverts to its original position every time you try to move it.

1. Right click on any area of the Desktop that is free of icons.
2. Place the pointer over "Arrange Icons By."
3. Make sure that the Auto Arrange option is not checked; if it is, click on it to uncheck it.

On chapter 6 you will learn how to create shortcuts, on the Windows desktop, of the programs you use often, so that you can open them right away after turning on your Windows based personal computer.

How to arrange the icons on the Windows Desktop

Adding a shortcut to programs/ or files you use frequently to the Desktop might help you become more productive by allowing you to find them faster, than if you have to open them from the Start menu, or even from the Windows Explorer.

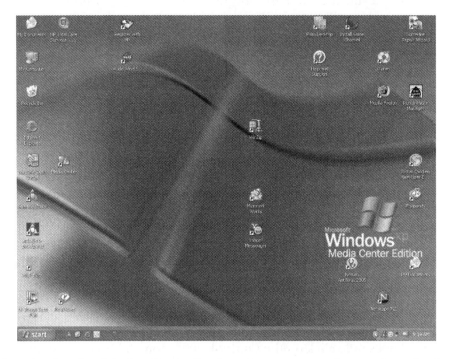

But the drawback is that if your Desktop becomes too cluttered—as in the screenshot you see above—then finding the right icon you need to work with might take you longer than looking for it on the Start menu.

In chapter 9 (Learn to Store and Retrieve your computer work in Windows) you will learn how to save a file to the Desktop, and in chapter 6 (Using computer Programs in Windows) you will learn how to add a shortcut to a program you use often to the Windows Desktop.

 When you are moving icons, try not to place them on top of each other. For example, never drag an icon over the Recycle Bin, as doing so will delete it.

If you are not able to find an icon you have already added to the Desktop, it might be necessary to rearrange the icons there. Doing so will allow you to see any icons that you have unintentionally moved out of view.

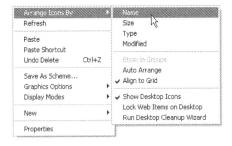

Follow these steps to rearrange the icons on the Desktop:

1. Right click on any part of the Desktop that is free of Icons.
2. In the dialog box that opens, click on Arrange Icons By, and then click on Name, Size, Type, or Modified.

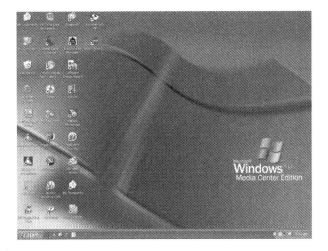

Now you will see the icons organized (lined up on the left side of the screen), on the Windows Desktop, according to your preference.

In Windows XP, there is even a setting that allows you to hide all the icons on the Desktop—perhaps the idea is that if a minor is using the computer, he will not be able to open your programs and delete important files.

Such a scenario can also be avoided by using the Windows XP User Account program, as explained in Chapter 5, to open limited user accounts for each person who has access to your computer.

Follow these steps to hide the icons located on the Desktop:

1. Right mouse click on any part of the Desktop that is free of icons.
2. Place the mouse pointer on Arrange Icons By, and uncheck Show Desktop Icons by clicking on it.

Now the Desktop icons are hidden.

It is easy to revert to the previous view (to show Desktop icons) with just a few clicks of the mouse. Simply follow the instructions above and re-check Show Desktop Icons, to see the Windows Desktop display the icons that were there before you hid them.

It is not recommend that you make these changes on a computer you are using temporarily, as the next user might not know how to undo this change to show the hidden icons.

The Windows XP Start Menu

The Start menu is the paneled-menu that opens up when you click on the Start button or when you press and hold the *CTRL* key and then the *Esc* one. This menu usually opens from the lower-left side of the screen, although it will open from a different corner if you've dragged the windows taskbar there.

From the Start menu you can accomplish most of the tasks associated with the use of your Windows based PC, such as opening programs or maintaining computer files.

To open the Start menu, click on the Start button. A Window will open and show you two panels, each loaded with icons. These icons represent shortcuts to programs that you can open with a single click of the mouse.

If you've just moved to Windows XP, from a previous version of the Windows operating system, such as Windows 98 or 2000, then you've noticed that the Start menu in Windows XP is slightly different than the one you are used to. And in this chapter you will learn how to change the look of the Windows XP Start menu, to the Windows 98 classical style.

The different working areas of the Windows XP Start menu

On the Start menu, you will find most of the icons you need to use with your Windows based personal computer. Please refer to the next graphic and read the labels in it, to familiarize yourself with the different areas of the Start menu.

The left panel of the Start menu shows the programs you use often, and the right side programs to manage the computer and your document files.

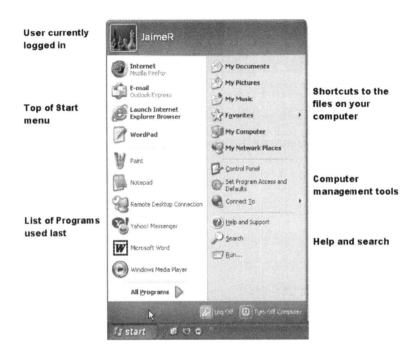

To work with these two panels, that comprise the Start Menu, after clicking on the *Start* button, place the mouse pointer, **under** the *All Programs* line. To access the program you wish to use, simply move the mouse pointer until you find its icon and single click to open it.

On the top of this panel you will also see the name of the user, on this example JaimeR, currently logged into the computer.

In Chapter 6, Using Computer Programs, you will learn more on how to open and close programs and also how to add a program to the top of the Start menu so that it can be open from there.

How to switch to the Classic Start menu in Windows XP

Windows XP offers many enhancements over previous releases of Windows, one of which is the new Start menu. You may, however, not welcome this enhancement if you have gotten accustomed to the classic Start menu used in older Windows versions. Luckily, Microsoft has designed a way to run Windows XP while still using the classic Start menu.

To begin changing the look of the Windows XP Start menu, to the classic Windows 98 look, right click on the *Start* menu button (almost always located on the left lower part of the computer screen) and then click on Properties.

These are the steps to change, as you can see on this screen capture, the look of the Windows XP Start menu to the Classic Start menu look:

1. When the Taskbar and Start menu Properties dialog box window opens, click on *Classic Start Menu.*
2. Now click on Apply, to make the Change. Close this window.

Bear in mind that from now on, after you click on the Start menu button and then on Programs and drag the mouse pointer to the right (to find a program you need to open), that you might only see a short list of these programs. To see them all: Take the mouse pointer to the bottom of the last program shown on the right panel, find the double arrows, and click on them.

If you switch to use the classic Start menu, your programs will still open with a single click of the mouse, just as they do when you open them from the regular Windows XP Start menu.

One way to tell if you are using Windows XP (besides the background picture), as opposed as a different version of Windows, is the label on the side of the Start menu (that opens up when you click on the Start menu button). In this case, it reads "Windows XP Professional."

Bear in mind that, in a computer used by a few people (and each one has his/her user name), that this change only affects the way the Start menu looks and behaves when the user who made the change uses it. For instance, if on your home computer you have two people using the following screen names; Jane01 and Paul01. Now if Jane01 follows the steps of the previews page, to change the look of the Windows XP Start menu to the Classic one, then when she logs in to the computer by clicking on the Jane01 icon on the Windows XP welcome page, and she clicks on the Start menu, it will look as the Classic Start menu, but when Paul01 logs into the computer, by clicking on the Paul01 icon on the Welcome page, the Start menu he will see will behave and look like the Windows XP Start Menu one.

If you want to return to use the regular Windows XP Start menu, follow the steps outlined on the previous page and select Start menu instead of Classic Start menu.

The Windows XP Taskbar

This is a long blue bar that runs along any of the computer screen's sides (because you can choose which side to place it along). It is present in all the different versions of the Microsoft Windows operating system.

The main function of the Windows Taskbar is to provide you with information about the programs that are currently running on your computer.

On the left part of the Windows taskbar you can see the Start button; in the middle is a blue bar. Every time you open a computer program, the name of the program will be shown on this blue bar, as a reminder that the program is currently running.

On the right side of the Taskbar you can also see some additional information, like the time, on an area called the Systray. This part of the Taskbar contains icons for programs that run at all times while the computer is on (such as antivirus scanner programs).

On the next screenshot you can see the footprint that a program leaves on the Windows Taskbar after it has been opened. In this case, the footprint reads "8 Microsoft Word fo . . ."

Such a footprint is especially useful to find the program you were working with when you click on the minus sign (located in the upper right corner of a window) to minimize a program. This action temporarily hides the program from view, but its footprint is still visible on the task bar.

If you wish to work with the program again, you can simply click on its footprint to bring it back into view. Likewise, a program that is not minimized but is hidden behind another program can be brought back into view by clicking on its footprint.

If you have too many different programs open, at the same time, not all of their footprints can be displayed on the blue Taskbar, and the Taskbar will create a virtual second page. You can access this page by clicking on the arrow down symbol to see the second page of program footprints.

How to use the Taskbar button grouping

Another improvement of Windows XP, over previous versions of Windows, is its Taskbar button-grouping feature. If you have many instances of the same program open, this feature stacks them on the Taskbar under a single label, when they don't fit across the working area of the Taskbar.

For example in this screen capture the number 8, seen next to the "W" (for Microsoft Word for Windows), notify you that there are eight instances of the Microsoft Word for Windows program open.

In this graphic you can see eight instances of Microsoft Word, and each one represents an open document. To work with one of these documents:

1. First click on the program label, that reads "Microsoft Word . . . ".
2. Now a list will open up. Click on the document you wish to work with. (In the example, this is "Letter to Janice.") If you haven't saved and named a document file yet, it will read DocumentX, where X is a number.

You can also quickly close the document files in a group by right clicking on the group label and then selecting *Close Group*. If there are still documents you haven't saved, the program will give you the option of doing so before it closes.

To move the Windows Taskbar to a different side on the computer screen, place the mouse pointer over the Clock (on the extreme right), or any other area of the Taskbar free of icons, now press and hold the left mouse button, and then drag it to the side of your choice. This works equally well, regardless of whether or not you have Windows 98 or Windows XP.

How to hide/show the Taskbar

The Taskbar can be set automatically to hide itself behind the edges of your computer screen when you are not using it. This feature, which temporarily frees the part of the screen normally occupied by the Taskbar, can be enabled or disabled as you wish.

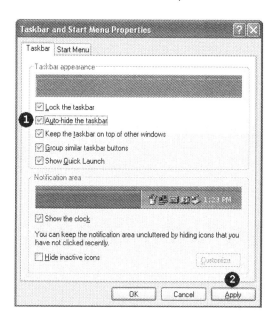

To enable it, open the *Taskbar and Start Menu* Properties dialog box window in the following way:

1. Right click on the Clock, which is located on the Systray at the right-hand side of the Taskbar. Then click on the Properties option.
2. Now check "Auto-hide the taskbar."

To stop the taskbar from hiding itself, return to the *Taskbar and Start Menu* Properties dialog box window and click again over "Auto-hide the taskbar", to remove the checkmark.

On the Taskbar Properties dialog box there are other settings you can work with, such as; click on *Lock the taskbar* (if is not already selected), so that it cannot be moved to any of the sides on the computer screen, or click *Group similar taskbar buttons* (which is enabled by default), so that every time you open an instance of a program you've opened before, the next instance will be stacked vertically on the Windows Taskbar, under a single program label.

Using Windows when the taskbar is nowhere to be found can be a little frustrating for the novice, and even for an experienced Windows user unfamiliar with this feature.

If the Windows Taskbar is hidden but you need to work with it, take the mouse pointer toward the outside of any of the sides of the screen. The Taskbar will then pop up.

Once the Taskbar becomes visible, as you can see on the next screen capture, you can work with it the regular way. To hide it again, just move the mouse pointer away from the Taskbar.

Notice on the screen capture of this Windows Taskbar, that it opened from the topside of the screen, because it was previously moved there. Notice also that its size is twice the regular size, because it was resized. To resize it back to the normal size, take the mouse pointer over to the side closer to the windows desktop, until it turns into a double arrow, now press and hold the left mouse button and then drag the Taskbar back to its original size. To drag it back—to the lower part of the computer screen, take the mouse pointer over to the System tray (see the clock), now press and hold the left mouse button, and drag it down or to any other side of the screen you want to move it to.

Steps to add the Quick Launch toolbar to the Taskbar

Quick Launch is a very useful toolbar that was added to the Taskbar starting with Windows 98. It consists of icons that allow you to launch programs from the Windows Taskbar with a single click of the mouse.

Windows XP, by default, doesn't show you the Quick Launch taskbar.

To add the Quick Launch toolbar to the Windows XP Taskbar:

1. Right click on the clock located on the Systray, or on a space on the Taskbar that is free of icons.
2. Now place the mouse indicator over *Toolbars*. A new menu will appear.
3. Now move the mouse pointer left or right and down, and then select Quick Launch by clicking on it.

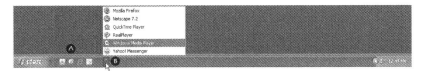

This is the way to launch programs from the Quick Launch:

A. If the icon representing the program you wish to use appears on this toolbar (see examples near the letter A above), simply click on it. The icon underneath the letter A is the Show Desktop icon.
B. Click on the guide, located near the letter B above and marked with the symbol >>, to see the rest of the icons available on the Quick Launch toolbar. To launch a program you see on this list just click on its icon.

One click on the *Show Desktop* icon and all your open programs will be hidden, so you can see your Desktop without much delay. Another click restores them just as you left them.

Chapter 2

Working with a Microsoft window

Introduction to a Microsoft window

A Microsoft window, from which the operating system Microsoft Windows takes its name, is a square or rectangular space with well-defined borders that you see on your computer screen. Windows are rendered on the screen in many different sizes, depending on their purpose.

Each window you see represents a program or process; for example, if your online-banking session is timing out for inactivity, a little window might open up to warn you that the online session is about to end.

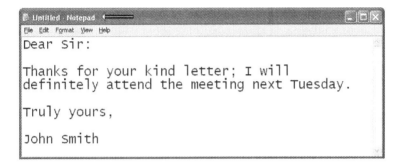

For example, a window like the one above will open on your computer screen when you launch the word processor Notepad, which is included with most of the different versions of the Microsoft Windows operating system.

An IBM compatible personal computer running later versions of the Microsoft Windows operating system, depending on the amount of memory Ram installed on the computer, can have many programs or processes running at the same time. And in most cases, each one o these processes will be rendered on your computer screen on their own window.

In chapter 6 of this book (Using computer Programs in Windows), you will learn how to switch back and forth between your open windows, using a process called multitasking; which is one of the main advantages of the Windows operating systems.

Ram stands for Random Access memory, and the more Ram you have the better (256 is good, but 512 is better). If you get more Ram, you will be able to work with more Windows at the same time.

The main parts of a typical Microsoft window

The chief advantage of using a personal computer with any version of the Microsoft Windows operating system is that, once you learn how to use one program, you will discover that it has similarities with other programs, even if they were written by different companies. This is because the main parts of a typical window look the same from program to program.

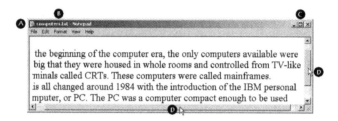

Follow the screen capture above to familiarize yourself with the main parts of a typical Microsoft window:

A. The control box: when you click on the upper left-hand corner of a window, a drop-down menu offers you the choice to restore, move, size, minimize, maximize, or close the window. To work with one of these actions, simply click on it.

B. The title bar is the horizontal bar at the top of a window. If you have several windows open, the title bar of the active window will be dark blue; title bars of the inactive windows will be light blue.

C. In the upper right-hand corner there are three symbols:
   - If you click on the minus sign, the window is minimized. This means that the window is hidden from view, and all you will see is its icon on the task bar. To restore the window, click on its icon on the taskbar.
   - To the right of the minus sign is a box that will have either one or two squares on it. If it has one square, clicking on it will cause the window to occupy your entire screen. If the box has two squares, clicking on it will make the window smaller.
   - If you click on the X sign, the window closes.

D. To work with the content that is out of view, click on the middle guide on either the Horizontal or Vertical Scroll Bars and hold the left mouse button, now move it up/down or left/right to bring it into view or click on the arrows at either end of each bar.

Bear in mind that when you type on your keyboard, this action only applies to the active window, or the more prominent one on your computer screen.

The working area in a window

The working area of a window is the space in which you can interface with the program it represents, in order to perform a task, such as; typing a letter with Microsoft Word or filling out an online form on a web page, using Internet Explorer.

The layout of the working area might vary slightly from program to program. In most word-processing programs, for example, you can start working in the working space at the center of the window right after the program opens; in some graphic programs, by contrast, you must take additional steps before you can begin work.

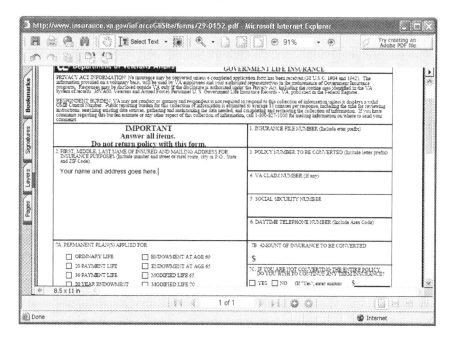

For example, on the graphic above, you can see on the working area of this window a Department of Defense form. This very particular form is found on the web, and was created with a special version of the Adobe acrobat program, and can be viewed with the Adobe Acrobat reader (which is a free program you can find on the Web). The document you are looking at on this Window will allow you to enter your information on this form before printing it out.

Note In Chapter 6, you will learn more about the different types of programs available for Windows, and how to perform such tasks as opening and closing them.

Different types of windows

While using a computer with Microsoft Windows, you will notice that each time you double click/click on an icon, a window opens. Some of these windows cover the whole screen and others are very small; some can be resized while others cannot. This is because some windows allow you to interface with them, while others might open for just enough time to show you a message and then close after a few seconds.

These are the three most common types of window you will see while working on any of the different versions of the Windows operating system:

- The program window (also know as the application window) visually represents a program on your computer screen. Generally speaking, this is the only type of window that can be both moved and resized, as you desire.
- The dialog-box window is a secondary type of window that opens on top of a primary program window. For example, when you choose to print from the File menu, a small window will open and prompt you to select the portion of the document that you want printed. A dialog box will close once you make a selection among the choices it offers you, or if you press the Esc key. Dialog-box windows can usually be moved but not resized.
- The Pop-up window is also a secondary type of window, that appears (pop-up) automatically while you are doing something else, like visiting a website. Like dialog-box windows, pop-up windows can generally be moved but not resized. And bear in mind that if for instance you are visiting a web site, for example the Amazon.com one, and you have Windows XP and the browser is blocking some pop-up windows you need to use to reply to an offer, then press and hold the CTRL key (while the page is loading), to temporally allow pop-up windows to open and display the pertinent information they have for you. And always keep in mind that clicking on Pop-up windows that open after visiting some web sites can be very harmful to your Windows based computer. Later in this book, in chapter 17, you will learn how to control these pop-up windows in Windows XP.

Bear in mind that the window that is open in front of all the other open windows is called the active window, and anything you type on your computer keyboard will be applied to it. The Title bar of the active Windows is dark blue; the Title bar of an inactive Windows is light blue.

 On chapter 6 you will learn how to work between the different windows you've opened, to complete your work.

Working with the different types of windows

The examples that follow will give you an introduction so that you can learn to recognize and work with the three main types of windows you will interface while using the Microsoft Windows operating system.

- The program window or application window

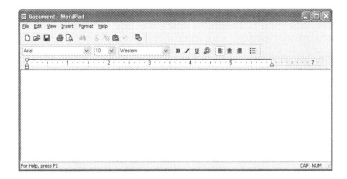

Program windows are the type of window you will see most commonly, as one opens every time you launch a program. The example above shows the window that will open when you click on the WordPad icon.

If your computer has enough Ram memory (like for example 512 Megabytes), you will be able to keep many different programs open at the same time; you can even have several instances of the same program open, and most importantly go back and forth between them.

For example, if you have a copy of the WordPad word processor open and decide you want to create a second document while you are still working on the first one, then you can click on the WordPad Icon again. A new instance of WordPad will now open in a different window.

 If you select to open a program, and its window is too small, then you can resize it to take more of the computer screen, following the steps outlined at the end of this chapter.

Once the program window opens, then you can work on it for as long as you want. If you've worked on a program (for instance creating a letter you want to save), then make sure you save it often.

When you are finished doing your computer work, then close its window in one of these four ways:

- By clicking on the File menu item and then on Exit or Close.
- By clicking on the "X" in the upper right-hand corner of the window.
- By clicking on the upper left-hand corner of the window and choosing Close.
- Alternatively press and hold the ALT key and then the F4 one, which closes the active window at the moment, or the window that is at the front of all the windows.

The next screen capture shows the window that will appear if you try to close a window, in which you were doing work, without first saving it.

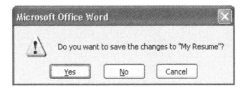

This is the way to work with this little window:

- To save your computer work, click on Yes. (If this is your first time saving the document, a new dialog box window will appear asking you what you would like to name the file and where you would like to save it.)
- To close the program without saving your work, click on No. You will lose whatever work you have done since the document was last saved. (If the document has never been saved, you will lose it entirely.)
- To return to work on your document, click on Cancel.

This dialog box will also pop-up if you start the process to shut down your computer, by clicking on the *Start* menu button, selecting *Turn Off Computer* and *Turn Off*, without first saving your computer work.

 In Chapter 9, you will learn the steps needed to permanently save your computer work to a permanent storage unit (such as the hard drive), and also how to retrieve it later.

- The dialog-box window

  This is the secondary window that opens over the program you are using, when you order that program to perform certain tasks (such as when you select to open a document, save a new document, or print a document).

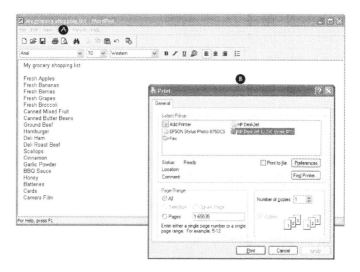

To learn how to work with a dialog box window open any program; for example open the Windows WordPad:

A. Now on the title bar of this program window, you will see; the name of the file (if you've chosen to save it already) and the name of the program this window belongs to.

B. For example, to invoke a typical Dialog box Window, click on the *File* menu item, and then select the *Print* option, now the Print dialog-box window opens over the Primary Window, to help you print your work.

A dialog-box window has to be closed before you can return to work in the program from which it was opened, by; a) Providing the information it is requesting, or b) By clicking on the "X" in the upper right-hand corner of the window.

If you open a dialog box by mistake, and you don't want to work with it, for example if you open the Speller in Ms Word, then you can close it by pressing the escape key (Esc).

It is also very important that you learn how to work with the different menu options found in some of these dialog-box windows.

These are some of the options you will find in a typical dialog box:

A. Tabs; which are useful to work in dialog boxes that have several pages of options. To move to a different page, just click on the appropriate tab for the option you are looking for. Alternatively, press and hold down the *CTRL* key and then press the Tab key to flip through the pages.

B. Pull-down menus; which have a small downward-pointing arrow next to them. Click on the arrow to see a list of the choices the menu contains. Once the drop-down menu is open, you can use the arrow keys on your keyboard to scroll up and down through the options.

C. Check boxes; which allow you to select options in a dialog box. To choose an option, simply click on the check box next to it. An X or a checkmark will appear, indicating that the option has been selected. To uncheck it, simply click on it a second time.

D. The spinner; which is a set of arrows on the side of a text box. Click on the up arrow to increase a value and the down area to decrease a value. Sometimes you can also type the value you want directly into the text box, like for example to change the font size.

If you want to try working with one of the different options found in one of these dialog box windows; open Word for Windows, and then click over Tools, then on Options. Now for example you can click on the Tabs (to see different pages of options), or open the drop-down menus.

The next graphic shows the dialog box window you will see when you select the print command from the File menu or from the Program toolbar.

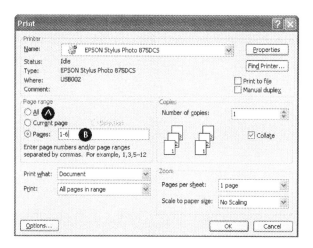

This is the way to work with the following options you will find on some dialog box window:

A. Radio buttons; which are a list of mutually exclusive options. If you see a dot next to an option, it means that option has been selected. You may only select one option from the list, by clicking on it.
B. Text fields; which allow you to type entries that aid the program in executing your request. For example, in the Print dialog box, you can enter the range of pages you wish to print.

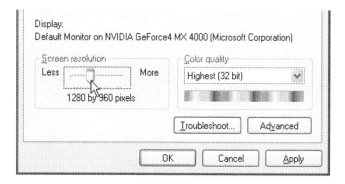

The slider is used to increase or decrease a value (for example, screen resolution). To increase a value, place the mouse pointer over the slider, and now, while you press and hold the left mouse button, move it to the right. Moving the slider to the left will decrease the value of the setting you are trying to change.

- The pop-up window

This is a different type of secondary window that is used—mostly by companies-, to send commercial advertisements to your computer. Such windows open automatically when you visit a website. Following the link in a pop-up window will usually direct your browser to the website of the company that is trying to sell its product to you.

You don't have to close a pop-up window to return to the work you were doing before it appeared on the screen, because if you want you can move it out of the way.

The graphic above shows a typical pop-up window. (This one opened after I visited the cnn.com website.) To reply to advertising on a pop-up window, simply click on it. This will cause a second window to open on your screen, and your browser will be directed toward a new webpage. To close a pop-up window, just click on the X in its upper right-hand corner.

If your computer has the second service pack of Windows XP, you can block most pop-up windows by activating an option on the Internet Explorer web browser (see Chapter 13). If you have Windows XP SP2 you can also temporary allow a pop-up window to open even if you have blocked pop-up windows, this way: Press and hold down the *CTRL* key while the page is loading (press the F5 key to reload the page). Once the web page loads you can release your finger from the CTRL key.

Never click inside a pop-up window unless you understand what it is offering you. Otherwise, it might install unwanted or malicious software on your computer.

Resizing a program window with the mouse

A program window that is not covering the whole screen can be resized (i.e., made bigger or smaller). If the window is covering the whole screen, you can click on the minimize/maximize button (it looks like two overlapping squares, located on the upper right-hand corner of a window) to make it smaller. Once it is smaller you can resize it or move it to another location. Double-clicking on the title bar of a window that is taking the whole screen will also cause it to occupy less than the full screen. To restore a window to its previous size, double-click on its title bar a second time.

Before manually resizing a window (that is not taking the whole screen), practice placing the mouse pointer over any of its sides or corners, then wait until the pointer turns into a double arrow.

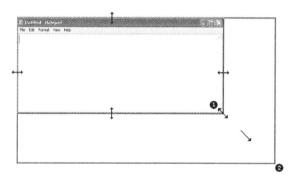

These are the steps to resize a Window that is not taking the whole screen:

1. To begin take the mouse pointer over any of the corners or sides, of any program Window. After the mouse pointer has turned into a double arrow, press and hold the left mouse button and then drag the corner or side until it is of the desired size.
2. To finish release your fingers from the mouse and the Window will stay on the new size. For instance if you close a program window -after resizing it, and re-open it again, then it should occupy the same space as it was occupying on the computer screen at the time you closed it.

Please remember that you cannot resize secondary dialog box windows or most Pop-up windows, and those types of windows can only be moved or closed.

Moving a window with the mouse

While using the windows operating system you might notice that the screen will get a little cluttered with different Windows, and at times the window you want to work with might be a little to the side of another window. Because of this, at times, you might need to move a window that is not covering the whole computer screen, to a different place on the screen.

The next screen capture below illustrates this process—in this case, moving an electronic-calculator program while you also work with a tax program.

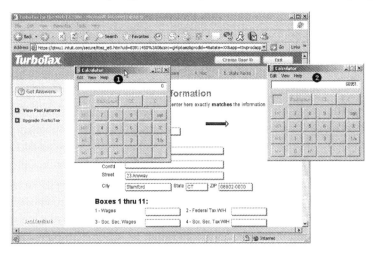

These are the steps, as you can see on this screen capture, to move the electronic calculator program, so that it doesn't cover the information you are working with at the moment:

1. Notice that when you open a Windows program, its ensuing window will open on top of any Windows currently open. To move it to another location on the computer screen, click on its title bar, and then press and hold the left mouse button down, now move/drag it to another place on the computer screen, finally lift your finger from the mouse button when you reach the desired location on the computer screen.
2. Now this Window is in a new location on the computer screen, out of the way of the work area of the windows you were using.

You can even drag a program window all the way to the right, hiding most of its content. On this example after moving the electronic calculator you will still be able to read the totals in it, otherwise you can switch back and forth between program windows by clicking on their icons on the windows taskbar.

Chapter 3

The Menus and Toolbars on a program window

Introduction to the menu bar and toolbar in a program window

In a graphical user interface, like the one used on the Microsoft Windows operating system, most of the actions required to perform a task (for example, opening a document) can be accomplished by using the mouse to click on a selection within the menu bar or on one of the toolbars in a program window.

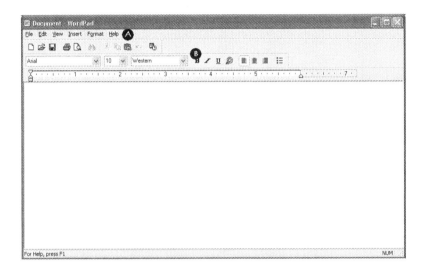

On this screen capture of a Microsoft WordPad window, you can see the location of the menu bar and its two toolbars.

A. The menu bar is composed of a list of names located at the top of most program windows. These generally include: File, Edit, Window, and Help. When you click on one of these names, a drop-down menu opens revealing another list of options, any of which can be selected by clicking on it.

B. Toolbars consists of a row of buttons that, when clicked, assist you in performing a specific task. For example, clicking on the "align center" button will center the text you are working on.

A typical program window can show you many different toolbars at the same time, like the Standard and Formatting toolbar that you see (if they are enabled) on the program window of any of the programs that comprise the Microsoft Office suite of programs (such as is the case in the Microsoft Excel 2003 program).

Using the menu bar on a program window

When you click on one of the names on the menu bar, a drop-down menu will open. For example, when you click on File, you will see a drop-down menu with a list of choices that, when clicked, allow you to command the program to perform various computer tasks.

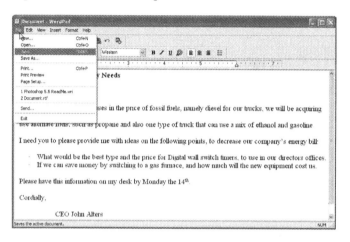

Once the drop-down menu opens, select one of its command options by just clicking on its name (for instance Print). Now in most cases, a new dialog-box window will then open over the main program window, presenting you with a different list of choices you can use to complete a task, such as printing your document.

Or if you prefer, you can also use the keyboard and the arrow keys to work with these menu items. For instance, if you wanted to Save a document you've been working on, you can press and hold the ALT key and the letter which is underlined on the File menu item (in this case the F) to open its drop-down menu (alternatively if you wanted to work with the Tools menu item, notice that the letter underline is the T, just press and hold the ALT and the T one to see its options). Once the drop-down menu opens, you can even navigate through all it's command/names by using the Down/Up arrow keys. When the choice you want to use is highlighted, such as the Spelling and Grammar ones locates under the Tools menu item, then press the Enter key to execute it or just click on it.

If you click on the wrong item name on a program toolbar, you can close the resulting dialog-box window by pressing the Esc key (located on the upper-left corner of the keyboard).

Standard item names on a menu bar

Some of the names of the items on a menu bar will vary from program to program, but others are standard in most programs for Windows.

In the next screen capture, notice that the menu bars on two different programs—Microsoft Word and Windows Notepad—include many of the same names.

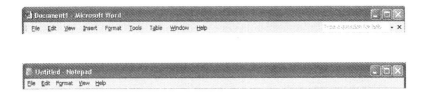

Here is a list of menu items, common to most Windows programs, as well as some of the tasks that they will give you access to (on the drop-down menu that opens up) when you click on their name:

- File: you are given the choice, among others, to create a new file, open an existing file, save a file, or print a file.
- Edit: you are given the choice to undo the last changes to your work, copy selections, paste selections to the same document or to another open document, or delete sections of your work. You can also find and replace paragraphs of text in word-processing documents.
- View: you are given the choice to add or remove certain panels of the window in which you are working; you could remove, for example, some of the toolbars.
- Format: this menu allows you to select a different font and paragraph preferences for word-processing documents.
- Help: when you click on the "About . . ." item on this menu, it will provide you with information on the version of the program you are using.

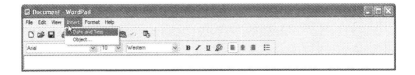

If you are not sure which menu item contains the task you wish to perform, then just click on a few of the names of the items on the menu bar (for instance Insert), to browse through the different choices available from the drop-down menus that open up.

How to use the new intuitive drop-down menus in Windows XP

In previous versions of the Windows operating system, when you clicked on a menu item its ensuing drop-down menu presented you with all its options. In Windows XP, by contrast, the drop-down menus adjust to the way you use them: the options you have used most recently will be at the very top of the drop-down menu.

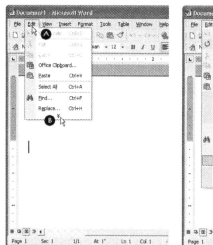 

Following this screen capture, you will learn how to use the new Windows XP drop-down menus in Windows XP:

A. Click on any item name on the menu bar to see its ensuing drop-down menu. In the example above, I clicked on Edit.

B. If the item/task name you are looking for (such as the *Go To* option, allowing you to jump to a different page in Word) is not visible, then place the mouse pointer on the double down-arrow mark at the bottom of the drop-down menu for a few seconds, to expand the rest of the choices on this particular drop-down menu.

C. Now you can see that the drop-down menu expands, showing you the rest of its options. On this example the Go To option now becomes visible.

Once the drop-down menu opens up, then you can single click on any of the options it presents to you, to execute a task. For instance if you've clicked over Edit, on most programs for Windows, and then on Select All, then all of the contents of the document or web page you are working with will be highlighted/selected.

The standard and formatting toolbars

As we saw earlier in this chapter, Windows toolbars are a set of buttons that, when clicked, perform some of the same tasks as the ones available from the drop-down menus. The standard and formatting toolbars are the two most widely used toolbars you will find in some Windows programs, including Microsoft Office. Using them, you can perform most of the commands needed to complete your work.

For instance when you click on these buttons (follow "A,B,C", on the graphic above) on the standard toolbar, you will be able to:

A. Open and Save files.
B. Print and Preview your work.
C. Cut, Copy and Paste a selection.

For instance when you click on these buttons (follow "A,B,C..", on the graphic above) on the formatting toolbar, you will be able to:

A. Change the writing section style
B. Change the font type
C. Change the font size
D. Bold, italicize, or underline text
E. Change the text alignment
F. Create numbered or bulleted list to highlight ideas

If you don't see one of these Toolbars on the program window you are working on; click over View, then on Toolbars, and finally click over Standard, or Formatting or any other you want to add to the program Window.

Tip

Leave the mouse pointer over any button (for a few seconds), and as you can see on the first graphic, it will show you its function. On the example, next to the button, it shows the word Paste.

Using the toolbars on a program window

When you click on any of the individual buttons on a particular toolbar, the program is instructed to perform a specific function. For example, when you click on the button that looks like a little disk, a window will open to help you save your work.

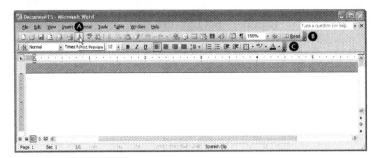

On this screenshot of Microsoft Word, notice the following:

A. When you leave the mouse pointer over one of the icons, without clicking on the mouse button, a little yellow window opens to show you the name of the task this particular button will help you complete when clicked on. In the screen capture above, the mouse pointer is on the Print-preview icon.

B. This is the Standard toolbar; from here you can perform some of the functions also found on the File and Edit menu items.

C. This is the Formatting toolbar; from here you can perform some of the functions available on the Format menu item.

These are the two main ways to format text, by:

- Clicking first on any of the formatting buttons. Now all the text you type from this moment on is applied the formatting options you chose. For instance if you click on the **bold** button, all the text you type from then on will be bolded.
- Selecting text you've already typed, which will be explained on the next page, then clicking on one of the formatting buttons, to change it's formatting.

Remember, that you must click on the **bold** button again or on any other option you've chosen (such as Underline or Italics) to stop formatting the text you are typing. These options are also reset when you close the program.

The example that follows will help you understand how to use some of the functions found on the formatting toolbar, to format text.

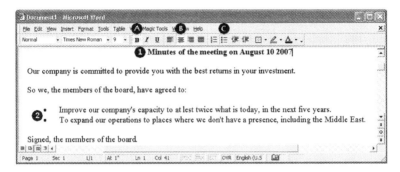

These are the steps to create a letter, with a centered title in bold letters and bullet points:

1. To begin, click on the Bold and on the align Center buttons (see "A" and "B").

   Now type the text you want to center and bold. When you finish click again on Bold and the align Center button to stop centering and bolding text, and press Enter to force a line break. Now you can finish your letter.

2. To create a bulleted list, click on the Bullets button (see "C").

   Now you can begin typing each bullet item (Press Enter after each one, to be at the beginning of a new bullet point). When you are done click on the Bullets button again, and then press Enter to force a line break, otherwise all the text you type will be bulleted.

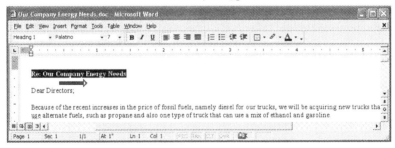

To change the formatting of text you've already written, select it this way; click before the first letter you want to change, then press and hold the left Mouse button and then move the Mouse in a sweeping motion until all the text you want to change is selected. Then click on the toolbar button option (for instance click on the "I" for italics) you want to use. When you are finished click on the same toolbar button again, to stop applying that particular formatting option to your text.

Troubleshooting toolbars

If after selecting to use a toolbar, you are still not able to see it, it might be due to the fact that the toolbar is staggered along the same line, under the menu bar, as another toolbar.

Notice on this screen capture that the Standard and Formatting toolbar are on the same line, under the menu bar. This makes it hard to click on some of the options available on the second toolbar (the formatting one), of which some buttons are hidden from view, like for example the one to change the type of font.

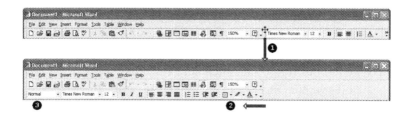

Follow these steps, guided by this screen capture, to align the Formation toolbar, under the Standard toolbar so that you can see its entire button lineup:

1. Take the mouse pointer along the staggered Toolbars, until it turns into a four-arrow symbol, and then press and hold the left mouse button.
2. Now drag the Toolbar, down first, then to the left until it is parallel to the Standard toolbar, and then finally release your finger from the mouse button.

This might not work right the first time you try it, but practice makes perfect (to move it again move the mouse pointer around the toolbar you want to move until it becomes a four way arrow). Also notice that if you move the toolbar over the work area, it becomes a floating toolbar. To bring this floating toolbar under the other toolbars, click on its top edge (it will look bluish), then press and hold the left mouse button, and them move it up until is parallel to the other toolbars.

Part II
Managing your Windows XP computer

Chapter 4

Programs included with Windows XP to Manage Your Computer and Its Resources

Intro to managing your computer and its resources

Using your personal computer might involve more than working with a few programs to type a letter or to send an e-mail message. At times you might also need to get some information that a regular program can't provide for you.

For that reason, Windows gives you an array of programs that you can think of as software tools to probe inside Windows and get the information you are looking for. For example, to find a file you've created, or to change a Windows setting.

Here are some such programs, all of which you will learn about in this book:

- The My Computer program, which allows you to work with the folders and files found on fixed or removable storage devices to which you have access from your computer. For instance Network drives.
- Windows Explorer, which also allows you to work with the folders and files found on fixed or removable storage devices available from your computer, but which presents information about them in a more intuitive way than the information shown on the My computer program (one folder at a time).
- The group of software tools found in the Control Panel. The most commonly used software tools in this group are; Add or Remove Programs, Printers and Faxes, Sounds and Audio Devices and Users Accounts.
- The Recycle Bin, which holds the folders or files you've previously deleted.

To give you a sense of how these programs are useful, here are some tasks you might need to perform, as well as the programs you can use to complete them with:

- To find a file whose location you aren't sure of, use the My Computer program or the Windows Explorer.
- To create a group of folders to better organize your work, use the Windows Explorer.
- To add a new user account, open the control panel and double click on the Users Accounts icon.
- To remove a program you don't need anymore, open the control panel and double click on the Add or Remove programs icon.
- To restore a file you've deleted, open the Recycle Bin, find it, and then select to restore.

Right now you might not need to perform any of these tasks, but you may wish to keep the above information in mind in case the necessity arises later.

The My Computer program

This is a program that opens when you double click on an icon, appropriately called My Computer, located on the desktop of computers running the Microsoft Windows operating system or on the Start menu. When you double click on this icon, a window opens; from this window, you can work with the folders and files found on the local and remote storage resources to which your computer has access.

Using the My Computer program, you can:

- View the contents of fixed and removable drives attached to your computer
- Work with your files and folders
- Open programs

On the above screen capture, you can see the usual location of the My Computer icon on the left side of the Windows desktop. In Windows XP, the appearance of this icon is slightly different from previous versions of Windows. Its main functions, however, are the same.

Note

If you have Windows XP and are not able to see the My Computer icon on your Windows desktop, then you can add it by following the steps outlined in the first chapter of this book.

Opening the My Computer program

To open the My Computer program, just double click on its icon on the Windows Desktop or single click on its icon if you see it on the Start menu. Once the My Computer window opens, you can begin working with all your computer resources (fixed hard drives and removable data storage media) as well as making changes to settings to the Microsoft Windows operating system.

You should learn to recognize these sections of the My computer window:

A. On this section of the My computer window, under *Files stored on This Computer*, you will see the names of folders, one for each one of the user accounts opened on the computer, that programs will suggest you use to save your work. One of these folders belongs to the user logged in (to find out the name of the user currently logged in click on the Start menu button, and its user name will be displayed at the very top of this menu). Everybody that uses the computer can also save his or her work to the Shared Documents folder. Additionally if you don't wish to use the suggested folder to save your work (the My Documents one), you can easily save your work to another location on the hard drive.
B. These are the fixed hard drives attached to your computer, on which you may save your work (see Chapter 9). Note that the fixed and the removable storage devices attached to your computer are assigned a letter, such as the "C:" drive.
C. These are removable storage resources, such as the CD-RW drive. They can be used to back up your work. You can also see an icon for a device called a USB drive (UDISK 20X (E:)). This drive belongs to a new class of portable storage devices, where you can also save your computer work.

Please notice that as you open and close various folders, the title of this window— visible on the blue bar at the top—changes to reflect the name of the folder that is currently open (right now on the example screenshot it reads My Computer).

Using the My Computer program to view the contents of fixed/ removable drives

When you double click on one of the aforementioned drive letters—in the example below, the Local Disk (C:)—your action is akin to opening a drawer in a filing cabinet to see what folders and files it contains.

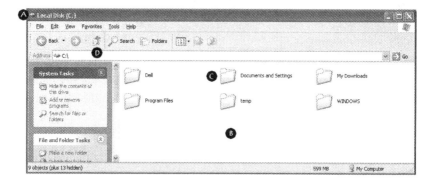

The screen capture above is a representative example of what you see in the screen that opens when you double click on a drive letter (on this example the C: drive) in the My Computer window. Note the following parts:

A. This is the name of the storage resource at the level you are working with—in this case, the local disk (C:).
B. In this panel you will see the names of the folders and files, found at the level of the folder or drive you are working with. On this example you can see the folders found at the beginning at the root of the C: drive.
C. To find your own work, double click on the folder Documents and Settings, and then click on the folder whose name reflects the user name you used to login to the computer. (You can find this name by clicking on the Start button; the name will appear on the top of the menu.)
D. Click on the up arrow, to return to the main My computer window or to work with a folder from which you opened this sub-folder.

You can also find your own work, if you've saved it there, by double clicking on the My Documents folder on the Windows desktop.

 Reading chapter seven of this book (Using computer Files and Folders in Windows), you will learn more about using files and folders to organize your computer work.

Windows Explorer

Windows Explorer is the primary file organizer and viewer available in all versions of Windows, since Windows 98. Windows Explorer allows you to work with your files and folders which you can also do using the My Computer program, albeit the information you see while using the Windows Explorer is presented in a more intuitive hierarchical-tree fashion.

To open the Windows Explorer, click on the Start menu. Place the mouse pointer over All Programs, over the Accessories group of programs, a little bit to the right and down, and finally click on Windows Explorer. When you open Windows Explorer this way, the default folder selected will be the My Documents folder.

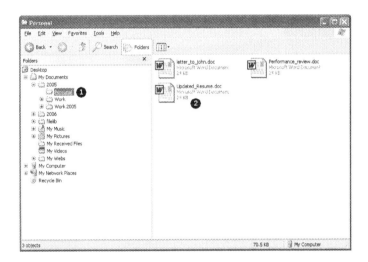

You can now navigate the folder tree to find your work as follows:

1. To begin click on the name of the folder, whose contents you want to work with. Its contents will be displayed in the right-hand panel of the window. In the example above, I clicked on the My Documents folder, the 2005 folder and finally on the Personal folder, to see its contents on the right panel.
2. To open a file, you see on the right panel, just double clicking on its name.

Reading chapter 8 (Guide to Windows Explorer), you will learn more about using Windows explorer, to work with the computer files you've saved to the storage resources attached to your computer

How to navigate the folders tree in Windows Explorer

You can also open Windows Explorer by right mouse-clicking on the Start button (located on the left side of the taskbar) and then clicking on Explorer. Opening the Windows Explorer this way is fast, but has the drawback that the location that appears immediately selected, after you've opened it, is at the level of the Start menu folder (read the name on the blue title bar).

These are the steps to navigate, if you have opened the Windows Explorer right from the Start button, to the right folder, which contains your files:

1. First click on the plus sign next to the My Documents folder, or on the name of the folder where you saved the files you are looking for.
2. In the My Documents folder, click on the folder where you think your work resides. (In this example, that is the 2005 folder.) The (+) sign, in front of a folder or drive icon, indicates that the folder or drive contains further hidden subfolders that you can see by clicking on the plus sign.
3. The contents of the folder you have clicked on the left panel will be displayed on the right one. To see the contents of a folder, which icon you see on the right panel, double click on it. To open a file you see here, just double click on it.

If you did saved the files or folder you are looking for to a different fixed or removable drive, then click on the plus sign next to My Computer, and then on the plus sign next to the drive letter (to expand its folders tree) that corresponds to the fixed or removable drive storage device where the information you are looking for was saved.

Managing your work: the My Computer program vs. the Windows Explorer

As you've seen on the previous pages, both the Windows Explorer and the My Computer program allow you to work with your files on the different fixed or removable drives connected locally or remotely to your computer (for instance the drives located on an office LAN or local access Network).

These two file management programs included with the windows operating system, are present in all the different versions of Windows, starting with Windows 98, and the main change is that in Windows 2000 and XP you can use the Thumbnail option to preview the digital photos you saved to your computer.

Here are the pros and cons of using the My Computer program:

- You can view one directory or folder at a time in its own window; to the computer novice, this can be very reassuring and easier to understand than a whole tree of folders. Bear in mind that in Windows 98, double clicking on the name of a folder causes it to open an additional My Computer window.
- You are less likely to move files or folders by mistake, from one folder to another.
- The con is that, using this method, it is very awkward—although not impossible—to move files to another location on the hard drive.

Here are the pros and cons of using the Windows Explorer:

- Using Windows Explorer, it is very easy to find the folder where you've saved your work. Click on its name to see its contents on the Explorer right panel.
- It is also easier to move or copy your files or folders to another location on the hard drive.
- The con is that a computer novice can easily move more files than he/she intended to, possibly rendering some programs inoperative.

In the end, it is a matter of personal preference. You may wish to use the My Computer program at the beginning and then switch to the Windows Explorer once you've gained more experience using the computer.

If you make a mistake while using one of these programs—for example, if you've deleted or moved a file you need—press and hold the *CTRL* key and then the *Z* one, to undo your error.

The Control Panel

The Control Panel is composed of a group of software tools to change the way Windows looks and behaves. The Control Panel is present in all versions of Windows, although in Windows XP some of these programs have changed a lot in comparison with Windows 98.

In Windows XP you can easily find the Control Panel under the Start menu.

This is the way to open the Control Panel in Microsoft Windows XP:

1. Click on the Start button to open the Start menu.
2. Now move the mouse pointer up and then to the right, and then click on the Control Panel menu item. In previous releases of Windows (such as Windows 98), place the mouse indicator first over "Settings", now move the mouse indicator to the right, and click on the Control Panel item.

This is an alternative way to open the Control Panel; click on the Start button, then move the mouse pointer to the right and then up over Run, and click on it. On the ensuing Run window, type *Control* and then press Enter to open the Control Panel.

These are some of the task you can complete using the Control Panel:

- Add Windows components
- Add or Remove programs
- Adjust the display options
- Adjust the mouse options
- Adjust the printer options
- Change the sound settings
- Remove programs
- Work with the local user accounts
- Work with the Printers and Faxes options

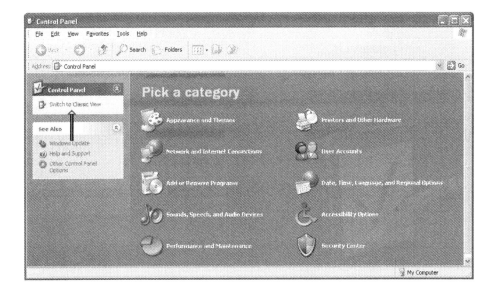

At times when the Control Panel opens in Windows XP, you might only see a few icons in different categories. To see all the icons on the Control Panel click on "Switch to Classic View". To open any of the programs found on the Control Panel then just double click on their respective icon.

If you have a Windows XP limited user account rights as opposed to an Administrative one, you won't be able to complete some tasks from the Control Panel, such as Adding or removing programs.

In the next graphic you can see all of the software tools available in the Control Panel to change your Windows settings. If you have used a previous version of Windows (such as Windows 98) then you will notice that some of these tools will be new to you, while most are the same and will work as before.

These are some of the tools you will learn about it in this book, and the chapters in which you will learn to use them:

A. To add hardware devices your computer doesn't automatically recognize, double click on the Add Hardware icon. See Chapter 15;Working with Hardware Devices in Windows XP.
B. To remove a program, double click on the Add or Remove Programs icon. See Chapter 6; Using Computer Programs in Windows.
C. To add or remove a user account, double click on the User Accounts icon. See Chapter 5; Working with Windows XP Local User Accounts.

Most of the software tools you see on the Control Panel were present when you bought the computer, and some were added later, when you installed a program, such as the Symantec LiveUpdate icon you see on the screen capture above.

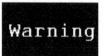

Bear in mind that if you work for a company, and they have an IT department, that you should not be using these programs to change the way your computer works.

The Recycle Bin

The Recycle Bin provides a safety net when deleting folders, files, or icons. When you delete any of these items from your hard drive, Windows places them in the Recycle Bin. In chapter eight of this book you will learn the steps necessary to send; Files, Folders, or Icons you don't need anymore to the Recycle bin.

Items you've deleted will remain in the Recycle Bin until you manually delete them, or until the disk becomes full and the operating system is forced to delete some of them.

In this screen capture you can see the Recycle Bin icon on the Desktop of a computer running Windows XP. This icon looks very similar in all the different editions of the Windows operating system. When the Recycle Bin is storing files (you've deleted), its icon changes to show you a piece of paper slightly sticking out. As long as an item you've deleted is still saved on the Recycle bin, then you can restore it back to your hard drive (shown in chapter eight of this book).

 Bear in mind that when you delete files or folders from removable media (such as a USB drive) or a network drive that they are not sent to the Recycle Bin, and cannot be retrieved later.

Chapter 5

Working With Windows XP Local User Accounts

Introduction to local user accounts in Windows XP

The enhanced security of the Windows XP operating system is implemented mainly through the use of different local user accounts. (The fact that these accounts are local means that they only provide access to the resources on the specific computer you are working, also called the Local Machine) These local user accounts are created so that each person who wants to use the computer can gain access to the Windows environment by clicking on his or her own individual user account name.

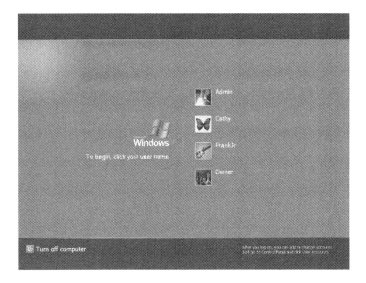

On this screen capture, taken just after turning on my Windows XP computer, you can see the typical Windows XP welcome screen, displaying the name of the user accounts allowed to use it.

Right after you finish setting up a new Windows XP computer, it is usually enough to click on the name of your user account to gain access to it. However, in order to take advantage of the extra security features that Windows XP offers, especially if unauthorized use of your computer concerns you, then it is also imperative to protect each of these user accounts with a password. The procedure for setting up user passwords is explained later in this chapter.

A Windows XP system with a single user account that is not protected by a password will never show you this welcome screen. Instead, it will proceed directly into the Windows desktop after you turn it on.

Working with user accounts in Windows XP

Ideally, on a personal computer with Windows XP or Windows 2000, each person who wants to gain access to the computer should use his or her own local user account when logging into it. The main advantage of logging in with your own user account is that the system creates a workspace for each user, to isolate his or her files from those other users.

To work with local user accounts in Windows XP, you must use the User Accounts tool, which icon is located in the Control Panel.

To open the Control Panel, follow these steps:

1. Click on the Start menu button.
2. Now bring the mouse indicator up (to the middle of the left panel), then over to the right, and now select "Run" (click on it).

3. Next click on the text field, type *Control* (you might need to use the backspace key to delete any text saved from a previous operation), then click on OK to open the Control Panel.

4. Once you've opened the Control Panel, double-click on the User Accounts icon to open the User Accounts software tool.

There are two types of relevant user accounts that a user with administrative privileges will be able to create:

- A Limited account, which is a restricted user account, which is ideal for school-age children. Users of these accounts are not able to see the files and folders of other users, and they are prevented from meddling with important system files.
- An Administrator account, which has administrative privileges or the power to add additional computer programs or hardware. Administrator accounts can also create additional user accounts and view the files and folders of other users.

Working in the User Accounts window

After you have opened the User Accounts software tool by following the steps outlined on the previous page, you can start working with local user accounts in Windows XP. This will allow you to create new user accounts, change a particular user-account type, and work with user-account passwords to protect them.

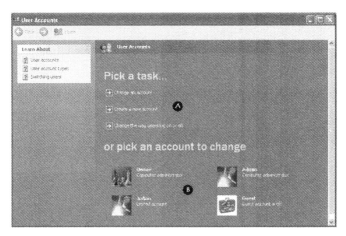

These are a few options to choose from in the User Accounts window:

A. Under "Pick a task," you can select from three different task choices, by clicking on it:
    - Change an account
    - Create a new account
    - Change the Way users log on or off.

B. If you want to make a change to an existing account, you can also click directly on the name of that account. All existing accounts are displayed at the bottom of the User Accounts window, under the heading "or pick an account to change."

Please notice the heading on the window that opens after you have chosen to change an account:

- If the heading says, "What do you want to change about your account?" then you are making changes to the user account you've used to log-in into the computer.
- If the heading says, "What do you want to change about [user name's] account?" then you are configuring the options of another local user account.

Creating a new local user account in Windows XP

To create a user account for another person whom you want to give access to your Windows XP computer, you must first log on to the computer using a local user account that has administrative privileges. Bear in mind that any user account you created at the time of the initial Windows XP setup was automatically given administrative privileges.

To start the process of creating a new local user account, open the User Accounts software tool by following the instructions on the previous pages. From the User Accounts window, click on "Create a new account."

To create a new local user account in Windows XP, follow these steps:

1. First type the name that you want to use for the new account, keeping in mind that you can use a combination of names and numbers (i.e., "John123"). To proceed to the next step, click on Next.
2. Now you must click on the desired account type you want to assign to this local user account. Please remember that if you have sensitive information on the computer that you want to protect from this user, and/or you are creating a user account for a child, you should probably select the "Limited" option.
3. To finish, click on "Create Account". This will create the local user account, which henceforth will be listed on the Windows XP welcome screen that displays after you turn on your computer. If you are given the option to make your files private from other users of the computer, then click on Yes.

Later on in this chapter, you will learn how to assign a password to these user accounts, in order to protect them (mainly their files) from other non-Administrator users.

Please be aware that normally, when you first power up a store-bought Windows XP computer, one of the first opening screens will allow you to create up to five user accounts for the people who will use the computer.

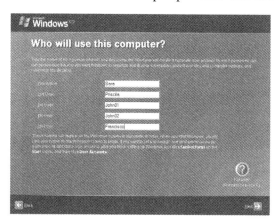

On this screen capture, you can see the Windows XP initial setup user-creation screen window ("Who will use this computer?"). To create local user accounts at this point, just type the names or the nicknames of up to five people to whom you would like to grant access to the computer via their own individual accounts. Please be aware that any user account you create at this point will have administrative privileges on this computer. Also note that access to these accounts won't initially be protected by a password. You need to provide at least a name here, so that a user account can be created under that name. Later on you can add additional user accounts. When you are done, click on Next to go onto the next step.

After you have done this and finished setting up Windows XP, remember later to do two things (Instructions for performing these tasks are provided later in this chapter.):

1. Protect these user accounts by creating a password for them.
2. Downgrade the permissions ASAP of these new user accounts, from Administrator to Limited.

The latest step is especially important if the accounts will belong to young children or other people who you'd like to share the computer with, to adjust their permissions from Computer administrator to Limited account.

Changing the account type of a user account

To change the permissions setting of a local user account, you must first be logged into the computer using a user account that has administrative privileges. (A user with administrative privileges can also lower the access privileges of his or her own user account, by changing his account type from an Administrator to a Limited account.)

To start the process of changing an account type, return to the User Accounts software tool, following the instructions provided earlier in this chapter. Once the User Accounts window opens, click on the name of the user account you want to change.

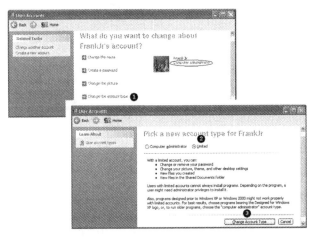

Once you have clicked on an individual user account, a window will open that looks like the top one of the two illustrated above. To change the account type of the user (which in this example was originally given Administrator privileges), follow these steps:

1. Click on "Change the account type."
2. Select the "Limited" option to lower the rights on this account. (This is especially important to do if you created user accounts for school-age children while doing the initial Windows XP setup) At this point, you could also change a Limited account to an Administrator account by selecting the "Computer administrator" option.
3. Finally, click on "Change Account Type."

If you have changed an account from an Administrator type to a Limited type, then the user of this user account will no longer be able to add or remove programs or make any changes to any other account, but will still be able to change his or her own password.

How to create a password for a user account

For a user account to be secure, it must be protected by a password. Ideally, a password should be a non-obvious string of characters, composed of a combination of letters and numbers.

To start creating, changing, or deleting passwords for any user account on your computer, first log on the computer with an Administrator account. Then:

1. Return to the User Accounts software tool, following the instructions provided earlier in this chapter
2. On the lower part of this Window, click on the name of the user account you want to work with.

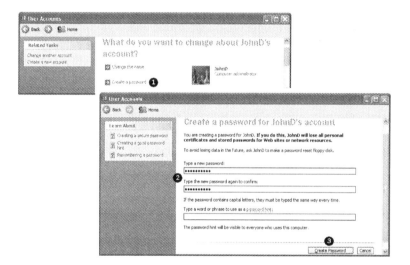

Next, follow these steps to add a password to this account:

1. First click on "Create a password."
2. Now type it under "Type a new password," press the Tab key and then type it again in the second field to confirm that this is the password you wish to use.
3. To finish, click on "Create Password." On the next page you will see the pro's and cons of creating a Password hint under "Type a word or phrase . . . ".

Any person with a user account can change his or her own password (by returning here and clicking on *Change the password*), but your user account must have administrative privileges for you to be able to create or change the password of a different user account.

Using password hints to recover your password

Adding a password to a user account can help increase user security, but it can also create problems by locking out users who forget their passwords. For this reason, it is sometimes useful to add a password "hint" (in the same window you used to add or change you user account password) so that if you forget it, the system can help you remember the password you used, by displaying a word or a phrase you chose.

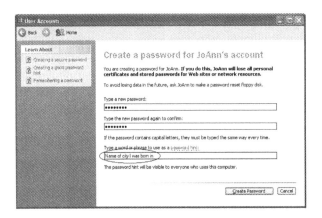

For instance, if you chose to use the word: "Memphis", as your password, them (while working on your password) click under "Type a word . . . ", and type your password reminder to be: "Name of the city I was born in" (Note, however, that for security reasons, it is best to have a reminder phrase that is meaningful to you and no one else.)

If you are at the login screen for your local account but you have forgotten your password, you can just click on the question-mark icon to see your password hint.

If this reminds you of your password, then click under *Type your password,* type your password, and then click on the arrow sign, to gain access to your Windows XP workplace. Password reminders can be very helpful and can save you a great deal of hassle, but the key is to use a password hint combination that is not too obvious.

Four examples of working with user accounts

To go over some of the things we've seen in this chapter so far, here are four examples of situations involving user accounts:

1. You've just finished setting up your new Windows XP computer, and during the initial setup process you created a local user account for one of your school-age children. And because this account was created during the initial Windows XP setup, it was automatically granted administrative privileges and is not yet protected by a password.
   - In this case you should reduce the rights on this account by changing its type from an Administrator to a Limited account. You should also ask your child if he or she want to use a password. If the answer is yes, create one by following the instructions on the previous pages. Users with a Limited account can work with their own password options.

2. On the initial welcome screen, you click on the main Administrator account, which is normally assigned the name "Admin," and the computer goes right into the Windows Desktop without stopping to ask you for a password.
   - If you want this account to be protected by a password, create a password for this account by returning to the User Accounts window.

3. One of your children has created a user-account password, but now he or she forgets the password and cannot get back into the computer.
   - To help your child, log back into the computer with your own administrative user account and change their password.

4. You forget the password to your own administrative user account.
   - Ask another user of the computer, if he or she has also a user account with administrative privileges, to change your password to something of your liking (you can later change your own password to something else). If no other user of the computer has administrative privileges, then you might try looking at your password hint by clicking on the question-mark symbol next to the login text field. If you still have no luck remembering your password, you may need to call a computer consultant to help you get back into your system.

Forgetting your password in Windows 2000/XP or even on the new Vista will prevent you from using your computer, so if you are forgetful write it down and store it on a safe place.

How to work with the logon and logoff options

In a computer shared by a few people, logging off and logging on in order to switch users can become tiresome. With this in mind, Microsoft created Fast User Switching, which is enabled in Windows XP by default. This feature allows different users to share a computer, switching back and forth between different user accounts that are logged in. (Note: this feature works only on home computers, not those wired in office LANs.)

To make changes to the way users log in to the computer, return to the User Accounts software tool. From this window, click on "Change the way users log on or off."

A. When the "Use the Welcome screen" box is checked, you will see the names of all the existing user accounts when you turn on your computer. Click on your user account, to gain access to the computer. Un-checking this box will hide their names and disable the Fast User Switching feature.

B. If you keep the "Use Fast User Switching" box checked, users will be able to keep their programs open while other users log on to the computer. For example, if you are typing a report and your child wants to check his or her e-mail, you can log off using the "Switch User" feature, select *Switch User*, the child can log on, check e-mail, and then log off. Then you can re-log back on and return to work without ever having closed any of your programs. If you uncheck the "Use Fast User Switching" box, however, programs will automatically shut down when users log off the computer.

C. If you make any changes on this screen, click on "Apply Options" before exiting.

WARNING: If you uncheck the "Use the Welcome screen", you will only see the name of the last person who logged onto the computer. This means that if you **forget** the name of your own user account, you won't be able to log back onto the computer until another user logs back in and visits the User Accounts window in order to **remind you** of the exact name of your own user account (for instance John12).

How to delete a user account

In Windows XP, you can create many different user accounts to accommodate all of the people whom you wish to give access to your computer. At any time, however, you can decide to delete some or all of these extra user accounts. The only accounts you cannot delete are the default local Administrator account and the one through which you are currently logged onto the computer.

When you want to delete an account, return to the User Accounts software tool and click on the name of the user account that you want to delete. After you do this, a new window will appear with the heading: "What do you want to change about [user name]'s account?"

From the available options, follow these steps to delete the account you have selected:

1. First click on "Delete the account."
2. In the next dialog box, click on either "Delete files" or "Keep files," depending on whether this user has some important files in his or her user folders that he or she would like to retrieve later.

If you want to delete the account of the user that is currently logged on to the computer, you must first log off to close the current user session. Then you can log back into a different account with administrative privileges, at which point you will be able to delete the undesired local user account.

Logging into a Windows XP computer

Now that we've reviewed the different aspects of working with user accounts, it's time for you to put your skills to the test by logging into your computer using your own user account, to practice following some of the tasks you read about it in this chapter.

For example, try changing your password, logging out, and then logging in again.

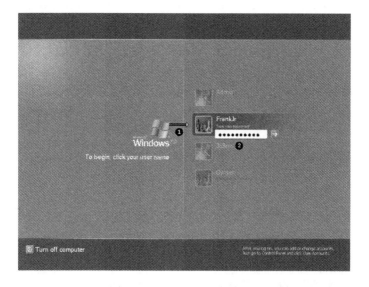

When the welcome screen is enabled, this is the way to log into a personal computer with the Window XP operating system:

1. First click on the icon with the name of your user account. If the user account is not protected by a password, then the computer will simply proceed to the Windows Desktop. If you've disabled the welcome screen, there will only be a small dialog box to type your user name, along with a box for your password underneath it.
2. If your user account is protected by a password, type it here and then click on the green arrow to gain access to the computer. Bear in mind that if the password you typed is wrong, you will be prompted to type it again.

From time to time, while you are away from your computer, the operating system will temporarily log you out and you will be prompted to log in again. To return to your account, follow the same login procedure to get back into your system.

Switching between user accounts

The process of switching between user accounts is different from the process of shutting down the computer for the day. When you switch between user accounts or when you log off a user account, the computer is still on, ready to accept the next login from you or from another user. Switching between users can be a convenient way to save time.

If, for example, one of your children wants to log onto his account for a few minutes to print a document, switching users will make this possible without requiring you to close any of the programs you have opened.

To switch between user accounts, follow these steps:

A. Click on the Start menu button and select "Log Off," then select "Switch User." Now the user who needs to login into the system should click on his or her user name. Then, when they are done, to return to your own workspace, ask the new user to do the same or simply to choose to "Log Off," returning you to the welcome screen. Now, to return to do your own work, click again on your own Local User account.

B. If you are concerned about losing any of your important files in the event of a computer crash, then you should not use the "Switch User" function. Instead, you should save your files first, close your programs, and simply select Log Off your user account. This process may take longer than switching users, but it will be safer for your data. Additionally, logging off instead of switching users will free up the memory that was being used by your programs, making the computer run more efficiently for other users.

It is important to remind users that when they are done using the computer for the day, that they should save their work and log off of their own accounts. If someone tries to shut the computer down, while some users still haven't logged off from their accounts, a dialog box will open with the warning: "Other people are logged into this computer . . ." It is still possible to shut down the computer at this point, though other users may lose any unsaved work on the documents they left open.

Safely turning off your personal computer

After you are done using the computer for the day, you can turn it off or you can leave it on overnight. Leaving the computer on at all times has the advantage of not requiring you to wait the next day for the computer's boot sequence, which is the startup process during which the computer checks its internal parts and loads the Windows operating system.

If you want to leave your computer on overnight, however, you should plug it in to a good power surge protector or, even better, to a UPS unit and power protector, which will provide a few minutes of battery supply in case the electricity in your area goes out. This will give you time to shut down your computer properly in an electrical storm, preventing it from shutting down abruptly.

Before turning off you computer, save any files you have been working on and close all of your programs. Then, to turn off your computer, just click on the Start menu and select "Turn Off computer."

This is the way to work with the different options on the Turn off computer window:

A. To put the computer to "sleep", just click on the "Stand By" or on the "Hibernate" icon. To wake it up, just press the power button, and notice that the programs you left open will be open waiting for your input.
B. To turn off the computer, just click on the "Turn Off" icon once.
C. To restart the computer, just click on the "Restart" icon once.

If you've failed to save the work you were doing using one of your programs (such as a letter you were creating using Microsoft Word), at the time you chose to Turn Off or Restart the computer, then you will be reminded to do so.

If the computer freezes up while doing any of these tasks (i.e., if 20 minutes have gone by and the computer still hasn't responded), hold down its main power button for a few seconds to force it to turn off.

Part III
Working with Programs, Files/Folders in Windows

Chapter 6

Using computer Programs in Windows

What is a Computer program?

A computer program (also called a "computer application") is a set of software instructions that allows you to order a computer to perform a particular function; for example, the program that helps you keep track of your business expenses on an electronic spreadsheet.

Each program, installed on the computer, is represented on the Start menu, the Desktop, the My Computer program or in the Windows Explorer by an icon or small graphic, appropriately labeled with the name of the program it represents.

Windows Media
Player

On the above graphic you can see the icon that belongs to the "Windows Media Player" program. Double clicking on this icon will open this program, which allows you to work with all the music files found on your computer, in addition to letting you sync this music with MP3 players.

These are the some of the most widely used types of computer programs you will find on a Windows-based personal computer today:

- Word processors, such as Microsoft Word. This type of program is mostly used to create documents like letters and work resumes.
- Spreadsheets programs, such as Microsoft Excel This is the type of program with cells in which you type numbers; this program can then add these numbers using formulas you create to produce totals.
- Databases, such as Microsoft Access. This is the type of program that allows you to enter information, like customer data, onto a database file that can be queried later.
- Web browsers, such as Microsoft Internet Explorer. This is the type of program that, in PCs or even PDAs connected to the Internet, allows you to surf the Web.
- Email clients, such as Microsoft Outlook Express This is the type of program that allows users with an e-mail account of the POP3/IMAP/GMAIL type, to: compose, send, and receive email messages.

Bear in mind that most of the programs written for use on personal computers, are geared for the manual entering of data by you its user, whether that is text or numbers. Other programs don't need much user intervention, such as the antivirus program that protects your computer against computer viruses.

Intro to using computer programs in Microsoft Windows

When you buy a new computer, it will most likely arrive with the new Windows Vista or even the Windows XP operating system installed, and you will notice many icons visible on its desktop. In most cases, each one of these Icons represents a program installed on the computer, ready to be used. (There may also be a couple of unrelated icons, when you turn on a new computer for the first time, that when clicked on will direct you to web sites with commercial offerings.)

Above is the screenshot of the Windows XP Desktop of a Dell laptop I used to write this book. As you can see, there are many icons on its Desktop.

To open any program whose icon is on the Desktop, such as the Microsoft Works group of programs, just double click on it. The computer you use might have more or less icons on the desktop, depending on the brand and how much you paid for it.

Not all of the programs installed on the computer have their icon represented on the Windows Desktop. Later in this chapter you will learn to add the icons of your favorite programs to the Desktop.

The main parts of a typical program window

The window that opens on the screen (when you click or double click on a program icon) is called the program window, which is the most important window you will see and interface with while using the Microsoft Windows operating system.

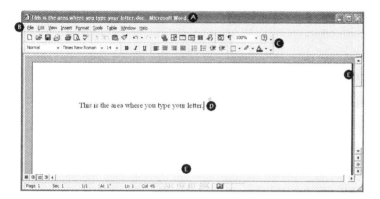

These are the main parts of a typical Microsoft program window (The above screenshot is from the Microsoft Word 2003 word processor):

A. This is the Title Bar; in a program window you will be able to read; the name you used to save your work and the name of the program it represents.
B. This is the main Menu Bar (note the labels; File, Edit, etc).
C. These are Toolbars (shown; the Standard and the Formatting one).
D. This is the main work area. Please note the blinking cursor, which gives you an idea of where the text you type will begin to show on the page.
E. These are the Scroll Bars; which are visible if the contents in the work area do not fit in the window. You can use them to move the hidden parts of a document into view.

One of the main advantages of using the Windows operating system is that, because completing some tasks on most programs for Windows is achieved in very similar fashion, once you learn to do something in one program, completing the same task in other programs is usually done the same way. For example, if you've learn to save a document using Microsoft Word, then you already have a good idea how to save the work you do while using Excel, because saving your work using most Windows programs is accomplish in the same way.

The blinking cursor

This is the bar like "|" character you see blinking (thereby the name blinking cursor) while in the working area of most programs that accept the manual input of text; such as in word processing documents, text boxes (for instance the text box of an online credit card application where you need to type your name) on some website, or even while naming a file. The main purpose of this blinking bar it to show you the exact point at which, if you were to type a letter or a character (such as the "#" sign), such letter or character will show (to the left of the blinking cursor) on the page.

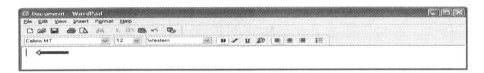

To see and follow the blinking cursor open the windows WordPad this way; click on the *Start* menu button, now move the mouse pointer up, and to the right over Run, and click on it. Now type the name *WordPad*, and press the *Enter* key. Notice that right after you **open** a word-processing document (such as WordPad), or even after clicking on a message text box, that the cursor blinks in its upper left corner.

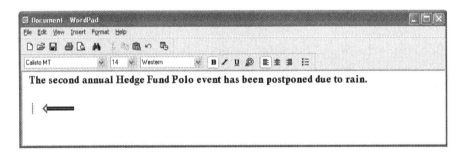

For instance type the sentence: "The second annual Hedge Fund Polo event has been postponed due to rain." Notice that as you type, the blinking cursor is always to the **right** of the last letter or character you've typed. Now press the Enter key twice to move the blinking cursor two lines down. Now the blinking cursor moved again to the **left** of the page (directly under the first letter of the first line).

Note

The only time you won't see (temporally) the blinking cursor, in one of the aforementioned situations, is when you've made a selection of text, or even after selecting a graphic.

How to change the position of the blinking cursor

As we saw on the previous page, the position of the blinking cursor will determine where on your document, the text you type will show. This most of the time is pretty straightforward: you commence working on a new word-processing document or a new e-mail message, which right away places the blinking cursor on the upper left corner of the page, and now you can type away. At times all you would want to do is: press the **Space bar** three times or even pres the Tab key once to move the blinking cursor a little bit to the right, to increase the indent of the first line in a paragraph.

These are keys you can use to move the position of the blinking cursor:

- The **Tab key**, that when pressed will move (each time you press it) the position of the blinking cursor to a preset position on the document you are working with. Bear in mind that if the blinking cursor is to the left of a word or line of text, and you press the Tab key, that that word or line of text will also move to the right. The tab key is ideal to move between text boxes, on web sites.
- The **Space bar**, that when pressed will create a space to the right of the blinking cursor. For instance after you type a word, press the Space bar to leave a space between the word you've just typed and the new word you are about to type. If the blinking cursor is to the left of a word or sentence, and you press the Space bar key, that word or paragraph will also move to the right.
- Use the four **Arrow** keys to navigate among text **you've written**, and even in some file management programs. For instance if you typed a letter, and forgot to write a word, then you can use the arrow keys to position the blinking cursor right before the point where you need to add the additional word. Now type it, and the next word will move to make room for the new one. The arrow keys cannot move the position of the blinking cursor to a place on the page where you haven't typed anything or pressed the space bar there before.

Alternatively move the mouse over the document you are working on, using the **Text select** pointer, and click **exactly right** before the letter where you want to commence writing (new text). For instance you can click before the letter you want to change *while* (before you click on save) in the process of adding a new post on the writing area of a web blog, such as Journalspace.

Or use the; Home (press it to return to the beginning of a line), End (press it to return to the end of a line), Page Down (press it to go onto the next page), and Page Up (press it to return to the previous page), to move the position of the blinking cursor in your documents.

The Insert, Backspace and Delete keys

Understanding how to use these keys while working in word processing type documents, text boxes on the web or even while naming a file, is very important, otherwise from time to time you might accidentally delete the work you've laboriously typed. Which are, the;

- **Insert** key. This is a key you can Toggle On/Off to overwrite/replace text with the new text you write. To enable it, just press it. For instance, if you need to replace the word "New York" with the word "Manhattan", then: a) place the blinking cursor before the first "N", and b) press the Insert key. Now start typing the word "Manhattan". But because the word "Manhattan" has one more letters that the word you are replacing (which is "New York") then you must press the Insert key again (after typing the last "a") to stop replacing text, otherwise you risk overwriting other words in the paragraph. There are two ways to know if the Insert key is enabled: a) if while working on a word processor, such as Word for Windows, on the status bar (at the bottom) it reads "Ovr" or overtype mode, and b) When the cursor is to the left of a word, and your typing deletes the letters to its right, then the Insert key is on. To disable this function, just press this key again. On a laptop computer keyboard this key will be labeled "Ins".
- **Backspace** key. This is a key that when pressed moves the blinking cursor one space back. Now if there is text, to the left of the blinking cursor, and you press it, then a letter is removed each time you press it. For instance if the cursor is blinking to the **right** of the word "Triangle", then pressing the Backspace key eight times will remove it.
- **Delete** key. Does exactly what its name implies, and it helps you delete, text, graphics or even files or folders (once they are selected). For instance if the cursor is blinking to the **left** of the word "Triangle", then pressing the Delete key eight times will remove it. To use it just press it. On a laptop computer this key will be labeled "Del".

Bear in mind that the Enter key also known as the return key, when pressed, moves the blinking cursor to the next line, creating a line break. If you press and hold the CTRL key and then the Enter key a new page break is created, and if you had (while working on a word processing document) a one-page letter before, then now you will have a two page one. Pressing this key will also help you work with some windows to answer a question posed by a dialog box window (such as is it ok to go onto the next page), and the choices are *Yes* or *OK* and *Cancel* or No. If you press the Enter key, then this is akin to clicking on the *Yes* or on the *OK* choice.

Working with computer programs in Windows

On the following pages you will learn how to open, work in, and close typical computer programs found on any Windows-based personal computer system. Even if you still have Windows 95 or Windows 98, and are not yet familiar with your computer, then you too can benefit from the instructions in this chapter.

There are many places on the computer from which you can open your programs, but most of the times you will find the program icons represented on either the Desktop or the Start Menu. You can also open a program from the My Computer program or the Windows Explorer, but this takes longer to do.

After a few weeks of using your computer you will become an expert on finding and opening the programs installed in it, but one of the most important decisions you have to make is selecting the right program to complete the project you want to work on.

Here are some examples of tasks you may want to complete, and the programs you can choose to do so with:

- You need to write your resume: Use a word processor, such as the Microsoft Word or WordPerfect, to create it.
- You want to retouch some of the pictures you've taken with your digital camera: Use an image/picture program, such as "Microsoft Picture It" or the program that was included with your digital camera.
- You need to create a running list of expenses with totals: You should use a spreadsheet program, like Microsoft Excel, to create a spreadsheet of your expenses.
- You need to find directions on the Internet: Use your Web browser, be that; Internet Explorer or Mozilla Firefox, to find them.

The advantage of using the Windows operating system is that you can work with many different programs at the same time (this is only restricted by the amount of available memory on your computer).

And later on in this chapter you will learn how to switch back and forth between the program windows you've opened, with very little effort.

Note

A typical computer bought at a computer store, will come included with most of the programs you will need to use, such as a word processing program, an Internet browser and an e-mail client.

Opening/launching a program from the Windows Desktop

When you turn on a personal computer with the Windows operating system, it will show you (unless you've programmed it to open a particular program first) the Windows Desktop right away.

Follow this graphic, of the Windows XP desktop, to understand how to open programs from here:

A. To open a computer program whose icon is on the Windows desktop, just double click on the icon with the name of the program. For instance if you want to surf the web using Internet Explorer, just double click on the "e" icon, action which will then open this Internet web browser.

B. To open a file (on this example "My resume.doc") you've previously saved to the Desktop, just double click on its icon. Now the program that you used to create it opens up, showing you the document you clicked on.

Bear in mind that when you choose to open a program it will open on its own window, which may take all or only part of the screen. If you've previously reduced the size of the program window for a particular program, and then closed it, the next time you re-open the same program its window should be of the same size as when you closed it.

The different areas of the Windows XP Start Menu

To work with the two panels that open after you click on the Start Menu: place the mouse pointer **under** the All Programs line (if you place the mouse pointer over the All Programs label, this will expand the complete list of programs installed on your computer).

Now you will, as you can see on the next screen capture, be able to see the programs and computer management tools accessible from here.

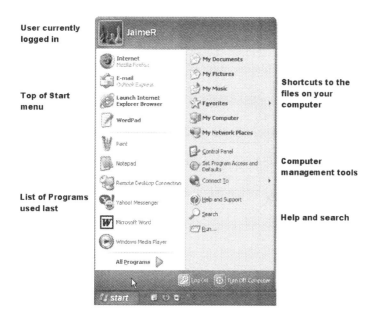

As you can see on this graphic, when you click on the Start menu button (Use this screen capture to familiarize yourself with the different areas of the Windows XP Start Menu), two panels open. That is unless it was changed to open in the Classical Windows 98 way.

To work with any of these programs just move the mouse pointer until you highlight the name of the program you want to launch, and then single click on it to open it. Remember that if you open a program by mistake, that you can close it by clicking on the X on its upper right corner.

The Start menu in previous versions of the Windows operating system, like Windows 98, opens differently, but once you click on the All programs group, opening programs is done the same way.

Quickly opening a program you've worked on recently

This is a new feature, only found on the Start menu of Windows XP, that gives you quick access to the programs you've open before, by placing the icons of the programs you've used last on the left panel of the new Start menu.

For instance if you've preciously opened the Microsoft Word 2003 word processor, then its icon should be listed on the lower part of the left panel of the Start menu. To open it again, do the following:

1. Click on the Start menu button.
2. Now move the mouse pointer up, over the left panel, and then click once over the Word Icon, or on any other program you need to work with.

The very top of this panel, above the dividing line, also contains the names of the icons of other programs that can also be opened from here. On the next page you will learn how to add the icons of programs you use frequently to the top of this menu.

Note   Bear in mind that as you open more programs, from the All Programs menu, that this list changes to reflect only the names of the programs you've used more recently.

Opening a Windows program from the "All programs" section on the Start menu

On a computer with the Windows operating system you will be able to open from the Start menu, starting from "All Programs," most of the programs installed on the hard drive, including the ones that might have been included with your personal computer system, and the ones you installed later.

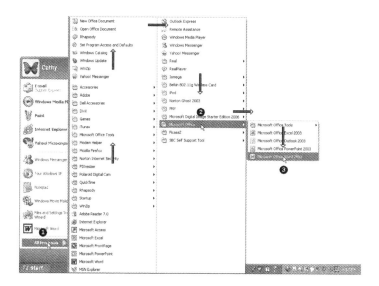

For example these are the steps to open a program, for instance Microsoft Word 2003 (if it is installed on your computer), from the Start menu:

1. First click on the Start menu button, then take the mouse pointer over "All Programs" and wait a few seconds, until you see its menu expand. In older versions of Windows click on Start, them Programs.
2. Now move the pointer to the right and then navigate through the menus to the Microsoft Office group (follow the arrows). On this example I moved the mouse pointer up, to the right, and then down. Bear in mind that if a name under the "All programs" list has a " ▶ " sign, then this is an indication that this is a group of programs that will appear when you put your mouse pointer over its name.
3. Now move the pointer over the Microsoft Office group of programs, then to the right, now a little bit down and click once over the Microsoft Office Word 2003 icon, to open/launch this program.

When a program opens up, it will be rendered on its own Window, and you will be able to start working on it right away—whether you are composing a letter with a Word processor—, or sending an e-mail message using your e-mail client program.

For example on the next screen capture you can see the program window that opens up when you select to open the Microsoft Word program.

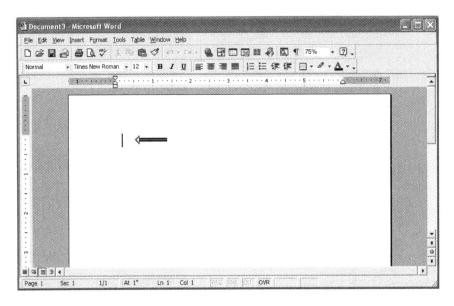

On this word processing program, the area in the middle (note the blinking cursor) is called the program's working area; it is akin to a virtual blackboard. On most programs that accept text, including on the areas on a web page in which you can type text (for instance an online credit card application), the blinking cursor indicates the location where your text will begin to show when you start typing.

Bear in mind that if the window of the program you've just opened overlaps the window of a program you opened previously, but you still want to use, then you can go back and forth between the two, or even between any other open program listed on the Windows Taskbar. This function is called multitasking, and is explained later in this chapter.

On the previous page you learned to open a program from the Start menu, but bear in mind that if the icon of the program you want to use is on the Desktop, then you can also open it from there.

Pinning a program to the top of the Start menu

In Windows XP you can add the icon of a program you want to use frequently to the top of the Start menu (Above the dividing line on its left panel), so that you can easily open it from there without having to search for its icon in the "All programs" menu or on the Desktop, every time you want to use it.

Here's how you display a program at the top of the Start menu:

1. First find the icon of the program you want to pin to the top of the Start menu, by looking for it from the All Programs menu.
2. Now right mouse click on its icon, and then select "Pin to Start menu."

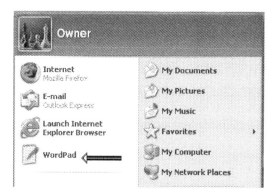

Now the program you chose is displayed among the pinned items in the area above the separator line on the top of the left panel of the Start menu. To open a program from the top of the Start menu just click on its name once. To remove it from the top of the start menu, just right mouse click on its name and select "Unpin from Start menu."

Adding a shortcut to a program on the Desktop

If you have dozens of programs, finding the one you want from the All Programs menu can be cumbersome. For this reason you might want to consider creating shortcuts to your frequently used programs on the Windows Desktop.

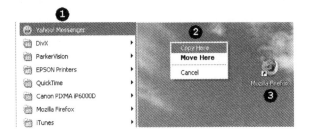

These are the steps to create a shortcut to a computer program:

1. First find on the Start Menu, under "All Programs", the icon of the program you want to launch from the desktop. When you find it place the mouse indicator over it. Now press and hold the right mouse button; then drag its icon away to any place on the Windows Desktop (free off icons).
2. Now release your finger from the icon, and left click on "Copy Here" or "Create a shortcut here."
3. Finally you can see the shortcut you've just created.

If there are any other open windows covering the Windows Desktop, then you must minimize or close them first, which can be done quickly by clicking on the "Show Desktop" icon on the Quick Launch Toolbar (next to the Start button). You will then be able to see the desktop right away so that you can follow the aforementioned steps. The steps to add the Quick Launch Toolbar to the Taskbar are outlined on Chapter one (Microsoft Windows XP basics).

Mozilla Firefox

For this example, I created a shortcut to the Mozilla Firefox Web browser, on the Windows Desktop. Ever since the windows Desktop is the first thing one sees after turning on the computer, then this program can now be quickly opened by double clicking on its icon there, without having to look for it on the Start menu.

Closing a Windows program

Once you finish working on a program, or when you want to stop using the computer, then save the work you've being doing (explained in great detail in chapter nine of this book) before closing its window. At the very least, you want to save the recent changes you've made, to a document you've already saved and named, before closing it.

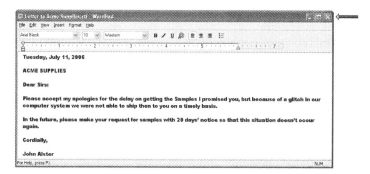

To close a computer program after saving your work (in some programs, such as a web browser, there is generally nothing to save), just click on the **X** on the right upper hand corner of the program window you were working with. You can also close a computer program by clicking over File, then selecting Close or Exit.

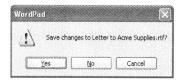

These are the steps to work on the Dialog box window that opens up when you attempt to close a program, without saving your work first:

- Click on *Yes* to save your work or just the changes to an existing document. If you haven't saved this document before, then you must also pick a name for it. This is explained in chapter nine of this book.
- Click on *No* to discard your work or, if you were working on a preexisting document, the changes you've made since the last time it was saved.
- Click on *Cancel* to return to work on the document.

If you ever need to leave your house in a hurry, and have many programs open, first save your work, then click on; the *Start* menu button, *Turn Off Computer* and on *Shut Down*, then all the open Windows will begin closing.

Switching among different open program windows

If you have too many program windows open, and want to switch back and forth to work with a different one that is open, then you can easily do so with just a few clicks of the mouse, or by pressing a few keys on the keyboard.

There are three common ways to switch between open windows.

1. When the other program window you want to work on is in view on the screen.

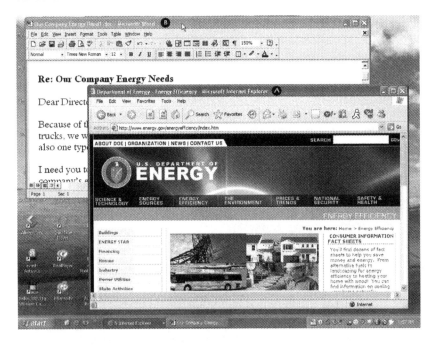

Please note the following, as you can see on the above image (in which two open windows are visible), while working with different program windows:

A. This is the active program window, meaning that it is the Window in front of all the other open windows. Please note that the color of its title bar (at the top), will be blue and also darker than the title bar on the other open Windows.
B. To switch to work with a different open program window that you can see, just click on its title bar or in its work area. In this example I clicked on the Word document, to bring it to the front.

2. When you cannot see the other program window you want to work with.

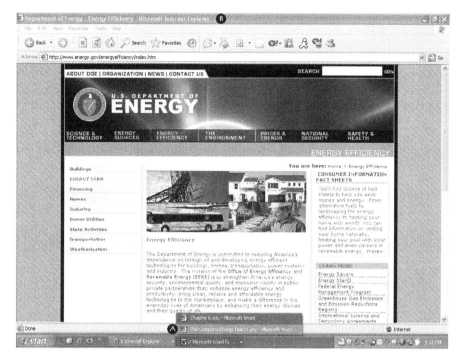

In the above image, a few program windows are open at the same time, but the active program window is taking up the whole screen. To use a different program (open in the background), bring its window to the front this way:

A. Click on the icon name/title of the other program you want to work with on the profile/footprint it leaves on the Taskbar. If there are too many open windows from the same program, then find the specific window you want to bring into view and click on its name (in this Example, I clicked on the "Our company . . . ") to bring it to the front.

B. You can also make the active window smaller so it's easier to see the other windows behind it; by just double clicking on the active window's title bar. Once the window you want to work is in view, click on its title bar to bring it to the front.

Or, if you want to move a window (that is not taking the whole screen), put the mouse pointer over the window's title bar, press and hold the left mouse button, and finally drag the Window to a new location on the computer screen.

3. When the program window you want to work with is out of view, you can use the keyboard combination ALT + TAB to bring it to the front.

This is a very useful feature that works well in all the different versions of Microsoft Windows,to switch among open windows. The screen capture below shows the typical square window that pops up when you use the ALT + TAB combination.

Here's how you switch between open program windows, using the ALT + TAB key combination:

- *Press and hold* the ALT key and then slowly tap the TAB key (while still holding the ALT key). Now you will see a dialog box with a list of Icons that represent your open Windows. When you tap on the Tab key you can see a round blue circle that changes position between the open programs each time you press the Tab key. You can also read information on the document that is selected to be open. In the example above you can read "Welcome to the Microsoft Corporate Web Site . . ." Lift your hands from the keyboard once the blue circle is over the Icon of the window you want to use.
- If you wish you could even go backward through the list of open Windows, pressing and holding the SHIFT key and then pressing the ALT + TAB keys. This is useful if you happen to have too many program windows open.

The main drawback of switching among open program windows this way (and even when switching among windows using the Taskbar) occurs when you still have not saved/named the document you are working with.

For example, depending on how many documents you might have opened; the unsaved ones on any one of these staggered lists will only show generic names. Such as: Document1, Document2, etc (for example if you are using Word for Windows). Because of this, you will need to open a few of these documents until you find the one that you are looking for. This can make switching between them very confusing.

Learning to select the right computer program to use for the project you have in mind

A computer with Windows XP or Vista installed or even one with a previous version of Windows (such as Windows 98), will put many different computer programs at your disposal. For this reason, for the novice, it might at first be a little confusing to choose the right program to complete the project you have in mind.

Here are some sample situations of computer projects you might want to complete, and the sequence and the programs you should use to complete them:

- To create a job resume, to be sent later (by e-mail) to a few prospective employers:

  1. Open a word processing program (such as Microsoft Word, WordPerfect, or the included WordPad) to compose your resume. Once you finish drafting your resume, save it (explained on chapter nine) and then close it.
  2. Now open your e-mail client program. If you have cable or DSL Internet service, use either the Outlook 2003 or Outlook Express e-mail client software. If you have AOL, use their software or you can even add your AOL e-mail account to your Outlook 2003 or Outlook Express client software (explained on chapter fourteen).
  3. Once the e-mail program is open, start composing the e-mail for the prospective employer, and then attach the resume file you created earlier (explained on chapter fourteen).
  4. Finally, send the e-mail message to prospective employers.

- To balance your checkbook:

  1. Use a program like intuit Quicken, which is one of the premier programs for this purpose (which is sometimes bundled with new computers so that people can try it). If it is on your computer, find and open Quicken.
  2. Now open the electronic calculator, a part of the accessories group of programs, and move it to the side, in case you need the calculator to figure out your expenses.
  3. When you are done with the program close it.

Today you can even balance your checkbook just by opening your Internet Web browser and visiting your bank's website, to sign up to use their online services. Later on you can even make payments online, which is a service that a lot of banks are offering free of charge, from the comfort of your own home.

- To create a wedding invitation letter, complete with directions:

  1. First open a word processing program (such as Microsoft Word, WordPerfect, or the included WordPad), then start composing your wedding invitation. Add the title and your information, finally save it (see chapter nine) to your hard drive.
  2. Now open your Internet Explorer or Netscape browser and visit the web site MapQuest by typing *http://www.mapquest.com* in front of the web browser address line. Follow the instruction to get driving directions to the place you want your guest to go.
  3. Once you find the driving directions, copy and paste (see chapter ten) these directions onto your word-processing letter.
  4. Finally print the letter if you intend to mail it, or save the letter to add it latter to an e-mail message as an attachment (see chapter fourteen).

- To download, edit, and print the photos you took with your digital camera:

  1. First connect the digital camera to your computer following the instructions that came with it. You can also use the Microsoft Scanner and Camera Wizard (see chapter sixteen).
  2. Now select the photos you want to download, to a folder of your choice on your computer hard drive.
  3. Later navigate to this folder and find the photos you want to work with (see chapter sixteen).
  4. If you want to edit them—to change the brightness or the size of the photo—you can use the graphic program that came with the camera, or you can use a program like HP Image Zone Express, which is free and can be downloaded from this URL; *http://www.hp.ca/portal/hho/ize/*
  5. Finally, when you are done retouching the photos, you can: a) save and print them using the same HP Image Zone Express software, or b) save and send them to friends via e-mail by using your e-mail program.

I should also remind you that for every program you can buy at a computer store, that there might be one that you can download and try for free on the Internet. You should check websites like the Nonags one at the URL; *http://www.nonags.com*, to see if you can find one of these programs.

 Remember to always follow the manufacturer's procedures when using a digital camera. And do not disconnect it while is copying photos to your hard drive.

- To find information on the Internet about a particular subject—for a school project, for example—which you will then copy and paste into a new document, to be e-mailed later to a teacher.

  1. First open a word processing program, then start composing your school project; add the title and your information, then save it (see chapter nine).
  2. Now open Internet Explorer or Netscape web browser and visit the site Google by typing *http://www.google.com* in the address line. If you already have a different search engine website in mind, just type that name in front of the address line. When using the Internet, always abide by the rules set by the website on how the information can be used.
  3. Type the information you'd like to find, and click on Search. Once you have it, use Copy and Paste (see chapter ten) to bring it into the word-processing document you created it during the first step. Edit it, and give credit to the source of the information (when credit is due). Save the document and then close it.
  4. Now open your e-mail client program. If you have cable or DSL Internet service, use either the Outlook 2003 or Outlook Express e-mail client software. If you have AOL, use their software or you can even add your AOL e-mail account to your Outlook 2003 or Outlook Express client software (explained on chapter fourteen).
  5. Compose the e-mail for your teacher or colleague and then attach the file to it (see chapter fourteen).
  6. Finally send the e-mail to the e-mail address of your teacher.

It is also important to check beforehand with the person who you are corresponding with, to ensure that they have the program you are using to create the work you are sending to them. Otherwise they might not be able to open/view the file you are sending to them. For example, if you are creating a budget using a spreadsheet made with Microsoft Excel, then make sure that the person (who will receive the file) has the Microsoft Excel program. If he/she doesn't, then they won't be able to open it.

Now if the person who you are sending a document, drafted using the Microsoft Word for windows word processing program, doesn't have Word, then it is still possible for your recipient to open it, as long as the file you are sending doesn't have any fancy formatting, using the WordPad word processing program that was included with your Window operating system, or even with a competing program such as WordPerfect, by just opening the file from the File menu (File and Open) and selecting, under Files of Type, Microsoft Word.

Installing a new computer program in Windows

The process to install/add a new computer program to your Windows computer is very easy to complete; just put the CD disk for the program into the CD drive, and follow the prompts to install it on your computer.

The main reasons why most programs need to be installed, as opposed to be run off of the CD they came on, are:

- The hard drive is much faster than the CD;
- The files on a CD are "read-only", but some programs need to update those files with your information;
- Once the files are on the hard drive you don't have to worry about carrying around (or losing) the CD.

The following example will highlight some of the steps needed to complete the installation of a computer program to your hard drive:

1. Start by pressing the eject button on your CD or DVD Rom drive to open it.

2. Now place the CD/DVD Rom disk on the CD/DVD Rom drive caddy, and close its door.

There are also other type of programs that don't need much space on your local hard drive called "Web enabled" programs: You only have to click on a very small file (called a Plug in) on a website, which will create an Icon you can use to access the program.

3. On most programs you will now need to accept the license agreement to use the software. Just click on the "I accept the agreement" prompt, then click on Next or Continue.

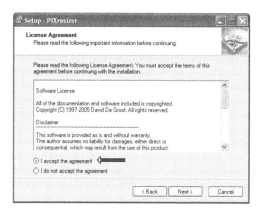

4. Now wait and follow the prompts; most of the time this involves clicking on the "Next" prompt as many times as it comes up. The program that you are trying to install might present you with different prompts, but the idea is the same; to bring the program into your computer hard drive so that it can be run from there, without you having to produce the install CD disk each time you want to use it.
5. When the installation is complete, click to accept the Reboot prompt.

Later on, when the computer finishes rebooting or restarting, you ought to see the icon that the install program created. It should be under the "All programs" menu, or, in the case of some programs, on the Windows Desktop.

To open/launch the new program just click once on its icon in the "All programs" menu, or if you see its icon is on the Windows Desktop (if the program or you has created an icon there), double click on it to open it.

Before purchasing a new computer program for an older computer, make sure that it is compatible with your system and the version of Windows it uses, because certain software has very stringed requirements and if your computer doesn't meet them you won't be able to run it.

 If the user account you used to login into the computer is of the Limited type, then you will need to ask a person with an administrator account to install the program for you.

How to remove a program you don't need anymore

Most computer programs take space on a permanent storage unit connected to your computer, most likely your hard drive. For this reason, you may from time to time wish to remove the programs you are not using—especially if your computer seems sluggish. Another reason why you might want to remove a computer program, from your Windows based system, is because is causing conflicts with other programs.

A program that has become dated and is no longer useful should also be removed—like a tax program that is only good for the current year.

To start the process of removing a program, click on the Start menu button, then move the mouse pointer up and to the right. Now click on Control Panel.

Add or Remove
Programs

Now double click on the "Add or Remove Programs" icon to open the next Window.

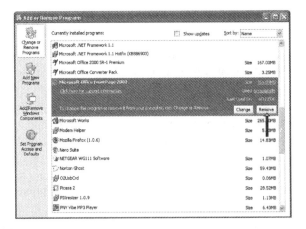

Now find the name of the program you want to remove and click on it to select it. Then click on "Remove" to start the process of removing it from your computer (bear in mind that you might be asked to produce the CD/DVD you used to install the program). Now follow the prompts to remove it, which may vary from program to program, which most of the times entails to click on Agree to remove the program. When this process if finished, restart your computer.

Components included with Windows XP

Windows XP offers you a whole array of programs included with the operating system. These are called Windows components, and they allow you to use the computer right away to complete differed tasks—like typing letters or organizing your computer hard drive using the Defrag program.

The four main groups of Windows XP components and some of their programs are:

Accessories:
- Calculator
- WordPad
- Paint

Games:
- FreeCell
- Solitaire

System Tools:
- Backup
- Disk Defragmenter

Communications and Entertainment:
- Volume Control
- Recorder
- Windows Media Player

Accessibility Wizard:
- Narrator overview.
- Magnifier overview.

To open any one of these programs, click on the Start button, now move the mouse pointer over "All Programs" (if you have a previous version of Windows click over "Programs"). Next over to Accessories and then over the name of the group the program you want to work with belongs. For instance take the mouse pointer over the System Tools group; to find the Disk Defragmenter program and when you find it click on it to open it.

Adding or removing a Windows Component

Most computers with Windows XP have most of the aforementioned programs installed by default, but if you find that the program you need to use is missing from one of the group of components you can install it on your computer. This is also accomplished by using the "Add or Remove Programs" tool in the Control Panel.

Here's the process to add or remove a Windows component. In this example we will remove and add the electronic calculator, which is a part of the "Accessories" group or windows components:

1. First click on the Start menu button, then take the mouse pointer up and to the right, and then click on the Control Panel icon. When it opens double-click on the "Add or Remove Programs" icon.
2. Now click on the "Add/Remove Windows Components" button, on the left side of this window, to open the "Windows Components Wizard."

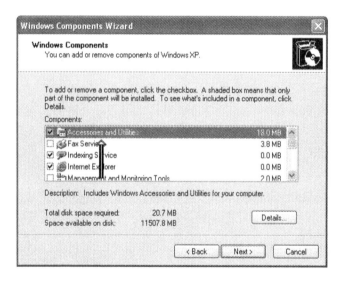

3. Now double click on the "Accessories and Utilities" group item because that is the group to which the Electronic Calculator belongs.

If a check box is shaded, then only some of its sub-components (under a particular group of windows components) are installed/ or selected to be installed. To add them all uncheck an item on this list and click on it again to add them all.

4. Now double click over the "Accessories" group, to open the following dialog window.

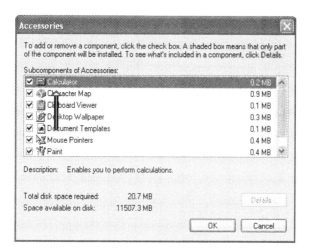

5. If you see a component that doesn't have a check mark, and you want to add it, simply click on the little box next to its name. If you want to remove a component, click next to the little box to remove its check mark.

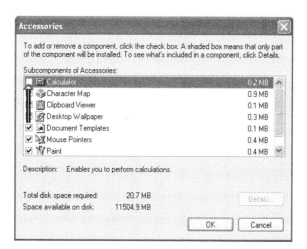

6. For example, if you wanted to remove the electronic calculator, just click on the box next to its name.

Don't remove a Windows component at a public place like a library, because the next person on that computer might need the program you've removed.

7. When you are done making changes click on "Ok" as many times as you need to in order to get back to the "Windows Components Wizard" dialog box.

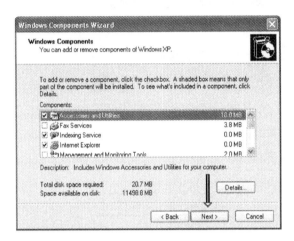

8. If you've made any changes to the Windows components then click on Next; otherwise, click Cancel. Now the component you wanted to add will be added, and the ones you wanted to remove will be removed.

At this point if you see a dialog box that prompts you to "Insert Disk," then insert your original Windows XP CD-ROM into your CD-ROM or DVD-ROM drive, and then click on "Ok." You can also tell Windows where you have your Windows installation files if you or someone has copied them to your hard drive. To do this, click on Browse in the "Files Needed" dialog box, and locate your Windows XP installation files. Now click on Open.

9. Finally, in the "Completing the Windows . . . ", click on Finish. If you did remove the Calculator, redo these steps and add it again.

Years ago computer hard drives didn't have much space on them. Because of this, many people used to remove Windows components to create space in the hard drive.

But on today's computer it doesn't make much sense to remove a Windows component because the hard drive can hold much more data than you can possible put there (unless you are making movies, and even then removing a Windows component doesn't clear enough space for even a one-minute movie clip).

Finding out the version of a program

The version release is a set of numbers assigned to a computer program when it is first released/ or even when it gets updated. A new number is assigned to a program (called the version release) every time the program is updated; this assignment can sometimes be nothing more than a single letter to indicate the version level or the year it was released. Microsoft Office 2003 is one example, and the name indicates that some changes were made from the previous version (2000).

To find out the version release of a particular software program you own:

1. Open the program you want to enquire about.
2. Click on Help, go down to the "About" line, and click on it.

The next graphic shows the result of this query for a copy of Microsoft Windows Messenger.

In this copy of the Windows messenger you can see that the version release is 4.7 (4.7.2009); this information might be requested by technical support people trying to help you with a software problem. You also may need this when you are deciding whether to upgrade the software you currently own.

For example, there is a program called Acrobat Reader, and some websites that use Acrobat documents might require you to have a certain version of this program. Follow the aforementioned steps on this or any other program, to find the version number installed on your computer.

Chapter 7

Using computer files and folders in Microsoft Windows

Introduction to using computer files and folders in Windows

A computer file consists of bits of data recorded by a computer program to your computer's hard drive or another permanent-storage medium. Each file is given a distinctive name, by you the user, and will serve as a record of the work you have done using a computer program. Once your work is saved as a computer file, to your computer hard drive or to a removable storage device, then you will be able to return to it at a later time.

Letter to DR. Donald L. Greer PhD.doc   19 KB   Microsoft Word Document   4/25/2006 11:48 AM

A file can be easily recognized by its name, which you chose at the time you saved it. In the example above, I have named a file "Letter to Dr. Donald L. Greer PhD". The file name, in Windows, can be up to 255 characters long.

A folder is a virtual storage unit where you can save your files. By separating files into different folders, you can better organize your computer work. The example below shows one possibility: organizing your work according to the year in which it was done.

2005   2006   2007   2008

This method of archiving your computer work can be especially useful if you have a business.

My Documents
  2006
    Personal
    Work

On the screen capture above—showing the folder for 2006—you can see how it is possible to divide your work further within a given year. You could, for example, create two additional folders within the 2006 folder—one containing personal files, and another containing files related to your work. You could then create additional folders within each of these folders: one possibility would be to create a different folder for each month of the year.

How computer files are created

You create a computer file whenever you use a program's save function. Other files are created automatically by some of the programs on your computer. These automatic files might include, for example, logs of failures or successes in connecting to the Internet.

Here are some examples of how files might be created:

- You open a word-processing program to type a letter and then choose to save it. The resulting file is an electronic record of the letter that can be opened at any time to make changes or to print the document.
- You take some pictures with your digital camera, and then transfer these pictures to your computer. Now they can be easily found and then accessed by opening the folder in which you saved them.

In general, there are two main types of computer files that you should know about:

- Program files
- Data files

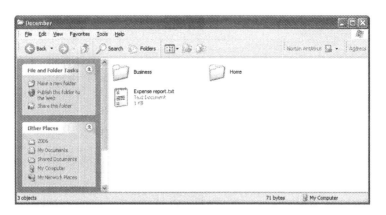

In the graphic above, you can see the two main types of objects you will work with while using Microsoft Windows. The folder like symbols (in yellow) represents computer folders (which may contain files and sub-folders); the other object you see here (named "Expense report") is an individual file. Please note that the "Expense report" file and the Business and Home folder are contained under the same December folder, who's name you can read on the title of this window.

The difference between program files and data files

A program file is the type of file that is needed for a program to work properly. At the beginning of the personal-computer era, some programs were composed of as little as a single file; a program today might be comprised of over a thousand files.

 Program Files

In Windows, the folder in which program files are placed by default (when you install a new computer program) is called, appropriately, the *My Programs Files* folder. (If you wish, at the time you are installing a program you can choose to save it to a different location on your hard drive, but I do recommend against this) In some versions of Windows, program files in the My Programs folder are hidden from view as a precaution to avoid their accidental deletion.

A data file is a file that you created using a computer program. Saving a letter in Microsoft Word will create a data file, as will downloading digital photos from your digital camera, to your computer hard drive.

My Documents

In a personal computer running Windows, the suggested folder for storing data files is the My Documents folder; under which you will also find three distinctive folders; My Music, My Pictures and my Received Files that you can use to better organize your computer files.

The main difference between data files and program files is simple. If you delete one or more program files, the program to which they belong may no longer work. On the other hand, if you delete one of your data files, the program used to create it will still work; you will simply have lost the work you did and saved to the file.

Now if you accidentally delete a folder with programs files and the program whom those files belonged ceases to work, then you can correct the problem by reinstalling the program from its original disk. The data files you already created using the program you've deleted should not be affected—the only exception being a situation in which you have deleted a program that mixed data files with program files on the same folder, in which case it may not be possible to recover the data files.

Creating a new data file

The process of creating a new data file is simple. Any time after you launch a program—even if you have not yet typed a single word—you can simply invoke the program's Save function. A dialog box will open, asking you what you would like to call the document (you can even use the the name the program is suggesting you use, which it takes from the heading of you document) and where you would like to save it. Once you have provided that information and clicked on "save," a new data file will be created.

For example, to create a data file using the program Notepad:

1. Click on the Start Menu, and then move the mouse pointer to All Programs.
2. Place the mouse pointer over Accessories, now to the right and down.
3. Finally click on Notepad to launch the program.

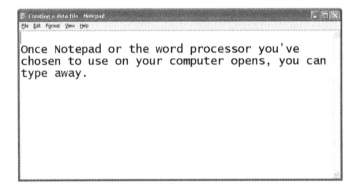

4. Now choose to save the document by clicking over File and then selecting Save. Now type a distinctive name for it (in front of File Name), and click on Save to create a new data file.

Once you save the Notepad document in the form of a data file with a distinctive name, it will remain available in the permanent storage device where you've saved it to, until you delete it.

Note

In chapter nine, you will learn all the different ways to save your work to a permanent-storage unit connected to your computer locally or to one (which you have access) on a LAN.

Recognizing a file by its extension

When a program creates a data file (after clicking on Save or Save As) you'd; given it a name and chosen where to save it to, the program automatically adds something called a file extension to the file name you chose. The file extension can be thought of as the last name of a data file. And it is useful because it makes the identification of files easier, by you and your computer programs.

Suppose you type a letter in Microsoft Word and saved it with the name "Doctor appointment date." After that name, Word automatically adds a dot "." and three letters—".doc", that identifies the file as a "word document."

Doctor appointment date.doc

The file extension can be useful in the following specific ways:

- If, while browsing the files saved in a folder, you see the file "Doctor Appointment date.doc" and double-clicked on it, the operating system will immediately recognize the file as one of the Word type. It will then launch Microsoft Word so that you can work on it.
- When you are searching for files, you can narrow your search parameters to include only files created by a certain program. If, for example, you wish to search only within your saved PowerPoint files, you can do so by providing the power-point extension (ppt) to your computer's search function, like this "*.ppt"

This is a list of common file extensions and the programs associated with them:

- .bmp; denotes a graphic file created with Windows Paintbrush.
- .doc; denotes a file created using Microsoft Word for Windows.
- .exe; is the extension of most program files on which your programs depend to work properly.
- .Jpg; is a type of graphic file, and is created by programs like Adobe Photoshop. Most digital cameras also create .jpg files. They can be easily manipulated once they are copied to a local hard drive.
- .txt; denotes a plain-text file, meaning a type of document that only contains text and no fancy formatting, for example the type of documents you create with a word processor like Notepad.
- .xls; denotes a file created with Microsoft Excel for Windows
- .ppt; denotes a file created with Microsoft PowerPoint for Windows

Being familiar with file extensions can be quite useful. You will be able instantly to ascertain whether your computer has the program required to open a particular file. If, for example, you receive an e-mail attachment with an .xls extension (for an Excel type of file) and you know that you don't have this program installed in your computer, then you should ask the sender to send you the information using a different program, or to print it and send it to you via regular mail.

If your computer doesn't display the file extensions when you look in your My Documents folder or any other file-management window, this probably means that the file extensions have been keep hidden (this is the default setting). You can easily change this setting by: double clicking on the My Documents folder on your desktop, then click on the Tools menu item, and finally over Folder Options.

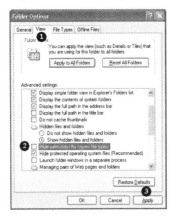

Using the dialog-box window that opens, follow the steps below to display the hidden file extensions:

1. Now click on the View tab.
2. Click next to "Hide extensions for known file types", to uncheck it.
3. Click on Apply, and then click on OK to close the dialog box.

Now you will be able to see the three-letter extensions for all your files when working in the My Computer program, Windows Explorer or the dialog box that open when you elect to Open or Save a file. If you can't see the file extension, while using one of the aforementioned programs, then click over the view menu, then on File Details.

Tip

When I write about a "file with the same name and file extension", you can replace "extension" with "type". For instance Word adds a .doc at the end of the file, so the .doc files are files of the Word type.

How to work with computer folders

A computer folder in a permanent storage device (such as a hard drive) has a purpose similar to that of a regular manila folder: it is a container that helps you organize your computer work so that you can find it later with relative ease. Although it is possible to save all your data files on the hard drive without placing them in folders, it is preferable, for the sake of organization, to use computer folders.

A computer folder can hold many different kinds of files: documents, music, pictures, videos, and programs files. Windows automatically creates some computer folders, like the My Documents folder, while other folders you will create.

The next graphic represents the icon of a typical Windows folder, which appears yellowish on the Desktop, in the My Computer window, or in Windows Explorer.

A computer folder stores files according to the following rules:

- Any one folder can hold as many files as the disk space on the particular storage device you are working with. Once you fill a folder up to the maximum capacity of the particular storage device you are working with, then you cannot put any more files into this particular folder or any other folder in the hard drive.
- No folder can contain two files with the same name and the same file extension, but **different** folders can contain copies of the same file. If you try to copy a file to a folder that already contains a file of that name and same file extension, the operating system will ask whether you want to overwrite the existing file with the new file.

For instance you cannot have two copies of your résumé, named Resume. doc, on the same 2005 folder, but you can create an additional sub-folder under the 2005 folder, called Personal and keep the same copy of your work resume there. On the next page I will expand more on how to store files (even ones with the same name), to different folders, to better organize and find your work later.

Folders are also knows as directories; if you are asked to create a folder on a specific directory, you are being asked to create a folder within a folder.

The method of storing computer files suggested earlier—by saving them to folders labeled by year, and divided into sub-folders organized by month—helps avoid the dilemma posed by the operating system's requirement that a folder might not contain two files with the same name and file extension. You may, for example, have ten copies of your résumé on your hard drive, corresponding to different times in your career. By placing them in different folders according to the year in which they were created, you can avoid the need to give each file a different name.

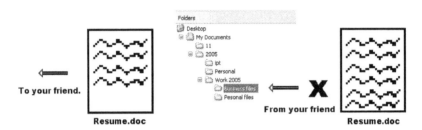

You can make use of a similar strategy if you and someone else plan to send a document back and forth to each other (via e-mail). Consider the following example:

1. You wish to send a copy of your résumé to a friend for editing. You attach the file Resume.doc, that currently resides in the "My Documents\work 2005\Business files" folder, to an e-mail message. This process is explained on chapter 14 (using the Outlook 2003 or Outlook Express e-mail clients).
2. Later on, you get the same file Resume.doc back—once again, attached to an e-mail message. Although the file has the same name, is different inside, because it contains the changes your friend has made.
3. If you try to save this edited Resume.doc file to the original folder ("My Documents\work 2005\Business files"), the operating system will return an error message, asking whether you wish to overwrite the original file. If you answer Yes, the original file will be replaced by the new edited file your friend sent you.

Now to preserve the original file, which you want to keep as a backup, save the edited file (with the changes your friend made) to a different folder in your hard drive or even to a removable storage unit. Bear in mind that when you have two version of a file with the same name (in different folders), that when you update one the other one doesn't automatically gets updated. Alternatively, you can save the new file to the same folder as the original file by changing its name slightly, at the time you are saving it: you could call it, for example, Resume1.doc. Just remember is newer.

The My Documents folder

This is the default folder for storing personal data files in Windows. In all the different editions of Windows, it is represented by a shortcut on the Desktop. Under the My Documents folder you will also find three distinctive folders; My Music, My Pictures and my Received Files, that you can use to appropriately save your music, your photos and the files you download from the Internet, or for any other purpose.

To open the My Documents folder and work with the files within it, simply double click on the My Documents icon on your Desktop (on this screenshot you can see it on the upper left corner). You can also access the My Documents folder whenever you are saving or opening document files from within a program on your computer.

You can create additional folders within the My Documents folder according to your needs: for example, you may wish to create folders called My Work, My Letters, and so on. Each of these folders can, in turn, contain subfolders; you could create, for example, folders for 2007 and 2008 within the My Work folder.

Although the operating system always suggests that you use the My Documents folder to store your work, it is also possible to save your work anywhere you choose on the computer hard drive

Creating a new folder

There are a few programs in Windows from which you can create a new folder (such as the Windows Explorer or even on the dialog box that opens when you select to save a document). Right now, you will learn to create a new folder starting from the My Documents folder.

First, double-click on the My Documents folder on the Desktop. A new window will open. In this new window, click on "Make a new folder" (on the left panel). You can also start creating a new folder by clicking over File, down over *New*, and then by clicking on Folder.

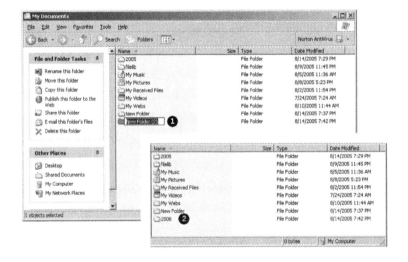

To create the new folder:

1. First click inside the "New Folder" cell. Once you see the cursor blinking inside it, you can delete the suggested name ("New Folder") using the backspace key and now type a name of your choosing.
2. Once you have typed the new name, click once outside the cell; the operating system will now accept the name you just typed.

If there is already another folder with the same name, at the same folder level you are creating this new folder, then you will be prompted to type a different name.

Navigating the folders tree

In order to fully take advantage of all that a Windows based personal computer has to offer, you must, in addition to be able to create new files and folders, learn to navigate what is called the folder tree on the Windows operating system.

The folder tree starts at the root of each drive on your PC—for example, the local drive (C:).

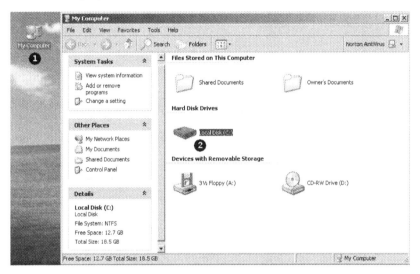

To learn how to navigate the folder tree, follow these steps:

1. First double-click on the My Computer icon, on the Windows Desktop. If you have Windows XP, and you don't see the My computer icon, then see chapter one to learn how to add it to the Windows desktop.
2. Now double-click on any of the drives, on this example there is only one drive, under Hard Disk Drives (in this instance the Local Disk (C:)).

Please think of this process as opening a virtual drawer, in which you might find another drawer, which depending on the way your computer is setup, might or not have another drawer, this with the purposed or separating and organizing your computer work.

Note

At times while you are navigating the folders tree, the right panel will turn blue, but no folders or files will show. Click on *Show the contents of this folder* to be able to see them.

From here on, most of the files and folders are organized in a logical way. Although you can create folders anywhere (for instance at the very root of a drive, such as the Temp folder on the next screen capture, which I created at the root of the C: drive), it is better to create data folders (where you will keep your work) only under the My Documents folder, so that later on you can easily find the files you saved there.

Below is the window that opens when you double-click on one of the drive letters in the My Computer window (the Local Disk (C:)):

Please notice the following information on this window:

A. On the blue bar at the top of the window, you can read the name of the drive or folder whose contents you are viewing on this window, in this case: the contents of the Local Disk C:

B. Notice the Documents and Settings folder. This is where most users will choose to keep their work. Double-click on this folder to find your files (assuming that you have been saving them there).

Please bear in mind, if you begin to look for your work this way (by double clicking on the My Computer icon first), that your work will appear (again if you've saved it under the My Documents folder and after double clicking on the Documents and Settings folder), right under the **user name** which you used to log onto the computer. For instance if you are using the user name JohnD, your files will be under the JohnD folder, although it is easier to just double click on the My Documents folder in your Windows Desktop, to find it.

If in doubt about the name of the user name currently logged in, then click on the Start menu button and read the label at the very top of this menu: this is the name of the user currently logged in.

After double-clicking on the user name, which is logged at the moment, on the Documents and Settings folder in, you will again be shown another list of folders, that correspond to the workspace or profile created by the operating system to shield your work from other users.

Now click on the My Documents folder, and then click on a few of the folder icons you see on the right-hand panel, to navigate them. Alternatively, you can also open the My Documents folder, by double-clicking on the My Documents icon on the Desktop.

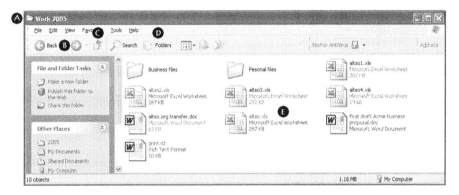

Following this screen capture, you will learn to recognize the different elements that will help you work with your files and folders:

A. Here you will see the name of the folder or drive whose files and folder are visible on the main panel to the right. In this example it reads (Work 2005)

B. Use these arrows to navigate the folder tree and return to folders *you've already opened*. Clicking on the left arrow will take you closer to the root level of the drive (or the My Documents folder), while clicking on the right arrow will take you one level away from the root of the folder tree.

C. Click on the up arrow, to return to the folder that preceded the contents you are looking at. The top level is the Desktop level; once you reach it, the up arrow is no longer available.

D. Click on the Folders icon to see folders and files using the same hierarchical view available in Windows Explorer (explained in detail in chapter eight).

E. In this panel you will see the files and folders contained within the folder whose name appears as the title of the window (in this example, Work 2005). To open one of these subfolders (yellow icons), and see its contents, simply double-click on its icon.

What is the path to a file or folder?

The path is the virtual address on a computer hard drive assigned to a file or folder by the Windows operating system, at the time you saved it or moved it. Most of the times you never have to think of the path of a file or folder, but this is very useful to know if you have to frequently exchange files with co-workers, by e-mail or by other means.

First draft Acme business
proposal.doc
Microsoft Word Document

C:\Documents and Settings\Owner\My Documents\2005\Business files

In the graphic above, you see a sample file, called "First draft Acme business proposal.doc," and also the file's virtual address on the computer, which can be broken up in the following way:

1. The first thing you see in the virtual address is C:\. This tells you that the file was saved on the C: drive, which is the first local fixed hard drive. (If you have more than one hard drive or a removable drive, this part of the address might read D, E, F, etc.—up to the letter Z.)
2. Next comes "Documents and Settings," which is the standard location for the files and folders of all the computer's users.
3. The third part of the virtual address refers to the name of the user, in this case Owner. If your user name were Charlie034, this part of the address would read \Charlie034\.
4. Next comes \My Documents\, which is a folder that Windows creates for the documents of a particular user.
5. Finally, there is a folder called 2005, under which there is also another folder called Business files, under which the file "First draft Acme business proposal.doc" is saved.

For instance if you wanted to open this file, after opening the program you used to create it (such as Word) click on File, then on the Open command. Now navigate to the My Documents folder (at this point is not important to think of the part of the address before the *My Documents* folder), the 2005 folder, the Business files folder, and then finally double-click on the First draft Acme business proposal.doc proposal file to open it. Alternatively you can also use the Windows Explorer or the My computer program, to find this file and open it. Chapter nine explains the process of saving and opening files in a lot more detail.

Finding and extracting the path of a file or folder

A modern computer is filled with thousands of files in many different folders. This great profusion of files at times might make it necessary to know how a particular file can be located—and that involves finding the path to it.

For example, you may want to find the path to a digital photo saved in your hard drive in order to send it to someone as an e-mail attachment, from your AOL software. To do so:

1. First right click on the name of the file or its thumbnail (if for example you are working with digital photos and that is how they are represented on the window you are working with), click on the *Properties* option.
2. In the dialog box that opens, you will see the word "Location," followed by the file path. Place the mouse pointer right over the file path (see the mouse pointer on the screenshot) and right click again, and then click on "Select all".
3. Now right click again on the path name, which is now highlighted, and on the dropdown menu, click "Copy". Alternatively, if you are using Windows Explorer, right click in front of "Address" and then select Copy, to copy the address of the folder at which level the file or files you want to send are saved.

If you are working with the files created by your digital camera, and they don't render on your computer screen like little thumbnails, click on View, and then click on Thumbnails. To see all the details for a file (like the date it was created), click over details, on the same menu.

Once you copied the path of a file, and for example you use American Online, is very easy to attach this file to a new AOL e-mail message. To begin open your AOL software, sign on to get a connection to the internet, and right away start composing a new message this way: press and hold the CTRL key and then the M one, or click on "Write" (on the AOL toolbar.)

These are the steps to use the path you previously copied, to find and attach a file or files to an e-mail message:

1. To begin click on Attach File, to open the "Attach File" window.
2. Now click on the cell in front of "File name", and then press and hold the *CTRL* key and then the *V* one, to paste the path of the file you want to send, and then press the "Enter" key, to see right away the contents of the folder, in which the file or files you want to send resides.
3. Now double click on the name of the file you want to send, to attach it to the e-mail message. If you want to select all the files saved on this folder, then press and hold the CTRL key and then the A one. If you only want to send a selected few, then press and hold the SHIFT key and then single click on the name of each file you want to send, and when you are done click on "Open". Finish the e-mail message, and then click on the Send button to send it.

If you have a POP3 e-mail account, which is the type of e-mail service you get with a regular ISP (like Cablevision Optimun Online), the process of attaching a file(s) is much easier to complete, just following the steps found on chapter 14.

If you select to copy (for instance a path), and then later select to copy something else, then the clipboard will produce on the screen (when you use Paste) the contents of the last time you invoked the copy command.

Chapter 8

Guide to Windows Explorer

Introduction to Windows Explorer

Windows Explorer is the primary file-management program (the other one is the My Computer program) found on every version of Microsoft Windows released after Windows 3.1. Using Windows Explorer you can easily view and manage the drives, folders, and individual files on your Windows personal computer. If your computer is a part of a local area network (LAN), then you can also use Windows Explorer to access files on folders on your network (provided you have the proper access).

Windows Explorer allows you to perform the following tasks:

- Create new folders to better organize your work. If, for example, you have a business with monthly budgets, you might want to create different folders for each year and also for each month you have done business, to save your work in, so that later you can find those saved files more quickly and easily.
- Copy files and/or folders from one folder to another to create backups or duplicates of your computer work, in case the original files are lost.
- Move files or folders from one folder to another. This function is useful when you are running out of space on your main hard drive and want to move data to a new hard drive, or when you want to move all the contents of a certain folder to another location on the same hard drive.
- Open programs or files. You can open files or programs by double-clicking on them in the Windows Explorer window. Programs files are identified by the ".exe" file extension. This can be especially useful when you cannot find a program listed on the Start menu. You can also open files you've saved. For instance a letter you wrote to a colleague that can just be opened by double clicking on its name, now the program that you used to create will be launched showing you the text of the letter.
- Delete files or folders to organize your computer and clear up space on the hard drive. If your computer seems sluggish, you may be running out of space on your hard drive. (Unlikely to happen on a new computer.) Should the need arise; you can use Windows Explorer to delete groups of files or folders.

The main difference between the presentation of the Windows Explorer included in Windows XP/2000 and the one included with Windows 98/Me is in the way you can choose to display files. For example, in Windows XP/2000 you can choose to see thumbnails (or little previews) of your digital photos files.

Additionally, it is just a matter of personal preference whether you decide to use the Windows Explorer or the My Computer program to manage your computer drives, folders or files. Whichever one you choose to use, will bring you the same results.

How to open Windows Explorer

To start working with Windows Explorer, you have to open /or launch it from the Start menu the following way:

1. Click on the Start menu button (almost always located on the lower-left side of your screen).
2. Now move the mouse pointer over to All Programs, then up and to the right until you reach the Accessories group, and then to the right.
3. Finally, move the mouse pointer down and then look for the Windows Explorer program icon. When you find it, click on it to open it.

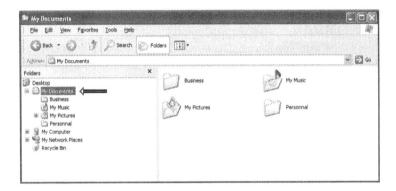

Right now, on this screen capture of the Windows Explorer window, the folder that appears selected in the left panel is the "My Documents" one. The "My Documents" folder is the main recommended repository in which you can save your work. If you choose, you can also save your work to any other location on a fixed hard drive, removable drive, or network drive to which you have access. On the right panel you will see the contents of the drive or folder selected on the left panel.

One of the nice features of Windows Explorer is its two-panel display function. When you click on a folder in the left panel, that folder's contents are displayed on the right panel. This allows you to see the contents of folders while still retaining a view of the complete hierarchical organization of your folders.

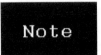

Note   Clicking on the Start button, then on Run, and then typing *Explorer* into its text field, and finally pressing the Enter key will also open the Windows Explorer.

Alternatively, to quickly open Windows Explorer; take the mouse pointer over the Start menu button, press the right mouse button, and then click on "Explore."

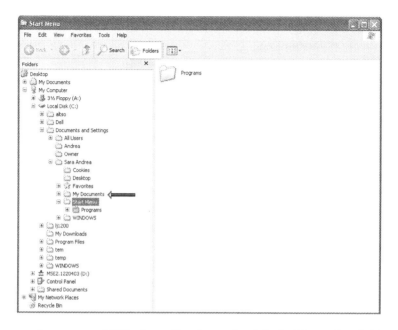

When you've opened Windows Explorer in this fashion, the folder that appears selected right away is the "Start Menu" one, in which you can see the subfolder "Programs", which contains most of the programs installed on your computer.

To work with your files, just click on the "My Documents" folder in the left panel, or on the name of the one that contains your files. The contents of the folder you chose will be displayed on the right panel.

In Windows XP and Windows 2000, a separate "My Documents" folder exists for each user name that you have created on your computer. If you log in as **User A** and save files to the "My Documents" folder, these files will be stored in a separate folder than they would be if you were logged in as **User B**. To keep them apart, the operating system creates a different "My Documents" folder for each local user account.

Bear in mind that other users with Administrative rights might be able to access your files from their own account. If this concerns you, read chapter 5 to lower their permissions to a limited account.

How to identify the different objects you see on the Windows Explorer window

Because of the fact that the Windows Explorer displays the complete hierarchical structure of the files, folders, and drives on your Windows computer, at times the information it provides can be a little intimidating. To follow the information on this page, open the Windows Explorer using the way shown on the previous page.

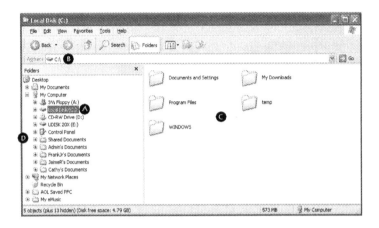

Please keep this in mind, when working in Windows Explorer:

A. Click on the minus sign (-) to the left of "Local disk . . . ", to hide this branch. Remember clicking on the Plus sign (+), un-hides a branch.

B. This is the Address Bar, where you can see the path or virtual computer address of the folder or drive that is selected in the left panel

C. These are the folders and files or both contained within the folder that you have selected in the left panel.

D. Now on the left panel you will see:
- The Windows Desktop. When you click on this icon you will see, on the right panel the same icons as what you see on your Windows Desktop
- The "My Documents" folder, containing any files you've saved there.
- The "My Computer" directory structure, which will display all of your fixed and removable drives such as the local disk (C:) and the removable storage devices, such as the (E:).
- "My Network Places," which provides access to any network resources (On a LAN) that you are authorized to access.
- The Recycle Bin, which holds the files you've deleted.

How to display the address bar in Windows Explorer

A new computer with Windows XP has the capacity to store thousands of files, such as word documents or digital pictures, on the local hard drive or on a removable storage unit. Because of this, at times it can seem daunting to find and use some of the files you have created and saved on your computer.

Let's say, for example, that you use American Online and want to send your children some of the photos you've taken of your vacation. You are able to see these photo files in Windows Explorer, but you can't find them from the AOL 9.0 program, to attach them to an email message. Now, if you knew the virtual address (or "path") of the folder in which these files were located, then it would be much easier to find them from your AOL email program. In order to find out the folder's path, you should use the Address Bar.

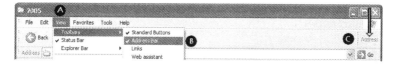

This is the way to add the Address Bar to Windows Explorer:

A. First click on "View", and then move the mouse pointer down over "Toolbars".

B. Now move the mouse pointer over "Address Bar" to select it (if is not already selected). If "Lock the toolbars" is selected in this dropdown menu, meaning it has a check mark, click on it to uncheck it.

C. If you are still unable to see the Address Bar, but instead see a label that says "Address . . ." at the right of the toolbar, then; place the mouse pointer over it (see the arrow), now **press and hold down** the left mouse button, and then drag this toolbar down and to the left until is parallel to the Standard toolbar.

Now you will see the complete path, or virtual address, of the folder you are working with. Click on this line, and then right mouse click on it, select copy. Now you can copy and paste the name of the folder, to the attach window to an e-mail messages using your AOL program (as shown on the previous chapter 7).

How to change the view options of files or folders

In Windows Explorer as well as when you are using the My Computer program or even while working on the dialog box window that opens when you select to save or open a file you can select to way you want to view the many folders and files saved on your computer.

These are the view options; you can use to work with your folders and files:

- Filmstrip, which will allow you to view picture files in a slideshow fashion. This view is offered only in the "My Pictures" folder or in folders that Windows XP recognizes as picture folders.
- Thumbnail, which will display small previews of your graphic files or big icons of your regular files.
- Tiles, which will display icons alphabetically across columns. Besides each icon will be the complete name of the file or folder it represents.
- Icons, which will display the icons of your computer files and folders alphabetically across columns.
- List, which will show you files or folders displayed alphabetically in a single column. This view allows you to see many more items at the same time.
- Details, which displays files or folders alphabetically in a single column, along with various pieces of information about each file and folder. Such as the file's name, size, type, and the date it was last modified.

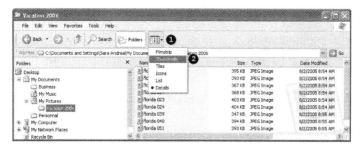

To change the view of files or folders:

1. First click on the view button on the Windows Explorer toolbar or on any other dialog box windows that has an icon similar to this.
2. Now click to select the view you want to use.

You can change the views of your files and folders, which is particularly useful when browsing for photos in Windows Explorer, as many times as you need to.

For example after opening the Windows Explorer and selecting the Thumbnail view for a folder that holds digital photos, they will be rendered as previews of those photos, that will make it easier to choose the one you want to work with.

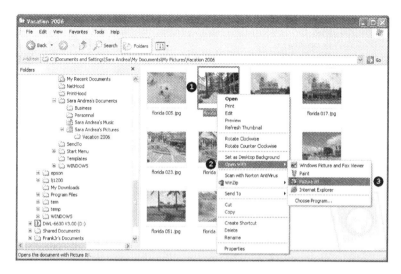

These are the steps to open photo files with a photo-editing program, to work with them:

1. To begin: find and click on the name of the folder (left panel) that holds the photos you are looking for and then right-click (on the right panel) on the particular digital photo you want to fix.
2. Now drag the mouse pointer down until it highlights the "Open With" option.
3. Finally mode the mouse pointer to the right, and click to select the program you want to use to edit this photo from the list that appears to the right. For this example I chose to use a program called "Picture it".

Instead of going through steps 2 and 3, you can also try to double click on the file, to see if the correct program to work with your digital photos will open automatically. Once the editing program has opened, you can edit it and or print it according to the particular instructions of that program.

If your computer doesn't have a special program to work with digital photos, then you can select to use the Windows Picture and Fax Viewer (to see and print them). You can also download the free HP photo-editing software, "HP Image Zone Plus," at this URL: *http://www.hp.ca/portal/hho/ize/home.php*.

How to widen or shorten the width of the columns you see when you are using the 'details' view

When you choose to use the "Details" view, the information for each particular folder/ or file will be displayed in columns, which appear side-by-side and are each of an adjustable width. For instance if the column width is too narrow, then widen it. If is too wide you can narrow it.

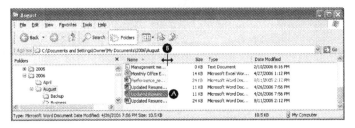

This is the way, to widen columns to see the complete information that they contain:

A. For instance this folder contains three files whose names begin with the same wording, "Updated Resume . . . ," but the column is not wide enough to display their full file name.

B. To see the hidden part of these files' names, widen the *Name* column. To begin, take the mouse pointer to the line that divides the column you want to widen or shorten. When the mouse pointer turns into a two-way arrow with a line across, click and hold down the left mouse button and drag the column divider to the right or left, depending on whether you want to widen or shorten a particular column.

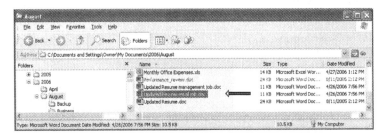

After widening the 'Name' field, you can now differentiate and find the file names you need to use. To open a file, just double-click on its name.

Click on the top of any column (on its label name) to sort the list of files you see under a column. For instance, if you click on the top of the column "Name", the file names (under the folder you've opened) are displayed in alphabetical order.

How to expand or hide folders in Windows Explorer

Please be aware that when you first open the Windows Explorer, some of the folders you want to work with might be hidden from view because they are stored within other folders (i.e., they are subfolders). To see a subfolder (a folder contained within another folder), you will need to learn how to expand the hidden folders.

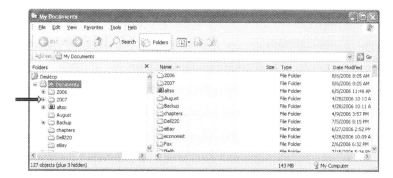

On this screen capture, you can see that there is a plus sign next to the "2007" folder. To expand this folder (or the folder you want to work with), to show the subfolders contained within it, just click once on the plus sign to its left.

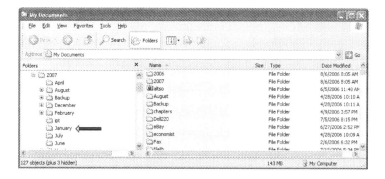

Now you can see the subfolders that are contained with the "2007" folder. If you've clicked on the "August" subfolder (which also shows a plus sign next to it), you will also be presented with the subfolders it contains. To **re-hide** the subfolders in this example, you just have to click on the minus sign next to the "2007" folder.

Note

Depending on how many folders and subfolders you've created on your hard drive, you might need to expand several folders to find the right subfolder whose contents you want to work with.

Working with computer files and folders using Windows Explorer

Now that you've learned how to find/show files and folders in Windows Explorer, it will be very easy to manage the data stored on your computer (in fixed hard drives, removable drives like disks or CDs, and on network drives on an office LAN).

On the pages that follow you will learn to:

1. Create new folders
2. Make a selection of files and/or folders
3. Copy a selection, of files and/or folders to another folder
4. Move a selection of files and/or folders to another folder
5. Delete a selection of files and/or folders

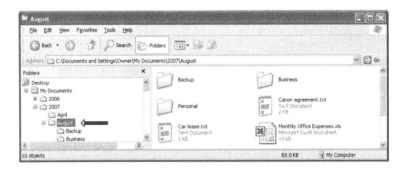

When working in Windows Explorer, it is always important to know where you are in the folder tree before working with your files. For example, on the above screen capture, the folder "August" is selected. So if you decide to create a new folder called "Acme," and the folder "August" is the one selected at the moment, then the new "Acme" folder will be created as a subfolder inside the "August" folder. As you can see, the "August" folder is inside the "2007" folder, which in turn was created inside the "My Documents" folder.

In this example, if you've saved files inside the "Acme" folder, then accessing them again will require several steps: You will first have to click on the "My Documents" folder, then on "2007," the "August" and then "Acme" folder before you can access the files you saved to this sub-folder.

Tip

Depending on the amount of work you do, it is easier to navigate four folder levels, than to look for a single file among a thousand you might have copied to a **single** folder.

How to create a New Folder

The first step to create a new folder, to store your files, is to click on the folder or drive under which you want to create it. You can think of it as an office cabinet with drawers (one drawer for each one of your drives, such as the C: drive), and in each drawer you've placed different manila envelopes (folders) to keep the letters you've written.

Notice on the screen capture below that the folder currently selected is called "August," meaning that the new folder will be created inside the "August" folder.

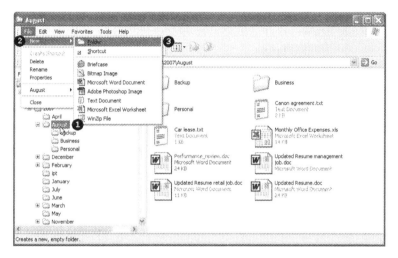

These are the steps, as you can see on this screen capture, to create a new folder:

1. To begin click on the folder name under which you want to create the new subfolder.
2. Now click on *File*, and then *New*.
3. Finally move the mouse indicator to the right and click on "Folder."

When new folders are created, the operating system initially automatically assigns them the name "New Folder, New Folder1" and so on. On the next page you will see the steps necessary to rename the new folders you've created, to a name of your choice.

Note

You can create as many subfolders as you want, but the more you create, the longer it will take to access them to save or to find your work.

After you select to create a new folder, a folder icon will appear in the right panel along with the label "New Folder." You should now rename it to your liking.

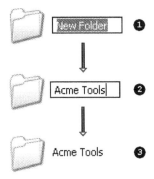

Follow these steps to name a folder:

1. Single click inside the "New Folder" label, and then use the Backspace key to delete the name shown. If the name inside the cell is not highlighted, **slowly** double-click on it until the name is bluish.
2. Now type the name you want to use for this new folder. Bear in mind that you cannot use a name that has already been assigned to another subfolder or even a file at the level of the folder in which you are working. For instance if you already named a folder, at the August folder level, Acme Tools, an now try to create a new folder under the August folder using the same Acme tools name, you will get the message; "A file with the name you specified already exist . . . '. If you must keep the folder name similar, you can use a number to make it different. For instance "Acme Tools1".
3. Finally, click outside of the folder to set the name for your new folder.

Once the folder is created, you can save any files you wish inside of it. If you don't give a name to the new folder you've created, then the Windows operating system will keep the suggested name, "New Folder." If you fail to rename it, then subsequent folders will be automatically labeled as: "New Folder (2)," "New Folder (3)," etc.

You can also rename an existing folder, this way; slowly click twice on the folder's name, press the right arrow key. Now use the backspace key to remove the extra letters, or just type additional letters or words to the name shown. You can even press the space bar, to leave a space between your letters.

How to select groups of files and/or folders

When using Windows Explorer, the first step before working with your folders and files (to copy, move or delete them) is to select them in the right panel. This can be done using the mouse, the keyboard, or both.

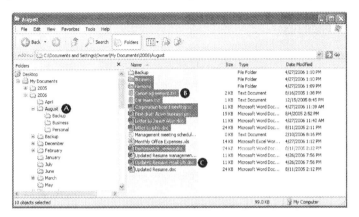

To make selections, as shown in the above example, follow these steps:

A. First click on the name of the folder (on the left panel) the files or folders or both you want to work with reside. Now you can see them on the right panel.

B. To select a group of consecutive files or folders: press and hold the Shift key, now click on the first file you want to select. Then click on the last file in the series you want to select, and lift your finger off of the Shift key. If the files you are trying to select are spanned across many pages, you must first hold down the Shift key, then click on the down arrow on the scroll bar until you find the last file or folder, and then click on it to highlight the entire selection.

C. To select non-consecutive files or folders, press and hold the CTRL key and then click on the files or folders you need to select (To remove a file from a selection click on it, to un-highlight it). To select a single file or folder, just click on it once.

After selecting a group of consecutive files, press and hold the *CTRL* key, and then click on other files that are non-consecutive, to add them to your selection.

Tip

After clicking inside the right panel, pressing and holding the *CTRL* key and then the *A* key will cause all of the contents of the folder you are working in to be selected.

You can also use only the mouse, in a sweeping motion, to select blocks of consecutive files and/or folders, even ones that are spanned across different pages under the same folder.

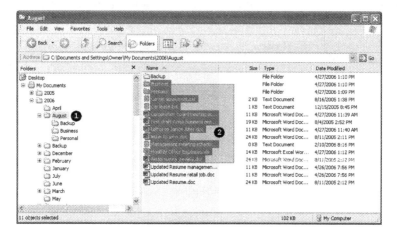

These are the steps to select files and/or folders using the mouse:

1. First locate and click on the name of the folder whose contents you want to work with, namely the files or folders you want to select, the contents of which will be displayed in the right panel.
2. Position the mouse pointer **outside** of the lower right side of the last file you want to select. While pressing and holding the left mouse button, move the mouse in a sweeping motion up and to the left, expanding the box that forms until all the appropriate files are selected. Finally, release the mouse button.

To deselect one or more of the files or folders you've selected, press and hold the *CTRL* key and then click on each one of the files or folders you want to deselect.

Using just the mouse to select files or folders can be a little more contentions for the computer novice, because you might **unintentionally** move files or folders from their current locations. If you think you've made a mistake, and unintentionally moved some files or folders to another folder, then: press and hold the *CTRL* key and then the *Z* one right away.

If you click anywhere on the left or right panel after you have selected a file or group of files, then they will be deselected and you will need to start this process over again.

How to Copy or Move a selection of files and/or folders to a different folder

On the previous pages, you learned to make selections of files and/or folders. Now you will learn to apply actions to these selections, so that you can performs tasks such as copying or moving them in Windows Explorer.

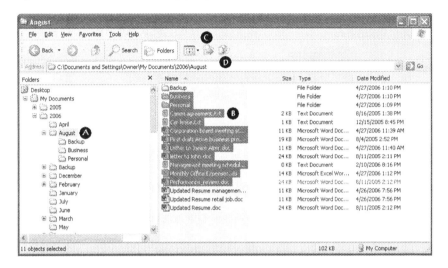

This is the way, as you can see on this screen capture, to start working on a selection to move or copy it to another Folder using the Windows Explorer:

A. First, in the left panel, select the folder that contains the files or the files and folders you want to work with.

B. Now, in the right panel, select all the individual files and/or folders you want to work with (as shown on the previous pages).

C. If you want to *move* the selected items, click over this button. Please bear in mind that once you complete the move operation, your selected items will only exist in the folder to which you have moved them. You can also click over the Edit menu item, and then click on Move to Folder.

D. If you want to *copy* the selected items, click over this button—a copy of these items will be placed in the new destination, and a copy will also remain in the original location. You can also click over Edit, and then click on Copy to folder.

Now a Dialog box window will open, and you will see **on the next page** how to pick the destination folder/directory for the selection you've chosen to copy or move using the Windows Explorer.

The final step of this process is to tell/show the Windows operating system the destination folder for the items that you are copying or moving.

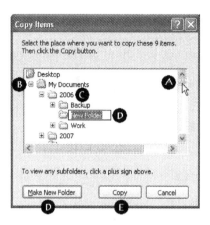

This is the way to finish copying or moving the selected files and/or folders:

A. First place the mouse pointer on the scrollbar guide (see the mouse pointer on this screenshot), click and hold the left mouse button, and drag the guide up until you can see the Desktop icon at the top of the list.

B. To expand folders and see their contents, click on the plus sign to their left. For instance if you want to copy/move the selection to the *My Documents* folder, click on the plus sign next to it to expand it. To copy/ or move them to a different drive (i.e., a drive other than the local C: hard drive), click on the plus sign next to the My Computer icon to see the list of available drives.

C. When you find the proper destination folder, click on it to select it. For this example I clicked on the 2006 folder.

D. If you so desire, click on "Make a New Folder" to create a new folder **under** the folder you've selected on **step C**. To rename it (the default name is "New folder"), while is highlighted or *bluish*, type the new name, and click outside of it. If not right click on it, and select Rename. Now type its name, and click once outside of it.

E. Finally, click on the appropriate button—"Move" or "Copy," depending on whether you are copying data or moving it.

If you have a previews version of Windows (such as Windows 98), and on the preceding step chose Edit and Copy, you won't see this little window. To proceed click (on the left panel) on the name of the folder you want to paste the selection you've made, click over the Edit menu item, and then on Paste.

How to add the "Move To" and "Copy To" buttons to the Windows Explorer toolbar

If you can't see the "Move To" and "Copy To" buttons on your Windows Explorer toolbar (in Windows 2000 or XP), then you can add them easily with a few clicks of the mouse.

To start the process of adding these two icons, you must open Windows Explorer and then the "Customize Toolbar" dialog box. To do this, first click over the "View" menu item, then bring the mouse pointer over "Toolbars," and then over to the right over "Standard Buttons", now bring the mouse pointer down and click on "Customize" to open the next dialog box.

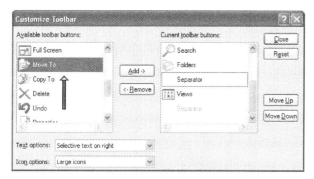

These are the steps, as seen on the above screen capture, to add the "Move To" and the "Copy To" buttons to the Windows Explorer toolbar:

- First click on the left-side panel of this dialog box, and then press the 'M' key a few times until you are able to see the "Move To" button on this list. When you find it double click on it, adding it to the Windows Explorer toolbar.
- Now also double click on the "Copy To" button, which should be next to the "Move To" button.

If you have an older version of the Windows operating system, such as Windows 98, the "Move To" and "Copy To" buttons won't be available to you. However, you can still move and copy files using Windows Explorer with the instructions that follow.

Note

In Windows XP you can also click over the "Edit" menu item and then, according to your desire, select the "Copy to Folder" or "Move to Folder" choices, instead of using the toolbar buttons.

How to Copy a selection of files and/or folders using a previous version of Windows

To begin copying files and folders or both in a previous version of the Windows operating system (such as Windows 98), first open Windows Explorer in the same manner shown earlier in this chapter, and then click on the drive letter or the name of the folder that contains the files and/or folders you want to work with.

In the next screen capture, notice I have selected the "Work" folder, because it contains the items I want to work with.

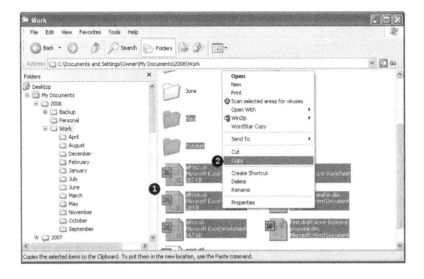

To copy files and/or folders from this point, you can follow these steps:

1. First make a selection of the files and folders or both you want to copy (as shown earlier in this Chapter).
2. Now right-click over your selection and then left-click over "Copy", to send it to the Windows Clipboard.

Or if you prefer, you can also click on the "Edit" menu and then click "Copy" to copy the selection you've made.

Be careful when you have files or folders selected, because you can; move them, or delete them by mistake. If this were to happen, then: press and hold the CTRL key and then the Z right away.

Now, to complete the copy operation, you must show the Windows operating system where do you want to paste the selection you've previously made.

These are the steps, as you can see on this screen capture, to finish pasting a selection:

1. First find and then click on the drive or folder into which you want to paste your selection.
2. Now right-click on the name of the folder you've selected, and then left-click over "Paste", to paste it. If you prefer, you can also open the "Edit" menu and then click "Paste" to paste the selection you've made.

This process also works equally well if you have Windows XP or Windows 2000, to copy files and folders from one folder to another, or from one folder to a removable storage unit, such a flash drive you bought to create backups of your important work.

Please bear in mind that fixed hard drives can and do fail from time to time. For this reason you might want to use this copy process to keep copies of your important computer data on a CD or a removable storage device.

 Be careful, when copying files from one location to another, that you don't overwrite (the operating system will warn you of this) newer copies of a file with an old copy, unless you want to.

How to Move a selection of files and/or folders using a previous version of Windows

To begin moving files and folders or both, first select the folder that contains the items that you want to work with, to see its contents on the right panel of the Explorer window.

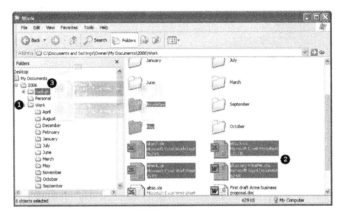

In the above screen capture, notice I have selected the "Work" folder, because it contains the items I want to work with. To move files and/or folders from this point, you can follow these steps:

1. First click on the folder that holds the items you want to move, to see its contents on the right panel.
2. Now make a selection of the work you want to move.
3. Next, left-click anywhere on top of it and immediately press and hold down the left mouse button. Now start dragging your selection (**don't lift your finger from the left mouse button yet**) toward the destination folder name (on this example I used the folder Backup). When the name of the destination folder is highlighted, lift your finger from the mouse button to move your selection there. If you make a mistake, and move the selection to the wrong folder, then press and hold the CTRL key and then the Z one (undo key combination) right away.

If you want to move a complete folder (yellowish object), then just click over its name and hold down the left mouse button to drag it over to the folder into which you want to move it to. If you press and hold the CTRL key while moving a selection, then this will work in the same fashion as the copy operation, and the selection of files you wanted to move will not be removed from its original location.

How to work with the "Confirm File" or "Folder Replace" dialog box

Earlier in this book you read that Windows will not allow you to have duplicate files with the same name and extension at the same folder level. The same holds true for folders, but they don't have a 3-letter extension.

For example, when you try to create/rename a file or folder with a name that has already been assigned to another file or folder in the same folder level, you will get an error message like the one above. To continue, just type a different name.

Now, because you can have files with the same name and extension (or subfolders with the same name) in *different* folders throughout your hard drivers, there is a chance that at times you might attempt to copy/move identically named files or folders into the same folder on your computer hard drive. For instance a folder you've created to save backup copies of your work.

Let say that trough the years you've created different copies of your resume (but always used the same name and the same program to create them), and keep them apart in different folders.

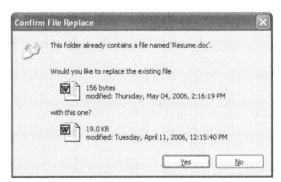

Now if one day you buy a removable storage device, and first move one copy of your resume there (from a particular folder), and later attempt to move a copy (found on a different folder) to the same removable storage device, then the operating system will display this message, and on the next page you will learn how to use it to avoid overwriting a more important copy of a file.

Please follow the next screen capture to learn to work on the "Confirm File or Folder Replace" window.

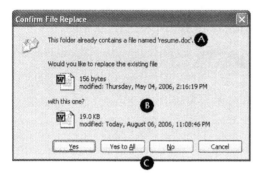

This is the way to work with the "Confirm File Replace" dialog box, to make sure you don't overwrite good files you want to keep:

A. To begin read on the top part of this window (Confirm File Replace) the name of the file or folder that you are trying to replace.
B. On the second part of this dialog box, you will see the size and the date the file or folder was modified;
    •   For the file or folder currently saved is under "Would you like . . . ."
    •   For the file or folder you are attempting to copy is under "With this . . ."
    If you are not sure which one has more value to you, then: click on **Cancel** and open them—on the original folder and on the destination folder, to see which one you want to keep. Once you ascertain this, then try copying/moving them again.
C. On the last part of this Dialog box you will see four choices:
    •   Click on "Yes" to replace the file or folder.
    •   Click on "Yes to All," if you are copying or moving more than one file or folder, to replace them all.
    •   Click on "No" to skip this file or folder and try the next one.
    •   Click on "Cancel" to close this Dialog box and stop moving or copying files.

It is important to make sure that you really want to replace a file or folder before clicking on the "Yes" button. Precaution is a good policy, and you can always click on "No," because once you click on "Yes", the file or folder currently saved on the destination folder is overwritten.

How to use the Send To menu

This is one of the Windows XP features that will save you time. For instance, using the "Send To" menu, from Windows Explorer or the My Computer program, you can quickly e-mail (providing you use Outlook or Outlook Express) a photo file with just a few clicks of the mouse.

Possible destinations for files sent via the "Send To" function include:

- Removable storage devices (for backup purposes)
- The Desktop
- Mail recipients
- The My Documents folder

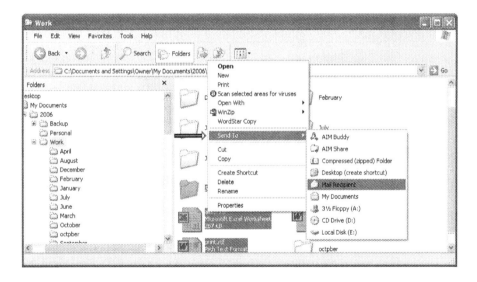

To use the "Send To" command, just right-click over a selection of files and/or folders and then select the "Send To" option, then move the mouse pointer to the right (or left). On the shortcut menu that appears, click the destination where you want to send the selection.

Once you do this, your selection will be sent to the destination of your choice. In this example, I chose the Mail recipient. This is especially useful for sending email attachments such as photographs/ or Microsoft Office documents (for instance the work resume you created in Word for Windows, and saved to your My Documents folder), using the steps outlined on chapter fourteen of this book.

How to delete a file or folder in Windows Explorer, My Documents folder or My Computer program

Deleting a file or folder is one of the easiest things you can do in Windows XP. The rule of thumb is, "If you can find it, you can delete it." However, depending on the type of user account you have (Limited or Administrator), you might not be able to delete other users' files or folders.

To begin deleting files and/or folders or both, first open the Windows Explorer, the My Documents folder, or even the My computer program, and then click on the folder or drive in which there are items you want to delete.

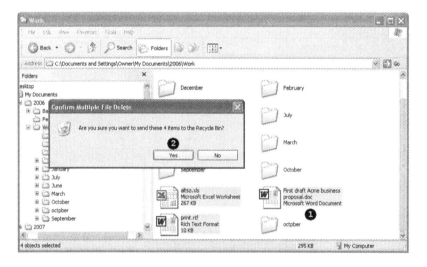

These are the steps, as you can see on this screen capture, to delete any items you can see in Windows Explorer:

1. Select the files and/or folders you want to delete.
2. Now press the "Delete key" to delete them, and then on the window that appears click on "Yes" to confirm the deletion. If you change your mind, just click on "No" or press the "Esc" key to close this dialog box.

If you accidentally delete a file or folder, then follow these steps (right away) to see if you can restore it: press and hold the CTRL key and then the Z one. Once you close the Window that you were working with, the CTRL + Z option is no longer available, but you can still check the Recycle bin as a potential way to restore the file.

Deleting Files, Folders, and shortcuts Icons on the Windows Desktop

To delete Files, Folders, and shortcuts Icons you see on the Windows Desktop is unfortunately very easy to do. You can even delete files from the dialog box window that opens when you choose to save or open a file, by just selecting it and pressing the Delete key on your computer keyboard.

And bear in mind that the files, folders or shortcuts sent to the Recycle Bin will remain there until you decide to permanently delete them. In the meantime, they will still take up space on your hard drive. While they are in the Recycle Bin, they can be undeleted and restored to their original locations.

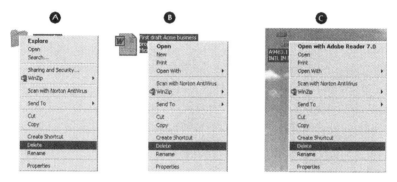

This is the way to delete files, folders, and shortcut icons, you see on the Windows Desktop:

A. To delete a folder, including all of the files in it, right mouse click on it and select "Delete." On the next prompt, click OK to confirm the deletion.

B. To delete a file, right mouse click on it and select "Delete." Again, you must click OK to finalize the deletion.

C. To delete a shortcut icon, follow the same procedure: Right mouse click, choose "Delete," and click on OK.

To permanently delete the contents of the Recycle Bin, right mouse click on its icon and select "Empty Recycle Bin." Finally, click OK to confirm. After you empty the Recycle Bin, it is next to impossible to recover the items that were in it.

Deleting files or folders on a brand new computer because you are concerned about hard drive space, is not crucial because your new computer has much more storage space than most people will use.

Restoring Items You've Sent to the Recycle Bin

Once you've deleted a folder, a file or a shortcut, it can be restored with a few clicks of the mouse to the original location from where you deleted it, provided that not too much time has gone by between the deletion and your attempt to recover the data. You might also be able to restore a folder or a file you've just deleted by mistake, this way: press/hold the **CTRL** key and then the **Z** one, right after deleting them.

To restore a file, visit the Windows desktop and double click on the Recycle Bin to open it, and see its contents.

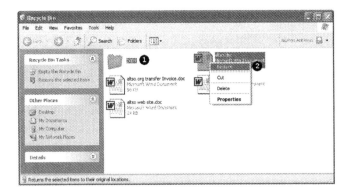

Follow these steps, once the Recycle Bin opens up, to restore the items in it:

1. Select the item or items you wish to restore:
    - To select a single item you want to restore, just click on it.
    - To select all of the items the Recycle Bin is holding: press and hold the *CTRL* key and then the *A* one.
    - To restore only a few selected items, press and hold the *CTRL* key and single click on each one of the items you want to restore.
2. Once you have selected the item or items you wish to restore, right mouse click on any of the selected items and click "Restore."

In the unlikely event that your computer system is running low on hard-drive space (one way to tell is that the computer is taking longer to finish tasks), then empty the Recycle Bin (explained on the previous page) to free more space in it.

Part IV
Guide to your everyday computer work in Windows

Chapter 9

Storing and Retrieving Your Computer Work in Windows

Intro to storing and retrieving your computer work

The process to store the work you do with your computer, to a permanent storage device (such as the fixed c:\ hard drive), is akin to storing paper files in an office filing cabinet, the main advantage being that stored files on a computer can be retrieved in seconds, as opposed to the several minutes it might take you to find paper ones.

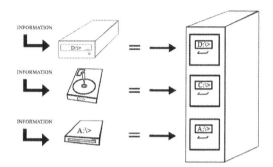

Now if, for example, your computer is equipped with a floppy drive, a hard drive and a CD Rom unit, then you can think of your computer as a virtual file cabinet with three drawers. (See the graphic above.) The first drawer will show the contents of each disk you insert into the 3 ½ floppy drive (A:\) (don't fret if your computer is not equipped with an A: drive, because they are being replaced as a means to carry files by USB flash drives of more capacity. They are assigned drive letters like E, G or F); the next drawer will represent the contents of the first fixed hard drive, which is always called the C:\ drive; and the last drawer represents the CD Rom unit. In a computer with a second hard drive, depending on your setup, the CD-ROM Unit might become the E:\ drive.

Remember to always save your important computer work as soon as you open the computer program you chose to create it in—for instance drafting a resume using Microsoft Word, as a power outage—or other unforeseen circumstances—will result in the loss of any unsaved work. Once you've saved your work in the form of a computer file with a particular name, it will remain available in the location to which you've saved it until you move it or permanently delete it.

Note
Ideally, each one of these virtual drawers should be organized (by you) into individual folders with descriptive names—for example, "February 2004 Letters."

The different buttons/areas that comprise the Save/and Open dialog box windows

To save and open files in Microsoft Windows efficiently, you should become familiar with the different buttons/parts found on the Save/and Open dialog box windows. These are the secondary windows that open up whenever you choose to save or open your work while working in a Windows computer program.

To see this dialog box window, open the WordPad program, in the following way:

1. Click on the Start menu button; now take your mouse pointer to All Programs. (In previous versions of Windows, click on Start, then Programs.)
2. Now move the mouse pointer to the right, over the Accessories group, and then down. Finally, click on the WordPad icon, to open it.
3. Once the program opens, click once on the File menu item. Next, click on Save. The "Save" dialog box window, which is almost identical to the "Open" dialog box window, should now open up.

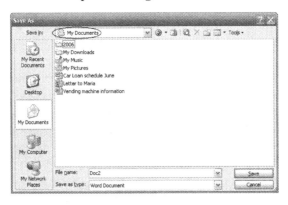

The first thing you should notice in this dialog box is the name of the folder as it appears in front of "Save in" if saving a file or "Look in" if looking for files you want to open. On this screenshot example it reads: My Documents.

The "Save As" dialog box window opens up the first time you are saving a new document, after invoking the "Save"/or the "Save As" command, to aid you in; a) Selecting a location on your hard drive (such as a particular folder) where you want to save your file, and b) To help you choose a name for your file. From then on, when you make changes to an existing file, and select the "Save" command, then this dialog box window won't pop up, unless you choose to save by clicking over *File* and then on "Save As". The Open dialog box always opens up when you select to open a file, by selecting the "Open" command.

To better understand this type of dialog box window, I will show you all the different ways you can use it—on the three pages that follow, highlighting on each one the different buttons/areas that you will use to complete the task of saving or opening files using your Windows programs:

• The **Save in** or **Look in** area.

A. This is the name of the folder, at which level you are currently working. For instance if you named a file "Letter to Maria", while in front of **Save in** reads: *My Documents* folder, and clicked on *Save*, the file would be saved at the level of the *My Documents* folder. Then to open that file later, navigate the folder three until in front of **Look in** reads: *My Documents* folder. Now find the file, and then double click on it to open it.

B. These are the names of the sub-folders and files found at the level of the folder whose name is in front of: **Save in** or **Look in**. To save your work to a different sub-folder, which name is visible in this area—for instance the 2006—then double click on its name. If the name of the folder you want to use, to save or to find your work, is not visible on this area, then click on one of the buttons on the left side (for instance the My Computer one) or click in front of **Save in**/or **Look in** to find it.

C. Click on this arrow to "go up" (i.e., go back) one level. For example, if you double clicked on one of the subfolders found under the "My Documents" folder—such as the "2005",—to work with its contents—and now want to return to the "My Documents" level, simply click on the up arrow button.

On the pages that follow you will learn to work with the other buttons/areas found on this dialog box window, to help you understand better how to use it to Store and Retrieve your computer work.

In the next screenshot you can see the list of different storage locations, you can save or open your work from that opens up when you click on the name of the folder you see in front of **Save in** or **Look in**.

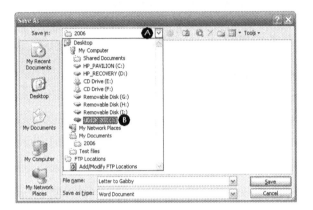

A. To begin click on the name of the folder shown in front of "Save in"—or, if you are opening a file, in front of "Look in"—to see the names of the different drives and storage resources available for saving and opening files.

B. On the ensuing list that opens you can select to work with the different storage resource, by single clicking over their name, such as:

- "Desktop": You will be taken to the level of the Windows Desktop.
- "My Documents": You will be taken to the level of the "My Documents" folder.
- "My Computer": You will be given access to all the resources available from your computer.
- "My Network": If you work in a LAN, clicking on this icon will show you the network folders you have access to.

For instance, if you decide to save a file, after choosing the *Desktop*, that (later on) to find and open it, you will need to return to the *Desktop*, by choosing it this way or by clicking on the *Desktop* button on the left side of this Dialog box window.

Bear in mind that, while saving or opening files, in some computer programs the dialog box windows that opens up will not have the same buttons/icons you see on the left side of this screenshot, and you will only work with this kind of drop-down-menu-list that opens up when you click on the name of the folder in front of *Save in* or *Look in* (if opening a file), as shown on this page.

- The buttons/shortcuts on the left side of the Save As/Open dialog box windows.

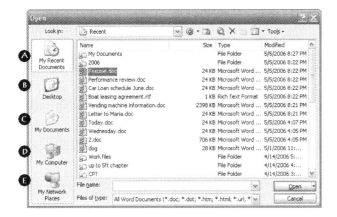

Here are the descriptions of these buttons/shortcuts. If you clicked on:

A. "My Recent Documents" or "History": You will be shown the name of folders, where you've saved files recently and also the names of those files. For instance if you are in the process to save a file, and see the 2006 folder there, you can double click on its name so that the new file you are saving can be grouped with others you've been saving to this folder. If opening a file you've worked with recently, then just double click on it to open it.

B. "Desktop": You will be taken to the level of the Windows Desktop.

C. "My Documents": You will be given access to the files and folders within the "My Documents" folder.

D. "My Computer" (not visible in older editions of Word): You will be given access to all the resources available from your computer.

E. "My Network": If you work in a LAN, clicking on this icon will show you the network folders you have access to.

On the previous page you saw how to find the J: drive (to save or open a file), which might be a removable flash drive you are using to save your work, by clicking first in front of Save in or Look in (if opening a file). Alternatively, you can reach the same J: drive by clicking on the *My Computer button*, to be taken at that level, and when you are presented with the list of drive letters, then just double click on the one assigned to your flash drive to work with it.

Storing your computer work permanently using the Save option

I can't stress enough that storing your work on a personal computer is akin to storing paper documents in a regular office filing cabinet. And once you save your work to a permanent storage location, then you will be able to find it later (unless is later moved or deleted) in the same location you saved it to.

This is the general process to save your work as a computer file in Windows:

1. Open the computer program you need to use, such as Microsoft Word.
2. Now click over *File* and then over *Save*, and then use the dialog box window (shown on the previous pages) that opens up to; a) Select the folder where you want to save your document, b) Choose a name for the file. Now click on Save. Alternatively draft the document first and select to save it later.
3. When you are done creating your work close the program, by clicking over File and then over Exit.

Now we will go over this process, to store a new document, step by step:

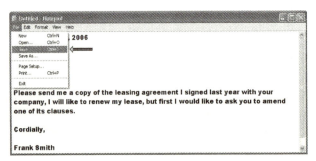

1. First click on "File" and then select "Save", as you can see on this screenshot, or press and hold the **CTRL** key and then the **S** one.

If you see this button (of a little Floppy disk), on a program toolbar, then you can also click on it to commence the process to save your work.

Now the "Save As" dialog box window (explained in the preceding pages) will open. In the pages that follow you will learn to complete the process of working with the different storage locations available from your computer, to save your work.

2. Now you must use the Save As dialog box window to tell your program exactly where—i.e., on the hard drive or in a removable storage location, an in what folder—to save your work. Notice on the next screenshot, in front of "Save in:", that if I choose to save a file it will be saved at the level of the folder "Work". If you want to save to a different drive or folder, then select it now, before clicking on Save.

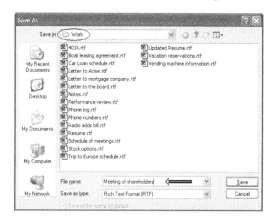

3. Now you must give your file a descriptive name and type it into the space to the right of the "File name:". With some programs you can also use the suggested name that the program chooses for your file (which is taken from the heading of the document you are working on). To start naming your file, first click on the space to the right of "File name:", now press the right arrow key and use the Backspace key to reduce part or the entire suggested name, and then type the name you want to use for your file. **Warning**: If you attempt to save your work using a file name with the exact name of a file currently saved at this folder level, then you will asked if you want to replace the file currently on the hard drive—which means overwriting the pre-existing file with the one you are saving. If you are not sure, click on No, then slightly change the name of the file you want to save. For example, if you get this message when you are trying to use the name "Résumé", and you want to preserve the original Résumé file, then just type a 2 at the end of the file to use "Résumé2" for your file.

Finally click on *Save* to permanently store your work, as a computer file. From now on every time you make changes to this particular file, click over *File* and then on *Save* or (if you see it) click on the floppy icon on a program toolbar, but bear in mind that, after you've named it, you will not see this dialog box window pop-up when you choose to save your changes. That is unless you use the *Save As* command (explained later in this chapter), to save it to a different folder/drive or to rename it.

At this point, as long as you haven't clicked on the Save button, you can even create an additional sub-folder to better organize/group the files you want to save. For example, if you've previously created a folder called "2006," but you don't want to keep all your work files and personal files mixed together, then create two sub—folders; one called "Personal" and another one called "Work"—both within the same 2006 folder, using the Save As dialog box window that opens when you select to save your work as a computer file.

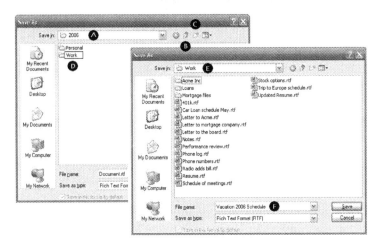

This is the way to create subfolders, using the 'Save As" window:

A. This is the name of the folder at which level you are currently set to save.

B. Click on this green arrow up, to return one level up, to find another sub-folder in which you prefer to save your work.

C. Click on this icon ("Create new folder") to begin creating a new subfolder, under the folder name currently shown in front of Save in:.

D. Now click on the highlighted "New folder" name, and use the backspace key to remove it. Now type a name for it, and click once outside it. Repeat this process to create as many folders as you want to create. To use this new folder, to save your files, double click on it. In previous versions of MS Office, if a little window pops up right away: type the new folder name and then click on OK to use it right away. To return to the folder, from which you created this folder, click on the arrow up button.

E. For this example I double clicked on the new "Work" folder, to use it.

F. Finally click in front of "File Name", and type a descriptive name for the file you want to save, and click on **Save** to store it as a computer file.

Later on to make changes to this file, return to the same sub-folder where you saved it. Once you see the name of the file, double click on it to open it again.

When to store your work using the Save As option

Often times you might create, or receive a file from your company, called a Template. This is a pre-designed document for a particular purpose—one that you'll want to use multiple times as a base to create another document. A time-card for recording employee's times and services rendered is but one example.

For instance, after opening a Template file which you need to preserve, and in which you now need to work, don't use the "Save" option right after inputting the information that it asks from you. And instead use the "Save As" option, which; a) Preserves the original file (without the new information you've just typed) and b) Creates a copy of the original file, with the new information, and for which you will pick a different name as the original file. To begin this process, click on "File", and then select "Save As", instead of "Save".

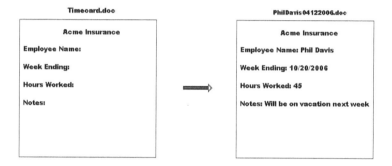

In the graphic above you see two documents: On the left, you see the original copy of a time-card on a computer file called: Timecard.doc, created to allow employees to electronically account for their time. On the right a copy of the original file, that was personalized, with the changes done by an employee with the information for a week of work, and saved with a different file name.

The procedure to accomplish this is simple: 1) Each week the employee opens the same original file (called **Timecard.doc**), 2) **Immediately he or she clicks** on File and then on the **Save As** command, and 3) Gives it a new name, for instance using a combination of his name and the week worked. He then fills out his work information for that week. Now notice the new file name: "phildavis0822005.doc"

Alternatively if you want to preserve the original file, but don't want to change its name; make the changes you need to do to a file, and then save it right away to a **different folder** on your hard drive. This process also assures that you still have an original file (for instance the file: résumé. doc), in the original folder you opened from.

To practice saving using "Save as", open any word-processing program such as the included WordPad and then type a sample letter with the exact wording of the template file on the previous page. Now click over "File" and then over "Save", give it the name: Timecard, click on "Save", and then leave it open.

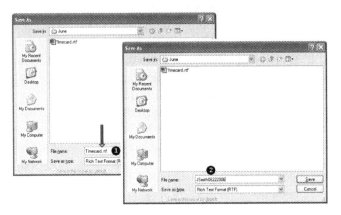

These are the step-by-step instructions, to use the Save As option:

1. Fill in the info requested on the sample template, click on File and then on *Save As* (instead of plain *Save*). To delete or change the file name shown, while is highlighted (bluish), press any key (for instance the Space bar). Otherwise press the right arrow key.

2. Now notice the position of the **blinking cursor** (use the *Backspace* key to remove text to the left of it, and the *Delete* one to the right) to change its position use the arrow keys, and then type the new name for it. For example, if this is a weekly time card, type the name, the week, month, and year. Adding just a number or a letter at the end of the current file name shown (to change it), such as "Timecard1", will suffice to protect the original file. Finally, to save it, click on the "Save" button.

This is particularly useful if you have a basic résumé that you modify from time to time, to suit a particular job opportunity. To that effect, to preserve the original résumé: a) Open the original basic résumé and now click over File and then on "Save as" and rename it right away, b) Customize it. Once the new file has a new name, to save the changes on the new resume file you can use the regular "Save".

Caution: While renaming files, try to preserve the 3-letter file extension (if you see it). For instance to rename: Test.doc, click on the space before the dot "." or use the left arrow key to position the blinking cursor before the dot ".", because most computer files won't open (without extra steps), if you change or delete their file extension. Bear in mind that you can also use the "Save As" process to work with files of different types, not just word processing files, such as Excel files or even graphic files.

Let's say that you took an excellent digital photo of your grandkids. Now you want to, using a graphic program, make some changes on the brightness or on the contrast of this photo, but want to be able to go back to the original one if the changes you make damage it. To begin open the original file that holds the photo, and right away use the "Save As" command (click on File and then on **Save As**), and save the photo file with a different name (to change its name is enough to add as little as one letter or a number to create an additional copy of it). Now open the copy of the name of the file, making all the changes you want to make. This insures that if later on you want to return to the original copy, it will be there safely filed on the original folder you've saved it to.

jan2006 096.jpg   jan2006 096a.jpg

For instance note on this screenshot; a) An original file (named "jan2006 096.jpg"), and b) A copy of the original file, which I saved using *Save As* to the same folder, albeit using a name that is different by just a single letter; "Jan2006 096a.jpg" (notice the **a** at the end), which allows it to be saved alongside the original file.

After a while, as you can see on this screen capture, if you've used this process right, you will have many files on your computer (even on the same folder), with similar names. For instance on this example these four files start with "Resume . . . "

Extra info on naming and renaming computer files

Bear in mind that when you commence the process of saving your computer work in Windows, most programs will offer you a suggested name you can use. And those programs take the suggested name from the heading of the document you are creating, or from a set name dictated by the program, such as: Untitled-7.tif. It is up to you to accept the suggested name for your file or to use one of your own choosing.

Ⓐ **Car expenses for the month of January.doc**

Ⓑ Car expenses for the month of January.doc| ⟸▬
Car expenses for the month of January|.doc

⬆

Ⓒ Car expenses for the month of Januarya|.doc
Car expenses.doc

Please note the following points when naming or renaming computer files:

A. Note, as soon as the **Save As** dialog box window opens up, in front of **File Name:,** the suggested file name will appear highlighted. If you press any key, other that the arrow keys, it will be deleted. To recover it, press and hold the **CTRL** key and then the **Z** one right away.

B. To use the suggested name click on Save. To change it; click on the file name shown, press the right Arrow key (lower right hand of the keyboard) or single click after the letter you want to add a letter to or remove a letter. If you see the three-letter file extension (for instance .doc), press the Left or Right arrow keys to place the blinking cursor before the dot ".". To use part of the name keep pressing the left arrow key until the cursor is blinking at the right of the last letter from which you want to start adding letters to the file name (to change it). Press the Backspace key to remove text to the left of a letter, and the Delete one to the right.

C. Adding a single letter (like an "a" or a "w") or a number to the end of the middle of the file name is enough to change its name (before the dot "."). On this example I removed most of the name of the sample file, using the Backspace key and now the file name reads "Car expenses.doc". Finally click on "Save".

If you are using Save As to preserve a template file, then you **SHOULD** definably give the file a new name. This again can be achieved by adding as little as a number or a letter at the end of the current file name.

Retrieving your computer work using the Open option

After you've chosen to save a file to a folder in your hard drive or other storage device from which you have access from your computer, the file will remain saved there; ready to be opened at any time (until you delete it or move it).

These are some of the ways to open a file saved to your computer in Windows:

- Open the computer program you used to create it, such as Microsoft Word, and then select the open command by clicking over File and then on Open, find the folder where is located, and then double click on its name to open it or single click on its name and then click on the Open button to open it.
- Open the Windows Explorer or the My computer program, navigate to the folder you've saved your file to, and then double click on its name to open it.
- If the file was saved to the Windows Desktop, or a shortcut was made there, then double click on its name to open it. You can also double click on the My Documents folder, to see the folders/files saved under it.

For instance, open the Windows Explorer, and navigate to the folder or subfolder where you've saved a file to.

When you find the file you are looking for (on this example the file "Letter to Tom.doc" on the August subfolder), double click on its name to open it.

Please note on this screen capture that the file "Car Photo" doesn't show a valid file extension (see chapter seven), so double clicking on its name won't open it, but that you can still open it by opening a compatible program first (Note that the name "Car Photo", suggests it is a graphic file). This way: 1) find a graphic program on your computer, an open it, 2) click on File and then on Open, and navigate to the folder where the file resides, 3) click in front of Files of Type and change it to "All formats" or "All Files (*.*)", and 4) now find the file and double click on its name to open it.

As you saw on the previous page, the most common way to open a computer file is to open first the program you used to create it. If the file was sent to you attached to e-mail messages, then you can ascertain, by looking at the file extension (as explained in chapter seven), what type of program will open it.

This is a list of the most common file extensions, and the names of the programs you will need to use to open files of this type:

- .bmp. Use the Paintbrush program
- .doc. Use Microsoft Word for Windows.
- .jpg. Use any graphic program installed on your computer, such as Adobe Photoshop.
- .xls. Use Microsoft Excel for Windows
- .ppt. Use Microsoft PowerPoint for Windows

This is the initial step to open a file using the "Open" file option, after opening the program you used to create it or one that is compatible with it:

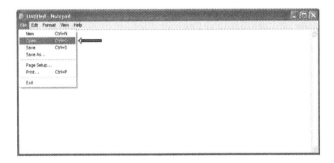

1. First click on "File" and then select "Open", or press and hold the **CTRL** key and then the **O** one.

- If you see this button (of a little Folder), on a program toolbar, then you can also click on it to commence the process to find/open your files.

Now the "Open" dialog box window (explained in previous pages) will open up. In the pages that follow you will learn to complete the process of working with the different storage locations available from your computer, to open your work.

2. Now the Open file dialog box window opens up, and you can begin looking for the file you need to find, to open it.

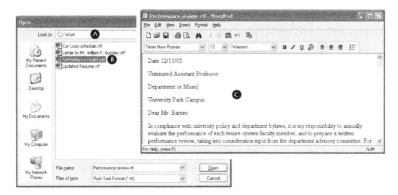

This is the way to use the Open file dialog box to open a file in Windows:

A. To begin return to the folder where you previously saved the file you need to work on. Look at the name beside "Look in:" or click on the buttons on the left side of this dialog box windows (shown earlier) to navigate to the folder where you've saved the file you are looking for. In chapter seven you will also find an excellent guide on how to navigate the folders tree.

B. Once you find the selected file, in this example "Performance review", double click on it to open it. If you single clicked on the File to select it, then click on the Open button, to open it.

C. Now your file should open. If you make changes to the file, then you should save them by using File + Save, or alternatively press and hold the *CTRL* key and then the *S* one, or click on the Floppy icon on the program Toolbar (if the program you are working with has one).

Or navigate to the file, using the Windows Explorer or the My Computer program, and when you find it double click on its name to open it.

Keep in mind (while looking for your files) that if for instance, you've previously created a: *Work* folder under the *2006* folder and another *Work* folder under the *2007* one. And at the time you saved a file, in front of **Save in** it read: *Work*, and now when you return to the *Work* folder (under the 2006 folder), the file is not there, that is probably saved on the *2007\Work* folder. So navigate to the *Work* folder (under the *2007* folder), to find and open it.

It is also important to know, when you are looking for the files you want to return to work with, that at times they might not be readily visible on the Open dialog box window, even if you're looking in the right folder where you saved them to.

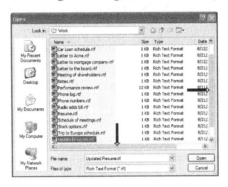

For instance if the scroll bars are visible—see the arrows in the above screenshot—then this means that there are more files, folders or information to be found by just shifting the contents of the Open dialog box window. To see the hidden files or folder you are unable to see on this window, click on the blue guide on the vertical or the horizontal scroll bar then hold the left mouse button, now move it down/up to see them. Or click on the middle panel (where you see your files and folders), and then press the PageDown/Up key to see them.

Sometimes you still may not be able to see the name of a file you are looking for. If this is the case, then try to open it this way:

1. Click in front of "Files of type:", and then select "All Files (*.*)".
2. When you see the name of the file you are looking for, whose icon might look different from the ones that you see on this window, then double click on it to open it.

If the file still doesn't open, then your program might not be compatible with it. This is usually the case with files, that you've received attached to e-mail messages. Chapter fourteen provides some tips on how to avoid some compatibility problems, when sending and receiving computer files attached to e-mail messages.

Opening files from the Desktop, My computer program or the Windows Explorer

As we saw earlier you can also open a file from your Windows Desktop, the My Computer program or the Windows Explorer window by double clicking on its name. Now the program used to create the file or one that is compatible with a file you received, will open displaying the contents of the file on its working window.

For example, let's open the Windows Explorer—chapter eight of this book has an excellent guide to learn how to use it—to find a file and open it.

To open the Windows Explorer, right mouse click on the Start menu button, then select Explore.

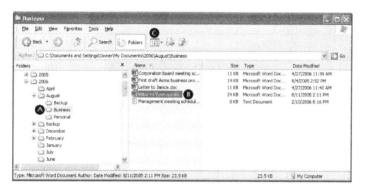

Once you have the Windows Explorer open, navigate to the Folder where the file you are looking for is located, and then open it this way:

A. This is the folder where the sample file is located.
B. Now you can start looking for the file you want to work with (in this example we're looking for "Performance review"). Once you find it, just double click on the file name and it will open. If this is a file that was sent to you in an e-mail attachment, and you don't have the program that created it, the file might not open at all.
C. If you are looking for a file by the date it was created, click on the View menu, and select Details, to see additional information (the date, for example). If you are looking for a particular digital photo, you can select Thumbnails to see a preview of the photos in this folder.

Bear in mind that sometimes, when looking for files you've saved, that you might need to look on several folders before you find them.

Opening documents you've worked on recently

Creating document files in Windows is very easy: You open the program, you choose a name for the file, and you save it. But looking for the file later can be cumbersome, especially if you are in a hurry and don't remember where you've saved it.

Luckily, Windows allows you to go back to work on the files you've worked on recently with only a few clicks of the mouse.

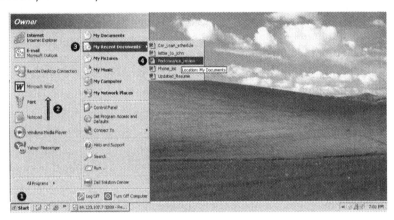

To access a list of your recently used documents, do the following:

1. Click on the Start menu button.
2. Move the mouse pointer up.
3. Now move the mouse pointer to the right over "My Recent Documents"
4. From this list click to select the name of the file you want to work on. If you've deleted or moved a file, then you will get a message that the file cannot be found.

If you don't see this option on the Start Menu, right mouse click on the Start button, and then select Properties. Now click on Customize, then click on the Advance tab. Make sure the "List my most recently opened documents" is checked. To clear the contents of this list, click on "Clear list".

Note

The list of the previously used computer files constantly changes, meaning as you open files, some names will be moved off this list, so that only the most recent ones you've opened will be listed here.

Some programs, such as Microsoft Word and Windows WordPad, also keep a very short list of the files you've worked on recently in their File menu. This list changes every time you open a file; because of that you will only see the names of the files you've opened recently.

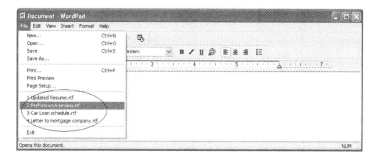

To see the list of the documents you've worked recently in Windows WordPad, or in most of the Microsoft Office programs:

1. Open Word or WordPad (if that is the word process you use) and click on File.
2. At the bottom of this dropdown menu, you will see a list of their file names.
3. To return to work on a particular file whose name you see on this list, just click on it.

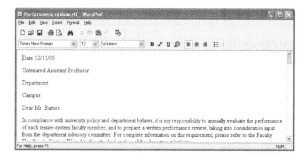

When the document opens again, it should read exactly as it did the last time you saved it. You can now make any changes or print the file. But if you've deleted or moved these files to another location, then the program will return a message that the file cannot be found.

In Windows XP it might be necessary to place the mouse pointer, on the double arrow sign (on the drop-down menu that opens), to expand it, and see the rest of the items on this menu.

Finding a file using the Search or Find options

If you don't remember the name of the file you're looking for, or the location where you saved it to, then you can use the Windows Search program to find it. If you have a different version of Windows, such as Windows 98, this option will read "Find" instead of "Search," but the steps that follow will be similar.

First open the search window by right mouse clicking on the Start menu button, and then clicking on Search or Find.

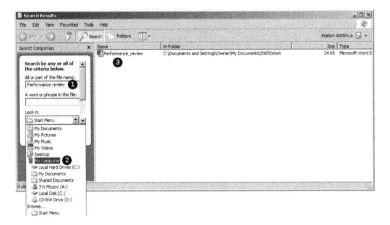

Now follow these steps, to find a file you've saved or copied from another computer:

1. Click on this space, and type the name (or part of the name) of the file you're looking for. For this example I typed "Performance review".
2. Click under "Look in:" to broaden the search, and then click on "My Computer" or on the drive where you think it is located. Then click on Search.
3. If the search program finds it, you will see its name on the right-hand panel (on this example it found a file name "Performance review"). Just double click on the file to open it.

Bear in mind that if you've worked with a file, that at different times you've saved to different folders (using the same name), that this program will show you a list of names with the same name and extension, but that are located on different folders throughout your storage resources, then you might need to open a few of these files to find the right one you need to work with.

Changing the default location to work with files in Microsoft Word

The default location to work with files is the folder name that always shows up beside "Save in:" or "Look in:" when you want to save or open files in Microsoft Word or any other program. You can change this designation in Microsoft Word, and in a few other programs by following their individual instructions.

To change this setting in Word, open Microsoft Word, click on Tools on the menu bar, and then click on the Options button on the dropdown menu. When the Options menu dialog box opens, click over the File locations tab. Then double click on Documents. Now you can change the folder path where you prefer to save or start opening your work from.

On this screen capture you can see clearly that the default location to work with files is the "My Documents" folder, because this is the name of the folder beside "Look in:" To change this setting to the "2005" folder, all you need to do is double click on it, then click on "OK" to close the "Modify location" dialog box.

Finally click on "OK" to close the "Options" dialog box. Now when you open Microsoft Word and choose to Save or Open your work, the folder path that it shows you in front of "Save in:" or "Look in:" (if opening files) will be the one you chose in this exercise.

This is only a suggested path. You can always select, manually, to save your work to another folder or to navigate to another folder to open a file.

The importance of backing up your computer work

You should never assume that the work you do on a personal computer will always be there, forever and ever. From time to time a computer might suffer a power surge that destroys its data, or you (or someone else with access to the computer) might accidentally delete a very important file. A computer virus could also attack your computer.

The question that you have to ask yourself is: What will you do if one day you need a very important file or be asked to look for a file, and the file is nowhere to be found, deleted/gone?

This is what I recommend:

- If you work at a company, meticulously follow the file backup process your IT department recommends. If you don't know what their suggestions (or policies) are, then ask!
- If you are a small business owner, find and hire an IT professional that can help you devise a disaster recovery plan to help you keep your business afloat in case your main computer crashes.
- If you are a home user you can use commercially available programs (like Nero Burning software) if you have the proper equipment on your computer (a CD or DVD writer), to back up your files.

- Be very cautions when working with files. On this screen capture you can see a message about deleting a file, which asks if you want to send the file to the "Recycle Bin". You might see this message if you are in Windows Explorer, My Computer, or another place in Windows, and accidentally select to delete a file. If this is not want you wanted to do, use the ESC (escape) key to close this dialog box, or click on "No".

For instance while writing this book I created backups of the chapter, by e-mailing them to my own e-mail address. This assured me if I my computer crashed, I would be able to retrieve my work by logging onto my e-mail account. The process, to attach and download files using e-mail, is explained on chapter 14 of this book.

Backing up your work to CDs or DVDs in Windows XP

If you don't have a dedicated software backup program (such as Nero Burning), then you can use Windows XP to create backup copies of your computer-created files—as long as your computer has the necessary hardware. But bear in mind that Windows XP, is only able to save your work using CD-R or CD-RW drives and not with DVD drives. To write to DVDs you need; a DVD writer, and software (such as the Nero Burning one.)

To begin, open the Windows Explorer by right mouse clicking on the Start button, and then select Explore.

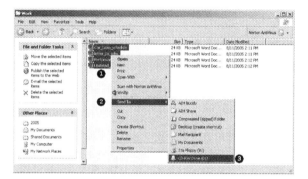

Now navigate to the folder that contains the file or files you want to backup, and then follow these instructions to send them to your CD writer:

1. Select the file or files you want to save:
   - To select one file or a folder, just click on it.
   - To select a group of contiguous files you want to backup, click once on the left panel on the name of the folder in which the files you need to backup are contained. Now click on the right hand panel, press and hold the Shift key, then click on the first one you want to select, and then click on the last one. Now lift your finger from the keyboard. If the files you need to select are hidden behind the window, then click on the guides on the vertical scroll bar, while still holding the Shift key, until you find the last one you want to select and then click on it to highlight the entire selection. To select non-contiguous files or folders or both, click on the first one, then while pressing and holding the CTRL key, single click on all the additional ones you want selected.
2. Now right mouse click on any of the selected files or folders, and move the mouse pointer over "Send to".
3. Finally move it to the right or the left (right, in this screen shot), and down to select the CD writer unit. Now left click on it to select it.

These files are now in a temporary place, ready to be copied to your CD. Now insert a CD-R or CD-RW disk (this depends on the type of drive you have on your computer) into the drive unit on your computer. You can use a new one, or one you've used to copy files before. But if this doesn't work then you might need to produce a new disk.

Double click on the My Computer Icon on the desktop, to start the process of writing these files to your CD.

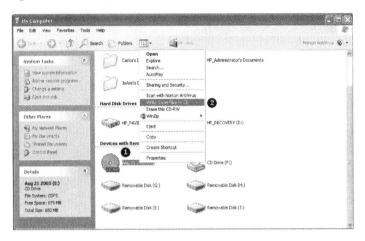

When the above window opens you will be able to write your files using these steps:

1. Right mouse click on the drive letter of the drive you want to use to burn your files. For instance the D drive. It should read CD-RW.
2. Now drag the mouse pointer, up or down, and click on "Write these files to CD". If you need to erase a CD-RW disk that already has info on it, click on "Erase this CD-RW". When it finishes erasing, you can repeat these steps and click on "Write these files to CD".

If the operation was a success, then the message; "You have successfully written your files," will pop-up. If you were to need any of these files later, then you can use the instructions in chapter eight (Guide to the Windows Explorer) to copy them back to the hard drive or to any other place you choose.

To find out if your computer has a CD-R or a CD-RW writer, then please read the documentation that came with it. If your computer lacks one of these drives, then you can also upgrade most computer systems by buying a new one at Circuit City or any other electronic store.

Chapter 10

Learn to share data between open programs

Introduction to Data sharing in Microsoft Windows

One of the main advantages of using the Windows operating system is the ease with which one can share data—for example, text and graphics— between open programs. This task can be accomplished by pressing a few key combinations on the computer keyboard, or with just a few clicks of the mouse.

The main process to complete this task is called Copy/Cut and Paste, a feature that allows you to copy or cut a selection of text or text and graphics from an open window and then paste it onto another line/page in the same window you are working on, or even to another line/page in a totally different open window.

These scenarios give you an idea of how you can share data amongst open programs using Copy/Cut and Paste:

- You are browsing a website using Internet Explorer; on the page you are visiting there is a quote you want to use for a school paper. Using the mouse, highlight the quote, select to copy it, and finally paste it on a page on a Word document running in another open window.
- You are using Word to create a flier to advertise your business. You want this flier to show ten copies of your name and phone number so that people can contact you, but you don't want to type this information ten times. In fact, you only need to type the information once. Then you can use the mouse to highlight your name and number, copy them, and paste them on the same document as many times as you wish—without having to retype them.
- You are composing a very important e-mail, and wish to write it first in Microsoft Word because of that program's better spell-check. Once your finish your letter, highlight it, copy and paste onto your e-mail message.
- You are looking at a document—be it a webpage or an open Word document—and decide to use a picture from it. Using the mouse, you can right click on the picture, copy it, and paste it onto another page on an open Word document or any other program that can accept graphics.

Bear in mind that Copy/Cut and paste only works among programs that are open and running in their own window, and if the program you want to paste the data (be that text or a combination or text and graphics) to is not open at the moment, then open it, to transfer the selection (using Paste) you previously selected and copied.

 **Note**

After following these steps to share a selection of data, the resulting data will be an exact mirror copy (with a few exceptions) of the original selection.

Basic info on how use the Copy/Cut and Paste process in Windows

To share data, text and graphics or both, between open windows, you must use a process called Copy/Cut and Paste. This process is made possible by a program that runs in the background, called the Windows Clipboard, which has a temporary virtual bin whose contents change every time you select the Copy/Cut command.

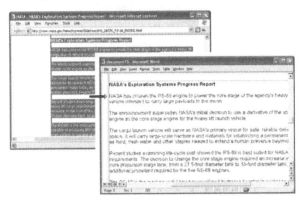

These are the general steps you must follow to use Copy/Cut and Paste, to share bits of data between open Windows programs:

1. To begin use the mouse or keyboard, to make a selection, of as little as a single letter to as much as the whole document you are looking at (on this example I copied a web page from the Nasa website). Now the selection you've made must appear highlighted, such as this; **Highlighted selection**

2. Now you must select to copy it, to the Windows Clipboard, using the copy command. If you select to cut a selection (by selecting *Cut*), then the selection is removed from the document you are working on. But keep in mind that you cannot remove/cut data from some windows/programs (such as web sites), unless is something you've written in a text box.

3. Finally Paste the selection, to another location/page on an **open** document running on a different window—for this example I am using Microsoft Word-, or you can even paste it anywhere on the same document you are working on.

If you followed these steps correctly, then now you will have an exact copy of the original selection you made, on the place you choose to paste it to, such as on this screen capture example, were I made a selection of text from the NASA's Exploration Systems Progress Report, copied it, and then pasted it onto a Word processing document.

The Windows clipboard

The windows clipboard is the program that every time you select to Copy or Cut a selection, receives the data that you've copied/cut and holds it temporally. Now this selection will be ready to be pasted into any open windows program by just invoking the Paste command.

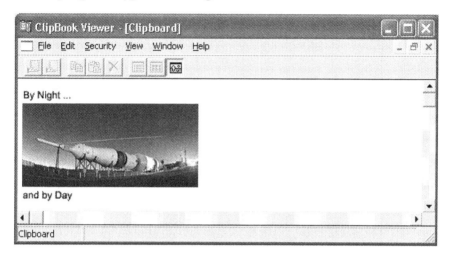

On this screen capture of the Windows Clipboard, which you never have to open and functions automatically as a bin that holds copied selections, you can see that right now is holding a photo (I copied there) I found on a Nasa Web site.

When using Copy/Cut and Paste, try to remember these guidelines:

- You can paste graphics and text onto a word-processing program that accepts both—for example, Microsoft Word for Windows.
- You can copy/cut and paste graphics from one graphic program to another; for example, you can copy or cut some parts of a graphic from Microsoft Paintbrush and paste them onto another window running another copy of Paintbrush.
- You can't paste text onto programs that accept only graphics (such as Microsoft Paintbrush) or graphics onto a program that only accepts text (such as Notepad). To paste text onto some graphic programs, you must first create what is called a text box, in which you can type text.

The contents of the clipboard change every time you select the Copy/Cut command, and are permanently erased when you turn the computer off.

Steps you need to follow to complete the Copy/Cut and Paste process

The Copy/Cut and Paste processes are very easy to learn using the instructions that follow in this chapter, and with a bit of practice in no time you'll be an expert at using them to complete your everyday computer work.

To complete these processes you will use either the *mouse* or the *keyboard or both*, and in most cases using one or the other will be a question of personal preference.

These are the general steps to use Copy/Cut and Paste:

1. To begin this process make a selection, be it a piece of text or a combination of text and graphics, of;
    *   As little as a single letter, using the mouse or the keyboard.
    *   Everything you see in the active window by clicking over *Edit* and then on *Select All*, or press and hold the *CTRL* key and then the *A* one.
2. Now Copy/Cut the selection, in one of the following ways:
    *   By putting the mouse pointer over the highlighted selection, right-clicking over it, and clicking over Copy or over Cut.
    *   By clicking over the Edit menu and selecting Copy or Cut.
    *   By pressing and holding the *CTRL* key, and then the *C* (to copy) or the *X* one (to remove/cut the selection). Now click outside the selection.
    Bear in mind that you cannot cut selections from fixed information on websites or other locked documents, such files of the PDF type.
3. To choose the target destination;
    > Switch to the target window, unless you want to paste to the same window you made the original selection, by bringing it to the front, and place the mouse pointer exactly where you want the selection to be pasted, and left click once. Otherwise the data on the clipboard will be pasted, beginning at the blinking cursor.
4. Finally invoke the Paste command (after clicking on the Target window)—in one of the following ways:
    *   By right-clicking on your document and selecting "Paste" on the dropdown menu.
    *   By clicking on the Edit menu and selecting "Paste."
    *   By pressing and holding the *CTRL* key, and then the *V* one

When, throughout this book, I write: press and hold the *CTRL* key, and then to type an additional word (for instance the letter *C* to copy a selection), that you should keep holding the *CTRL* key down, until you press the additional letter, to finish the instruction. When you finish the desired task, for instance to Paste a selection, release your finger from the *CTRL* key.

A little extra info on making selections with the mouse and the keyboard

Before we go into using the Copy/Cut and Paste process in more detail, please type a letter in your word processing program or visit any web page, to get better acquainted with the process of selecting text. For this example I used the Exploring Activity 1: "Getting Started in Mars . . ." text, I found on a JPL web page.

Exploring Activity 1: Getting Started in Mars Exploration

Purpose: To probe students' understanding of Mars and to have each student create a Mars Journal.

Key Concepts:

• Mars is a neighboring planet.
• Mars has a variety of landforms many of which are similar to ones found on Earth.
• Spacecraft have visited Mars and returned images and data.
• Journals help people record and organize their thoughts and are valuable tools in scientific research.

This is the way to use either the mouse or the keyboard, to select text:

A. Using the mouse you can select text, this way;
   1. Take the mouse pointer to the very *beginning* or the *end* of the text/word you want to select.
   2. Now click and hold the left mouse button, and then move the mouse (in a sweeping motion) until all the text is selected. As you can see, on this screenshot, you can do this in either direction. By moving the mouse from left to right (if you clicked at the beginning of the text) or by moving from right to left (if you began at the end of the text).
   3. To finish lift your finger from the mouse button.
B. Using the keyboard, you can also select text: for instance, a comment you made on a web-blog (**before** you've clicked on Submit/Save), this way:
   1. Take the mouse pointer and click right before the first letter of the text you want selected or after the last letter you want to select. Please notice the position of the blinking cursor. It should be blinking to the left of the first letter or to the right of last letter you want to select.
   2. Now, while pressing/holding the Shift key, tap the right arrow key to select from left to right until all the text you want to select is selected. Alternatively, if you clicked at the *end* of the word/paragraph, to select from right to left then tap the left arrow key.

Please practice using these two different ways to select text, and bear in mind that both of these processes will yield the same results, and at times it will come down to a matter of preference, whether to use the keyboard or the mouse.

Step by step examples of how to select text or graphics or both

As you saw earlier, the first step in the Copy/Cut and Paste operation, is to make a selection of text or graphics or both, to be Copied later to the Windows clipboard. Once you've made a selection, it should appear selected or "**highlighted**".

Please follow these examples of the different types of selections you can make, and the steps to highlight them.

To select:

- A few lines of Text, in a letter or any other open Window using the mouse.

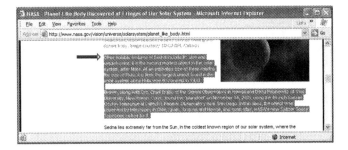

Follow these steps to select a few lines of text or text and graphics, the example above is from an article on the Nasa web site about a mysterious planet-like body orbiting our Sun, using the mouse:

- To begin, place the mouse pointer just before the very first letter of the paragraph or word you want to copy. (In this case, the word is "Pluto," so place the mouse pointer just before the "P.")
- Now click on the left mouse button and hold it down. Now, while still holding the left mouse button, move the mouse pointer in a sweeping motion across the text until everything you wish to copy is highlighted. When all the text or the text and the graphics you want selected is selected, lift your finger from the mouse button.

If after you finished making a selection, the *whole* selection of text or graphics you need to Copy/Cut is not completely highlighted, then you must click anywhere on the page, and return to your document to highlight it again.

- A single word or a complete paragraph, in a letter or any other open Window.

Follow these steps to select a single word or a complete paragraph; the example above is from the Smithsonian National Zoo Fujifilm Giant Panda Habitat web site, using the mouse:

A. To select a single word double click on it, or until the word is selected.

B. To select a whole paragraph, triple click anywhere within it. In some Windows programs, such as Word for Windows, position the mouse pointer to the left of a line of text, and select it by just clicking once.

You can also select as few as a single letter in a word, to replace it or move it (which might be useful in the case of a symbol, like for example the "@" symbol), this way:

1. Take the mouse pointer to the space *right before the letter you want to select.*

2. Now click, and notice the blinking cursor. Make sure it is located before the letter you want to change, now press and hold the left mouse button, and then move the mouse a little bit, until the letter or symbol is selected. To finish lift your finger from the mouse.

If you make a mistake while making a selection, such as moving a block of text to another part of the document you were working with, then invoke the Undo function this way: press and hold the *CTRL* key and then the *Z* one (you can also click on the menu bar over Edit, then Undo) right away, because if do further work on the document, the undo function might not work to restore a previous step.

- All of the text or all of the text and the graphics on a document (for instance from a letter you've created or a web page you are visiting).

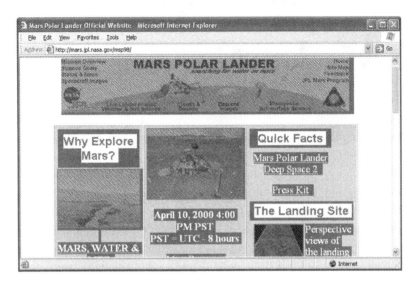

To select all the contents of the window you are looking at, such as this web page on the Mars Polar Lander, click anywhere inside the page and press and hold the *CTRL* key and then the *A* one, or click over Edit and then on "Select All".

Please be also warned that when you are finished highlighting text or text and graphics on a Word processing or any Graphic kind of program *you are creating work on*, and *you press any key* on the computer keyboard (for example the space bar), the computer will understand this action as your desire to replace *all the items you've selected* with the value of the key you've just pressed. Because of this from time to time you might hear people telling you that they don't know where the letter they were working on went.

For instance, let's just say that you have a 20-page long word processing document selected (highlighted), and you pressed the "U" letter on the keyboard (even by mistake). This action will instruct the program, to replace your entire 20 pages with the single "U" letter you've just typed. If this were to happen to you, then press and hold the *CTRL* key and then the Z key (undo) *RIGHT AWAY* to recover the part of the document that was replaced by mistake, with the value of the key you've just pressed.

How to Copy /Cut a selection to the Windows Clipboard

Once you have a selection highlighted, select the Copy command to send it to the electronic clipboard (If you select to Cut the selection, instead of copy, then it will be permanently removed from your document); where it will be ready to be pasted onto any open Window program, providing that the Windows program can accept the information on the Clipboard (as shown on the Windows clipboard page).

Additionally once a selection is on the Windows clipboard (which contents won't change until you select the Copy or Cut command again, or when you power down the computer), it will be available to be pasted onto another Windows program as many times as you need, without you having to repeat the copy command again.

These are the four ways to use the Copy/Cut command on Windows:

- By clicking over the Edit menu on the file menu of the program you are working with, and then selecting the Copy option. If you select Cut, the selection is removed from the original document.
- By clicking on the Copy or Cut button on a program Toolbar.

For example, as you can see on this toolbar in Microsoft Word 2000, if you have text or graphics or both selected, and you:

A. Click on this button (Cut) to copy the selection to the Clipboard; this action also removes it from the original location.
B. Click on this button (Copy), and the selection will be copied to the Clipboard

If you select to Cut the selection by mistake (you really meant to click on the Copy button), then press and hold the CTRL key and then the Z one **right away** (Undo) to recover the selection you lost, because if you continue working, then the program might lose track of the change you want to undo.

Bear in mind that some programs (such as the Windows Notepad) only allow you to undo the very last change you've made. Although in others, such as in Microsoft Word, you can undo a few of the steps you've taken while composing a document, by pressing and holding the *CTRL* key and then slowly tapping the *Z* key until you reach the change you want to Undo. This will work as long as you don't close the document you are working on.

- By selecting the Copy option on the menu that opens when you press the right button of the mouse over a selection you've made. On this menu you also have the option to select Cut, to remove the original selection from your document. Although the later only works to remove selections from documents that you have a right to change, like is the case with your own letters or graphic designs, because you cannot really cut information on a web site, unless is something you've written.

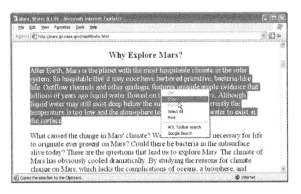

This is the way, as you can see on this example of a selection I made of information I found on a JPL web site, to copy it using the mouse:

Take the mouse pointer over the selection, press the right mouse button, and select Copy. Please note how on this example the option to Cut the selection is not available, because this is a read only web page.

- By pressing and holding the *CTRL* key and then the *C* one to copy, or the *X* one if you want to remove (Cut) the original selection from your document.

If neither the option to Copy or Cut are available, when you right mouse click over a selection, then that means that the items you've previously selected were accidentally un-selected, and now you should select them again.

Right after you finish copying a selection you should single click anywhere on the page to unselect it, so that it cannot be accidentally deleted, when you press any key on your keyboard.

How to copy a single graphic to the Windows clipboard

To copy a graphic object, such as a single photo you found on a Web site, or from one of your own documents, is very easy to do, and generally speaking, you don't need to select it beforehand, before copying it.

On the next screen capture, from a photo that Frances (Somesei on her Flickr account) took of the Washington Zoo 10 month old panda "Butterstick" (Tai Shan) with his keeper Cathy Morvick, you can see an example of how to copy a single photo, that you can later use in one of your own documents.

To copy a single photo is simple; just right-click on the image you want to copy and on the menu (that opens up) click on Copy. Please note that on this menu there will be other options you can take, such as "Save Picture As" to save the photo to your hard drive or "E-mail Picture", to attach the photo to an e-mail message (the later only works if you use Outlook Express or Outlook e-mail client, and it doesn't work with the America Online software).

Now, after you select Copy, the photo/graphic is sent to the Windows Clipboard, which will hold it, and it will be ready to be pasted to any Windows application, with just a few clicks of the mouse, or by just pressing a few keys on the keyboard.

 Always remember to give the proper credit to the source of the information/photos you find and use, even on school papers, which most of the time just involves quoting the place where you got it.

How to paste a selection you've copied to the Windows Clipboard

This is the last step to share data amongst open program windows, and is the easiest one to complete, providing you've strictly followed the select and Copy or Cut steps I outlined on the previous pages.

These are the final steps to Paste the contents of a selection, you sent to the Windows clipboard (for instance a photo you Copied following the instructions on the previous page) using the Copy/Cut Command, to the program of your choice:

1. First select/change to the destination window (using the Taskbar or the ALT + TAB key combination), unless the destination location is the same document you selected/copied/cut data from, to the **Program window** to which you want to paste the selection then:

   • Now place the mouse pointer on the exact place (page, line or paragraph) in your document, where you want to paste the data on the clipboard and **click on it** or use the arrow keys to move the blinking cursor there. Now the blinking cursor which looks like this; |, will indicate the point where the copied/cut selection is to be pasted.
   • If you've just opened a *new document*, and you don't select a beginning place to Paste to, then the Pasted information will be pasted starting at the very beginning of the document.

2. Now finally invoke the Paste command, which can also be done in four different ways:

   • By clicking on the *Edit* menu item, and then selecting the *Paste* option.
   • By clicking on the *Paste* icon on a program Toolbar.

   For example on the toolbar of Microsoft Word 2000, if you've copied something previously, and you:

   • Click on this icon (Paste), the contents of the Windows Clipboard will be pasted onto your document, beginning at the blinking cursor.

Now you can repeat the Paste command, as many times you want, and in each case you will get the same information from the Windows Clipboard, that is until you invoke the Copy or Cut command again, or shut down your computer.

- By invoking the Paste option on the menu that opens when you press the right button of the mouse on the document you are working on.

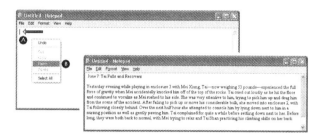

On this Screen capture you can see how some text (which I found on the Washington Zoo web site) is pasted onto the Windows Notepad, this way:

    A. This is the blinking cursor that indicates the beginning of where the selection will be pasted.

    B. Right click anywhere in the document, to which you want to send the contents of the Clipboard, now click on Paste.

    C. Now you can see the Pasted text, on the work area of Notepad. If you are working on a document, and you select to Paste again, then the same information will be pasted, beginning at the end of the information you've pasted.

- By pressing and holding the *CTRL* key and then the V one to Paste the contents of the Windows Clipboard, to the Active window, beginning at the blinking cursor.

Bear in mind that when you finish Pasting a selection of data you previously chose to Copy/ or Cut, from an open program window to a different one or even from one page/line in the same document you are working on to another one, that the resulting data will be an exact replica of the original selection you Copied/ or Cut.

There is a few exceptions to this rule; let say for example that you made a selection, on a web site (of text and graphics objects), copied it, and then opened the Windows Notepad to paste it into it. Now most of the original text will be pasted, but if they were are any tables or graphics (which Notepad cannot work with) on the original document, then they won't be pasted over onto Notepad.

Some real world examples of using Copy or Cut and Paste

If you already know how to use the Copy and Paste process, then you should move to the next chapter of this book, but you are still not sure of how to complete this process, then please use the following examples to get a better grasp of the Copy/Cut and Paste process to complete your every day computer work.

These are four different situations, of using the Copy and Paste command. For example:

- Paste the contents of the Windows Clipboard as many times as you need to.

> Larry O'Toole
> 2345 Summer Way
> Acadia, CT 06902
>
> Larry O'Toole
> 2345 Summer Way
> Acadia, CT 06902
>
> Larry O'Toole
> 2345 Summer Way
> Acadia, CT 06902
>
> Larry O'Toole
> 2345 Summer Way
> Acadia, CT 06902

For example to make return labels, open any Word processing, and type your name and address (once), select it, and Copy it. Now; a) Click outside of the document, to unselect it, and b) Press the Enter key twice to position the blinking cursor two lines below the first letter of the last line of your address. Notice that the blinking cursor should be flush to the left of the document. Now select Paste by pressing and holding down the CTRL key, and then the V key. Repeat this as many times as you need to (press the Return key twice each time you use Paste, so that the next address block is separated from the previous one). Later on you can print the resulting document, cut the addresses and then use glue/tape to affix them to your envelopes.

Or create a Help Wanted Ad, this way: 1) Type your name and phone number once on a line, and generate 10 or so instances of it using the same procedure shown on this page, and Print it, 2) Type your Ad, and print it, 3) Cut the Names/ Phone numbers and affix them sideways at the bottom of the Ad. Finally find a Kinko's copy place to make photocopies of your Ad. Using Word for Windows and Paintbrush you can avoid having to visit a copy center, but this is a little more challenging to the novice.

- To move parts of a document around, to improve it. For example on the following screen captures, of a letter I typed using the Windows Notepad, you can see the whole process of moving a selection of words in a letter.

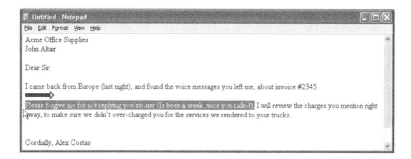

To begin with, I selected the words that begin: "Please forgive me . . . " (Shown highlighted) up to the comma. Now I pressed and held the *CTRL* key and then the *X* one (which achieves the same results as clicking over Edit + Cut), to remove this selection of words from the second paragraph.

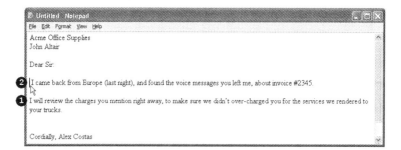

Now you can see, that the selection of words that begins: "Please forgive . . . " was removed. Now I must prepare the letter this way, before I invoke the Paste command, to bring it back to the first paragraph of the letter:

1. To begin I pressed the Backspace key to remove one space, until the letter "I" is completely lined with the left margin.
2. Then I took the mouse pointer right before the "I" on "I came back . . . " and clicked; to place the blinking cursor there.

Please bear in mind that the blinking cursor marks the point, where if you were to invoke the Paste command, in one of the ways shown earlier, the contents of the clipboard will be pasted.

Please note that when you use Copy/Cut and Paste, that the program automatically makes room for the Pasted data. For instance if you select and copy a twenty-page letter, and pasted it at the beginning of a one-page letter, now your one page letter will be twenty-one pages long.

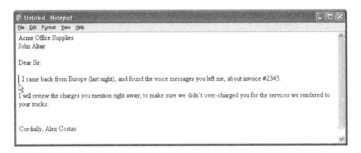

Now I pressed the Space Bar to add an extra space to the left of the "I", then pressed once the left arrow key to move the cursor one space to the left of the "I", to separate the last word of the line I want to paste here with the "I".

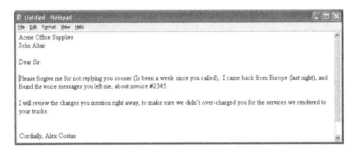

Now, to bring back the selection I removed earlier, I invoked the Paste command, by pressing/ and holding the *CTRL* key and then the *V* one. Clicking over Edit, and then selecting Paste accomplishes the same thing.

Finally you can see the finish letter, in which I moved a selection of words from one paragraph to another with the help of Cut and Paste, which would had also worked if I had had to move 50 pages or more from one end of a letter to another.

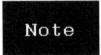

Do not close a file you been working, while using Copy and Paste or Cut and Paste to move data around, until you are sure that all your paragraphs are accounted for.

- To use text, you've composed using a word processing program, you want to Paste into a new e-mail message

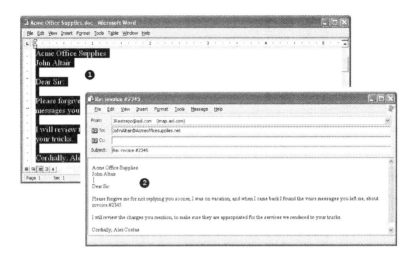

These are the steps to Copy and Paste text, from a base program (you chose because it has a good speller), to the body of an e-mail message:

1. Open Word, compose and proofread a message (press the F7 key to open the Spell/Grammar checker). Now press and hold the *CTRL* key and then the *A* one, to select it. Next press and hold the *CTRL* key and then the *C* one, to copy it to the Clipboard.

2. Now start composing a New e-mail message, in Outlook or with ANY e-mail client program you use, click on the main body of the message (white space), and then press and hold the *CTRL* key and then the *V* one, to paste it here. Now finish composing the e-mail message, adding the recipient addresses and then click on Send, to send it.

For this example I chose to create a new e-mail message using the Outlook Express e-mail client, but this will work just as well if you have any other e-mail client program, including the America Online software.

To review how to work with different windows at the same time revisit chapter 2 (Working with a Microsoft Window), and chapter 6 (Using computer Programs in Windows).

- To replace a selection of text

  Let say, for example, that Jane is typing a letter to her accountant to get a copy of last year income tax return, with his address, but somehow she now remembers that he has moved to another city. Plus she remembered that his office (a few months ago) sent her an e-mail with the new address (which Jane overlooked), or she find the new address on the web, and now wants to copy and paste it, to replace the old address on the letter she just typed to him.

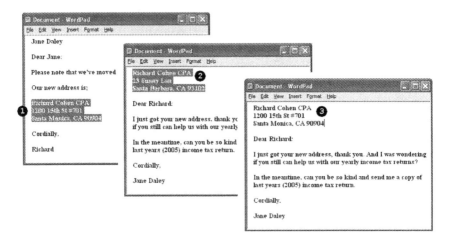

  These are the steps, to use Copy and Paste to replace a selection of text:

  1. This is the e-mail that Jane got, with the *correct address*. Now she selects it, and then presses and holds the *CTRL* key and then the *C* one, to copy it.
  2. Now she returns to the original letter she typed, with the old address, and now she selects (highlights) the old address, which she wants to replace with the correct one.
  3. Now she presses and holds the *CTRL* key and then the *V* one, to Paste it onto her letter, replacing the old address with the new correct one.

The main advantage of moving information this way, as opposed to re-typing it yourself, is that when you do these steps right, all the original information will transfer, so there is no chance that you will misspell something important.

Chapter 11

The Microsoft Windows Multimedia Experience

Introduction to the Multimedia Experience on Microsoft Windows

A Windows "Multimedia" computer system is the type equipped with the appropriate hardware and software, that allows its users to seamlessly experience movie and sound files. Most Windows computers in sale today are multimedia ready.

On a Multimedia-ready computer, you will be able to see images, hear sound, and experience full-motion video—either from files already on your computer, or from your CD's, DVDs, as well as websites (such as YouTube) you visit on the Internet.

There are a few basic requirements that a Microsoft Windows computer should meet to be able to take advantage of the full Multimedia experience:

- On the hardware side:

  - ✓ A good video card, otherwise movie files may not look very sharp.
  - ✓ A good sound card, otherwise the sound will be of poor quality.
  - ✓ A good set of computer speakers, preferably the type with volume controls on the speakers.
  - ✓ Enough available Ram memory—256 Megabytes is a good number, though you may be able to enjoy Multimedia files with less memory.
  - ✓ A CD or DVD drive unit.

- On the software side:

  - ✓ A digital media player, like the Microsoft Windows Media player.
  - ✓ The latest update to DirectX, which is a free Microsoft software add-on that makes Windows-based computers the ideal platform for running applications rich in multimedia elements (such as full-color graphics, video, 3D animation, and rich audio). To obtain this free software add-on visit the Direct X website at this URL: (*http://www.microsoft.com/windows/directx/default.aspx*) and follow the instructions to download the latest version.
  - ✓ The right video codec, which is an analog-to-digital (A/D) and digital-to-analog (D/A) converter for translating video and audio signals from the outside world to digital, and back again. On the last page of this chapter you will learn how to automatically download video codec's.
  - ✓ DVD decoder software, so that you can play your DVD movies.

Any computer you buy today will meet these requirements. But if you own an older computer that lacks a good sound or video card, it might be a good investment to replace both cards to improve its sound and video capabilities.

Opening the Microsoft Windows Media Player

The Windows Media Player is an intrinsic part of the Windows Entertainment group of programs, located under the *Accessories* group of programs.

You can open/launch the Windows Media Player, in one of the following ways:

- Place a music CD/ or DVD disk in the CD/DVD drive, now the Auto Play function should recognize its type and offer you a few choices you can take. Double click on the one you want to use. On this example I double clicked on: Play audio CD, to open the Windows media player.

Windows Media
Player

- If you see the Windows Media Player icon on the Windows Desktop, then double click it to open the program.
- You can also open the Windows Media Player from the *Start* menu, this way: to begin click on the *Start* menu button, now take the mouse pointer over to *All Programs* and wait a few seconds (In Windows 98 click on *Start*, then Programs). Now move the mouse to the right and up and until you find the *Accessories* group, then over to the right and down (or maybe up) until you find the *Entertainment* group. Finally take the mouse pointer over to the *Entertainment* group, and then click on the *Windows Media Player* icon, to open it.

Once the Windows Media Player opens you will be able to work with most of the different types of windows media files, but bear in mind that the Window Media Player won't be able to work with *all* Multimedia files (such as QuickTime files or Real Network ones).

Introduction to the Microsoft Windows Media Player

The Microsoft Windows Media Player, which is included free with the Microsoft Windows operating system, can be the center of all your Multimedia needs.

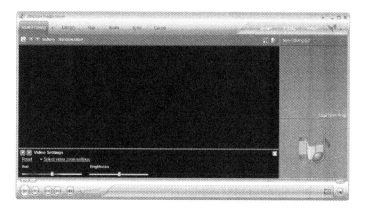

This is the main working window of the Microsoft Windows Media Player 10, which is still one of the best versions of this media player.

Using the Windows Media Player you will be able to:

- Listen to sound files—music on your own CDs, or Podcast files you've saved on your computer.
- Copy music from the CDs you own to your computer, using a process called "ripping"; which allows you to listed to music tracks on your computer without producing the original CD, or to download them to MP3 players.
- Watch movie clips of many different file types (Mp3, Mpeg and Avi, which are some of the most popular formats used).
- Make your own music CDs using music files you've previously copied/ripped to your computer.
- Listen to Internet Radio Stations.

If you don't have version 10 of this excellent media player, then you can get it for free, by visiting the Microsoft Windows media home at this URL; *http://www.microsoft.com/windows/windowsmedia/player/10/default.aspx* Once this web page loads click on *Download Now*, and follow the onscreen prompts.

The Features Taskbar on Microsoft Windows Media Player 10

The *Features taskbar* consists of different tabs running across the top of the Windows Media Player 10 window. When clicked, they present you with different options you can use to either work with media files or listen to content found on the Internet.

To use the Media Player, just click on the tab label/name. For instance, click on:

- *Now playing* to watch/listen video/audio files, you've opened. On the right side of this window you will see the names cued on the Playlist.
- *Library* to work with media files you or a program has added to the computer, to the default Windows Media files folder
- *Rip* to begin transferring your music CDs to your computer.
- *Burn* to burn music CDs from the music you've ripped.
- *Sync* to synchronize an MP3 player with your computer's Playlist.
- *Guide* to find movies, movie trailers, and TV shows.

On the right side of the player you will see the following tabs:
- *Music.* From here you can purchase music online.
- *Radio.* You will see a list of Internet radio stations.
- *Video.* From here you can purchase videos on the Internet.

To find music you might have added to your PC using a different media player: 1) Click on the Library tab, and 2) Click on + *Add to Library (lower part of this window)*, and then 3) Click on *By Searching Computer.* Now click on Search, to find it, and when the search is over click on Close

Working with the Video Settings/Playback/Volume Controls on Windows Media Player 10

At the bottom of the Windows Media Player 10 window you will find an array of controls you can use with your movie and music files. For instance, if you are playing a 5-minute movie clip, you can use the **Seek** slider to advance to the exact point in the movie you want to watch.

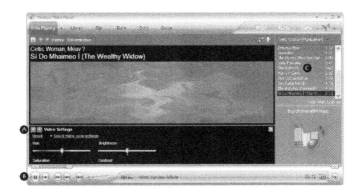

This is the way to work with the different windows media player settings:

A. Video Settings: Click on these arrows (left and right) to work with different settings (such as Graphic Equalizer), you can use to enhance your multimedia experience. Right clicking on these arrows and selecting the setting you want to work with, accomplishes the same thing.

B. The playback controls: These allow you to control basic playback tasks such as Play, Pause, Stop, Rewind, and Fast-forward for audio and video files. You can also adjust the volume here.

C. On the top right panel, notice the names of the tracks cued to play. To play a different one than the one currently playing, just double click on any name. To delete the items on this list, select them and press delete.

To use one of these slider controls, first take the mouse pointer over to the slider guide, now press/ and hold the left mouse button, and move the appropriate slider to the left or right. For example, to work with the sound volume, move the slider guide to the left to decrease the volume and to the right to increase it.

Ripping Music from Your Own CDs Using the Windows Media Player

The audio files saved on CD discs tend to be very large, so when you save songs to your computer (using the Windows Media Player), they are converted to a smaller format using a process called "ripping." And once you've ripped a song, you can play it over and over again (without producing the original CD) or even download it to a portable music device or MP3 player; using a process called *Sync*.

To begin open the Windows media player in one of the ways shown before.

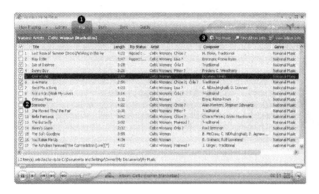

Now, place the music CD on the CD/or DVD drive and follow these steps:

1. Begin by clicking on the *Rip* tab. Now you will see the list of the songs on your CD; by default, all of them will have a check-mark, indicating that they are selected to be ripped. In this example there are two songs that are not checked because they were previously ripped (copied to your computer).
2. Please click on the squares beside any songs you don't want ripped. Click on the check box above the # 1, to unchecked all of the songs.
3. If the names of the songs don't show up (they read Track 1, Track 2, and so on), and you are connected to the Internet then click on *Find Album info* (before clicking on *Rip music)*, and Windows Media player will try to find their names. Finally click on *Rip Music*. (If you are prompted to choose the format for the files being created. Select "keep my current format settings.")

If you've inserted the music CD before opening the Windows Media player, then at the Audio CD dialog box window double click *Rip music from CD*, to start the ripping process right away. Note: Even after the ripping process is underway, you can still uncheck any un-ripped tracks you don't want copied to your computer.

Saving a Movie or Sound File to Your Computer

The general process to save movie or sound files you found on the Internet to your computer is very similar to the process to save photos, device drivers, or other types of files.

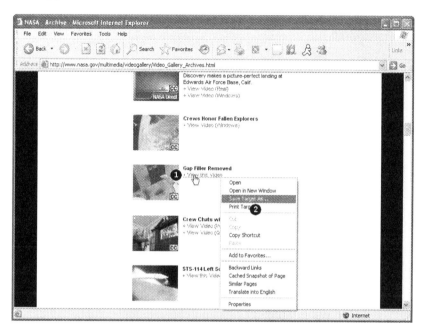

Here's an example of how to save a file from the NASA multimedia web site:

1. To begin find the movie/or music file you want to download, now place the mouse pointer over its name (wait until the mouse pointer turns into a little hand), and right-click on it.
2. On the menu that opens, click *Save Target As* to begin the process to save this file to your hard drive.

You can double click on the file to stream it directly from the Internet, but it often makes more sense to save the file directly to your computer. When a movie plays over the Internet, it can be choppy, whereas if you save the entire file to your computer to play it later, it should render/play smoothly.

When you double click on a media file, then the compatible media player should open: For instance if the file is of the ".wav" type, then the Windows Media Player should open rendering it.

Now you must tell the computer where to save the file, if you chose to save it, by using the options in the *Save As* windows. If you don't select a different folder than the one whose name you can see beside *Save in*—in this example it is *My Videos*—then the file will be saved at the level of the folder name shown there.

To save a movie or a sound file you found on the web, just follow these steps:

A. First read the name of the folder, as noted above. If the folder shown is not the one where you want to save this file, then click in front of *Save in* or use the buttons on the left side of this dialog box window to select a different drive or folder.
B. In front of "File name" you will see the name of the movie or sound file you want to save.
C. Finally click on *Save* to save it to your computer. After the file is saved, you can access it any time by returning to the folder where you save it and double clicking on its name or by opening the Windows Media player first, selecting File then Open, then finding it using the Open dialog box.

If you don't remember how to work with the different options in the *Save As* window, then please see chapter nine; "Storing and Retrieving Your Computer Work in Windows."

If you wish to, you can change the file name shown, this way: If the name is selected (if not click on it), press the right arrow key and then use the backspace key to remove part of it, or just type additional letters to it. For instance if the suggested name was space shuttle, you can add a # 2 at the end to make it spaceshuttle2.

Note

Although the suggested place to download videos is the *My Videos* folder (*My Music* for audio files), you can save a file anywhere on your hard drive, or even to an external USB flash drive.

Creating a New Playlist in Windows Media Player

One of the advantages of using the Media player is the ease with which one can create different Playlists or compilations of your music. To begin, open the Windows Media Player, and then click on the *Library* tab. Now click on the *Now Playing List* button (on the right side), and then click on the **Clear List** menu item. To begin, click on *Library Options* (top of next window), and then click on *Add to List on Double-click.*

To begin adding new music tracks to a new Playlist just do the following:

A. To look for music, single-click on the plus sign next to the name of the Album (under All Music) or any other category you wish to use to find music. To, if you enabled the *Add to List on Double-click,* add the complete album/genre to your Playlist double-click on its name.

B. Now you can see, in the middle panel, the music corresponding to the selection you made on the left panel. To add a single music track simply double-click on its name. To select contiguous items, click on the name of the first one, and (while pressing and holding the SHIFT key) click on the last one. To select nonadjacent items, press and hold the CTRL key, to click on the ones you want to add. Now, click and hold the left mouse button on any of the tracks you've selected, and then drag them over to the right panel.

C. On the right panel you will see the music tracks you've added to this Playlist.

To save your Playlist click over Now Playing List, bring the mouse indicator down and then click over Save Playlist As. On the window that opens, name your Playlist according to the choice of music tracks you've added to it (such as Dinner Music).

Listening to a Playlist You've Created

One way to work with your Playlist's is to click on the *Now Playing* tab. Notice that on the screenshot below it reads "Dinner music." To continue listening to a Playlist whose name you see there, click on the controls at the bottom left (such as Pause).

This is the way to listen to a different (other than the one shown) saved Playlist:

1. To begin, click on the name shown (see the arrow), or on Now Playing list.
2. Now bring the mouse indicator down, over Open Playlist.
3. Finally move the mouse indicator, to the left or right and click on the name of the Playlist. Now the Windows media player will begin rendering all of the tracks you've added to it; and it will stop when it reaches the end of the last track, or when you press the Pause or Stop buttons.

To repeat all of its tracks, press and hold the CTRL key and then the T One. To shuffle the tracks in the Playlist—so they play in random order—press and hold the CTRL key and then the H one. To remove a track from a Playlist (while you are listening to it), just right-click over the name of the track in the upper right panel, and then click *Remove from list*. If you click on delete, you will be asked if you want to "Delete from library only" or "Delete from library and my computer." Pick on the appropriate choice, and click *OK*. To add additional tracks to the Playlist, click on the *Library* tab, then on the *Now Playing list* label. Then move your mouse to select Edit Playlist, and click on the name of the Playlist you want to add tracks to. Now follow the same procedure you used to create the Playlist to add more tracks to it.

Listening to Your Music Files/Tracks or Watching Your Video Files Using the Windows Media player

The Windows Media player is ideal for playing video and music files you've saved to your computer—or for playing files you've found on the Internet.

These are four different ways to experience video or music files using your Windows computer:

1. Return to the Windows Media Player, click on *File*, and then select the *Open* command. If you cannot see the File menu item, double-click on the *Windows Media Player* name (shown next to the Windows logo).

    Now navigate to the folder you've saved your file to. When you see the file you are looking for, double-click on its name to open it.

2. To find music/or video files you've saved, double-click on the Music or the My Videos folder (under the My Documents folder), or open the Windows Explorer or the My Computer program.

    When you find the file you are looking for then just double-click on its name to open it.

Please note that in the above screen capture that there are two additional files next to the Windows Media player one: The one in the middle is a QuickTime movie file, and the one on the right is a Real Network file. At the end of this chapter you will learn how to obtain the free media players you will need to run files of this kind.

If you are having trouble opening or watching a video file, then you may not have the correct software add-on for the Windows Media player; these are called software Codecs. At the end of this chapter you will learn how to change your Windows Media Player settings to allow it to download codecs automatically.

3. To play a video or a sound file, you see on a web site, click on its link (while pressing and holding the CTRL key down).

Please note that on this NASA website some of the files have "Windows" in parenthesis. This means they are compatible with the Windows Media Player. To play it, just click next to +*View Video (Windows)*.

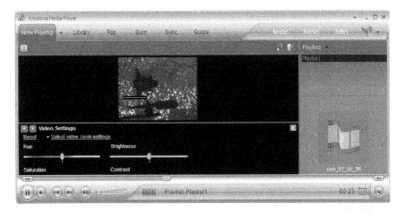

The movie you've chosen should start playing in the Windows Media player. To adjust the different Video settings, use the controls you read about on previous pages—if, for instance, you want to skip ahead in the movie or adjust the volume. You can also double click anywhere in the movie being played to bring up the *Full Mode* option, which makes the movie play in full screen. To return to a normal screen, just press the ESC key.

Please bear in mind that the Windows Media Player won't have any trouble playing the music you've ripped yourself, but it cannot play some files you've copied using a different music player, such as ".aac" or ".mp4.", created by the iTunes player.

4. To listen to the individual music tracks you've added just follow these steps:

1. Click on the *Library* tab to see all the music you've ripped or downloaded from the Internet using the Windows Media Player.

2. Next click on the plus sign next to *All Music*. Notice now that you can find music by clicking on the plus sign next to; *Album Artist, Contributing Artist, Composer, etc.* If you double click on any of the aforementioned categories, for instance Genre, then all the music filed under it will start playing. If you double click on just name of an album, artist, etc, all its saved songs will start playing.

3. Now if you single clicked on one of the aforementioned categories then you will see, on the middle column, the list of songs saved under it. To play a few of these songs, press and hold the CTRL key and then single click on each track you want to hear. Now click on one of the names selected, immediately press and hold the left mouse button and then drag the tracks to the right column, to listen to them.

If you single clicked on All Music, then all of the music in the Library will appear in the middle panel. If you double clicked on All Music, all of your saved music will begin playing. Please notice that each time you make a selection, it's saved tracks replaces the previous selection tracks shown on the middle panel.

Learning to Sync Your Music with an MP3 Player using Windows Media Player

One of the great features of the Windows Media Player is that it allows you—very easily—to download music from your library to a portable MP3 player using a process called Sync.

To start synchronize your music, open the Windows Media Player.

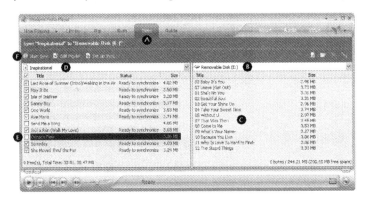

Here's how to use the sync process to download music to your MP3 player:

A. To begin click on the Sync tab.
B. Now connect your MP3 Player to your personal computer using the provided cable. Notice a label with something like "*Removable disk.*" If you don't see it, your MP3 is either not compatible with the Windows Media Player—in which case try using the software that came with it, or not connected to your PC.
C. If there are any songs, on the MP3 player, then they will be listed here.
D. Click on this line to **select** the Playlist or the Album you want to copy to the MP3 player. Use the PageDown/Up, down and up arrow keys to navigate this list. When you find it, click on it or press the Enter key.
E. You can click on any song to unselect it, if you don't want it on your MP3 player. It will be removed from the list of tracks to be downloaded.
F. Finally, to download the songs you've selected, click on *Start Sync*.

Note that if you delete a Playlist from your library, then the corresponding Playlist on your MP3 player will also be deleted the next time you choose to synchronize it with your computer, using this process.

Burning Your Own Music CDs from Music Tracks You've Ripped

Once you've ripped a few songs from your CD collection, then you can make your own CDs with the music saved on your computer. For example, if you've ripped music tracks from five different CDs, then you can make a CD that includes Track 1 from one CD, Track 3 from another one, and so on.

These are the steps, as you can see on this screenshot, to burn your own CDs:

1. To begin click on the *Library* Tab.
2. Now click on the plus sign next to All Music to look for each track you want to add to your CD, and click on either: *Album Artist, Contributing Artist, Composer, Album, Genre, Year Released,* or *Purchased Music* to see them.
3. For this example I clicked on the plus sign next to *Album* to see the list of all of the *Albums* saved there.
4. Click on the *Album name* you want to select tracks from. To select right away all of its tracks, right click on its name and then click on *Add to burn list.*
5. Now right-click on the name of the track you want to add to your CD.
6. Finally move the mouse pointer down to *Add To,* and then click on *Burn List* to add this track to the *Burn list.* Alternatively, you can right-click over a particular Playlist, in which you've added particular songs, and then select *Add to Burn List* to burn all of those tracks.

Repeat this process until you've selected all the songs you want to add to your CD. But keep in mind that if the message: "will not fit" appears next to any tracks you've selected, then those tracks will not be burned to the CD.

Now place a blank CD-R or CD-RW in your CD/or DVD drive. If you've changed your mind about any of the tracks you've selected, then click to clear any check boxes (on the left side of the screen) next to the songs you no longer want to burn.

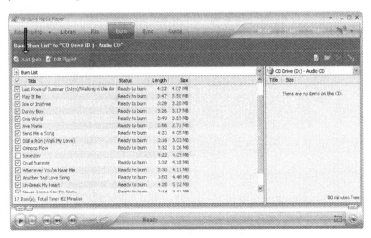

To start burning your CD just click on the Burn tab, and then on *Start Burn*. If any of the tracks you've selected to burn has a copy-protection feature, then the burning process will be halted, and you will see the following message:

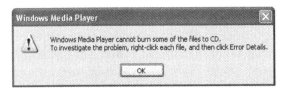

You may see this message if the song (you are trying to burn) is of a kind, not allowed to be burned. While you might still be able to listen to this music track from your computer, you cannot burn it to a CD. To proceed, just click on OK.

Now click on this box to remove/uncheck the song with the error; otherwise the burning operation won't proceed. Click on *Start Burn* again. When the Disk is ready you will be able to listen to the music in it on most newer standalone CD units.

Adjusting Your Computer's Volume

If you cannot hear sound on the speakers connected to your computer, it could just be due to the fact that the volume is all the way down, or turned to mute. This is easy to fix: You can adjust the volume from the control panel or from the Volume icon on the system tray—or you can use the volume control on your speakers (which is available in most newer computer speakers).

Here's how to adjust the volume from the system tray:

1. First click on the speaker icon to open the volume settings.
2. Now a small dialog box opens. To change the volume take the mouse pointer over the guide, and press and hold the left mouse button while you drag it up to increase the volume or down to decrease it. To finish click outside of it.

If you do not see the speaker icon on your system tray, then you can change the volume by working with the sound settings on the control panel (explained on the next page).

As you saw in Chapter 4 ("Programs included in Windows XP to Manage Your Computer and its Resources"), the control panel houses a group of programs that can be used to change your personal setting.

Using the control panel, here's how to increase or decrease the volume:

1. First click on the Start menu button.
2. Now take the mouse pointer up, to the right and then click on Control Panel
3. If you only see a few icons then you are in Category view. To change the Sound volume, click "Sound Speech and Audio Devices," then "Adjust the system volume." If, on the other hand, you see a plain background with many icons, double click on "Sounds and Audio devices."

Here's how to work with the volume settings:

A. If it is not already checked, click on *Place volume icon on the taskbar,* so that the Volume setting icon is always visible on the Taskbar.
B. To change the volume take the mouse pointer over to the guide (as shown above), and press and hold the left mouse button as you drag the cursor to the left to decrease the volume and to the right to increase it. When done making changes, close this window.

If the mute option is checked, click on it to uncheck it. If after adjusting the volume, you are still not able to hear sound, then check the connection from your speakers to the computer. Also check to see if the speakers are equipped with a volume knob; if they are, turn it to the right to increase the sound volume.

Troubleshooting Problems Viewing Movie Files in Windows

In Windows you will be able to play most of the movie files you find on the Internet as well as those that you receive from family, and co-workers. From time to time, however, these video files might be too choppy to watch, or even refuse to play. If a movie refuses to play, then this is usually due to the lack of a software component called a codec. On this page you will learn how to make sure your Windows Media Player finds/downloads them every time it needs a new one.

When you attempt to open a movie file and this dialog box appears (*Windows Media Player cannot play the file . . .*), then the player is most likely missing the requisite Codec.

There are two things you can do to correct the problem:

- Open the Windows Media Player and click on *Tools*, then *Options*. Make sure that the box beside *Download codec Automatically* is checked. If it is not, then click to check it
- Download the DIVX codec—one of the most popular movie codec's in use today—by opening your web browser and going to this website: *http://www.divx.com/divx/codec.php*. Now follow the instructions under "How do you get your hands on the free DivX codec for Windows . . ." to download it.

To download additional media players—QuickTime or Real Networks—open your web browser and do the following:

A. To get the free QuickTime movie player, go to this website: *http://www.apple.com/quicktime/download/win.html*. Click on *Free Download Now*, and follow the prompts to download this movie player.
B. To get Real Network's Real Player go to this website: *http://www.real.com/*. Click on *Free Download* and follow the prompts.

While you are on these websites downloading their free media player, they will try to sell you higher-end players. But you usually don't need to buy anything to download the free, basic media player they offer you.

Chapter 12

Learn to Print Your Work in Microsoft Windows

Introduction to printing in Microsoft Windows

Printing your work using your Windows-based personal computer system can be one of the most important and satisfying computer tasks you can master. And keep in mind that in Windows the general process of printing any document you are working on, almost regardless of the program you are using is the same (with only a few exceptions, mainly databases and some spreadsheets).

In this chapter, you will learn to send your work to a personal printer with efficiency, and to avoid some common problems associated with printing.

The process to print your computer work to a printer directly connected to your computer (such as this Epson connected to the Dell computer shown), or a network printer associated with a local-area network (LAN) is very easy to complete. This process is common to all versions of the Windows operating system:

1. While you are working in a program, select *Print* after clicking on the *File* menu item or by clicking on the Print icon on a program toolbar.
2. If you have more than one printer, you may now choose which printer will receive the print job. If you don't change the selection, the job will go to the printer set as the default one.
3. Finally click on OK.

In Windows all the programs installed on the computer share the same printers to which the computer is setup to have access to, and generally speaking you also don't have to wait for the printer to finish printing a job, before you can send an additional one to be printed, which will be sent to the Print queue, which organizes the print jobs in the order they were sent to the printer. As soon as the printer finishes a print job, it continues to the next one on the Print queue.

Tip Always keep some extra ink available for your printer, because if the ink runs out in the middle of a job, and you keep using it, then this might ruin some printers, making then incredible expensive to fix.

Printing from the file menu

Printing from the File menu is the most common way to send your work to a printer connected to your computer, or if you work on a LAN or local area network, to a network printer you have permission to print to.

But first, prior to printing your work, make sure that the printer you want to print to is turned on, ready, and stocked with the kind of paper you wish to use. (Bear in mind that some print jobs, such as the printing of digital photographs, require a special kind of paper.). And before you print save your work (see chapter nine).

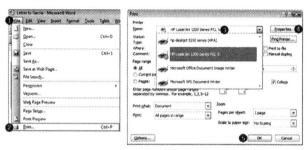

These are the steps to print your work from the File menu:

1. While looking at the document you want to print, be that a web page or a letter you've typed, click on the *File* menu item.
2. Now click on the Print option on this drop-down menu. In Windows XP, if the option to Print is not visible right away, it might be necessary to expand the drop-down menu, by placing the mouse pointer on the double arrow (at the bottom of the drop-down menu) so that you can see it.
3. On the Print dialog box window, click in front of Name to select a printer other than the default printer, if you so desire.
4. To change printer settings, click on the Properties field of the printer you wish to use and make the appropriate changes (e.g., if you wish to print using glossy paper). Close this window, to return to the Print window.
5. Finally click on OK to start printing your document.

The printer will now receive the print job, and one of two things will happen: It will complete the job, or it will fail to do so. If it fails to print, then it will be up to you to ascertain, based on the visual information you can gather (such as the paper tray is empty, which is solved by adding more paper) or by looking at the front light in front of the printer, why the printer could not complete the printing process.

Printing from a program toolbar

To print your work from the toolbar, single click on the printer button (indicated by the arrow on the next screen capture). To print a second copy of the same document, click again; each click will result in a copy of the same document.

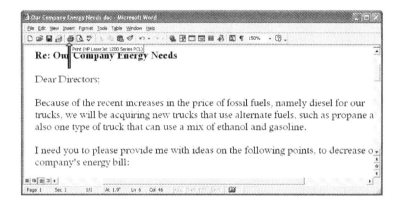

Disadvantages of printing from the toolbar include:

- Lack of control over what page range of the document you want to send to the printer: Once you click on the printer icon, the program will send the entire document to the printer, whether it is a one-page letter or a hundred-page legal brief. It's possible to cancel the print job after it has started, but if you have a fast laser printer it will print a lot of pages before you can stop it.
- Printing from the toolbar does not allow you to select the printer you wish to use. Suppose, for example, you wish to print a long webpage with many graphics on your laser printer but you have set an ink-jet printer as your default. If you click on the printer icon without selecting a different one, you will send the document to the color printer, wasting precious ink.

Because of this last point you may wish to confirm which printer will receive the print job, prior to clicking on the print button on the Toolbar. To do this, place your mouse pointer over the print button, without clicking over it. The name of the printer to which the document will be sent will now appear (see the screenshot, it reads "Print (HP Laser Jet 1200 series PCL"). If this is not the printer you want to use, click on File and follow the steps of the previous page (printing from the File Menu) to select the right printer. One you have done so, the printer you chose should remain your default printer until you close the program.

Using the print-preview option

Most Windows programs, mainly word-processing and graphics programs, function under a premise called WYSIWYG, short for "What you see (on the screen) is what you get (on paper).", which is pretty accurate, unless the printer you use is not capable of handling the information it receives from the program.

If you want you can preview a document (to see how it will look once printed), by clicking on *File*. Then, click on *Print Preview*.

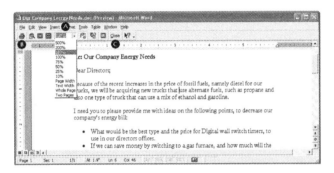

This is the way to work with the Print Preview window in Ms. Word:

A. To adjust how much of the document appears in the preview window, click on the zoom menu, and click on a different percentage to enlarge or reduce the preview setting of your document.
B. If you are happy with the preview of your document, click on the print icon to print it, but if is a long document and you only want to print a selected range of pages, then click on Close and see the instructions that follow on the next page.
C. To close the preview and return to your document, click on Close.

You can also zoom in or out of the document you are working on using the middle wheel of the mouse, this way; press and hold the CTRL key, roll the wheel away from you, the document is magnified (zoom in), if you roll it towards you, the document is minimized (zoom out). This tip also works in websites you are visiting.

In some programs, such as Microsoft Word, you will find an icon (on the toolbar) that looks like a magnifying glass over a blank page. If you click on this icon, it will also open the print preview.

Using the page-range settings to print only certain pages of your document

This setting, available when printing from most Windows programs, is one of the most useful features you will find in the Print dialog box window. It will help you save ink and paper.

To use the page-range settings, you have to invoke the *Print* command from the *File* menu instead of the print icon on the toolbar; by clicking over *File* and then selecting the *Print* command.

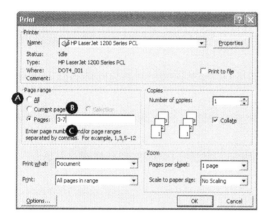

This is the way to work with the Page range options:

A. The default setting is *All*, on this Print dialog box. Meaning if you click on OK, without making any changes, to the print range, all of the pages on the document you are working on will be sent to the printer.

B. If you choose "Current page," and click on OK, only the page you are currently looking at will print.

C. To select more than one page but less than the complete document, click on the white space in front of "Pages". Now type the page range you wish to print. For example, if you want to print page 10 as well as pages 12 through 15, type the following: "10, 12-15.". Now click on OK to print them.

The fields on the page-range section of the Print dialog box are called radio buttons—they are a list of mutually exclusive options, of which you can select only one. When one of these options is selected, it will have a dot in the middle.

How to cancel a print job

From time to time your printer might refuse to print your work. There are a variety of reasons for this, such as a shortage of paper or ink. Or you might have sent a job to a printer by mistake, and now want to cancel it.

In cases of printer error or accidental printing, you may wish to cancel the print job. To do so:

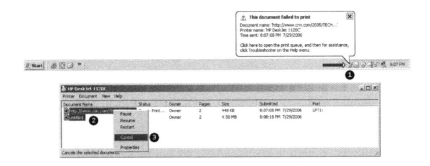

1. Remove the paper from the printer tray and wait until it gives you an error signal. Double click on the printer icon (located on the system tray), and then turn off the printer. If you can't see the printer icon on the System tray, then open the Printer and Faxes software tool in the control panel (instructions on how to do so are outlined on the next page), and double click on the name of the printer you want to work with.
2. Clicking on the printer icon will have opened a window that displays the printer queue. You may now select the jobs you wish to delete. If you wish to select only one job, simply click on it. To select more than one job, hold down the shift key while clicking on all of the print jobs you wish to delete.
3. Finally, right click on the selected jobs, click on Cancel, and press the Enter key to delete them.

Now turn the printer back on, and try to print again, to see if it works properly. If the printer has some of the front lights on, for instance out of ink lights, then use the printer manual to find out what they mean (namely which type of ink it needs).

Tip

It is recommended that you fan the paper, to remove the static cling, before adding it to the printer; otherwise from time to time the paper will cause paper jams inside the printer.

How to change the default printer

The default printer is the primary printer to which your programs will send print jobs to every time you select to print. For this reason, you should select as the default printer whichever printer you use most frequently. (If you have only one printer, you need not concern yourself with this choice, and may skip this section). Bear in mind, however, that if you ever add an additional printer to your system, you will be asked (while installing it) whether you wish to designate the new one as the default printer.

To select or change the default printer, you will need to open the Printers and Faxes dialog box from the control panel. To do so:

- To begin click on the Start menu button, then move the mouse pointer up and to the right and then click over the Control panel icon, when this window opens double-click on the Printers and Faxes icon.
- In previous releases of Windows, like Windows 98, click on the Start menu button and then place your mouse pointer over Settings. Now move the mouse pointer to the right and down, and click on the Printers and Faxes icon, to work with your installed printers.

Once the Printers and Faxes window opens up, you may change the default printer:

- A. Notice that the current default printer has a check mark near its icon.
- B. If you want to set a different printer as your default, right click on its icon, then click on "Set as Default Printer."

The default printer designation can be changed as often as you need to. In the meantime you can always use a different printer, than the default one, by clicking over *File* on the program you are using, then selecting the *Print* item, and then clicking in front of *Name* (to see the list of printers available), and finally clicking on the name of the printer you want to temporarily print to.

How to remove a printer from the Printer and Faxes window

If you want to delete a printer from your printer list, you can do so by returning to the Printer and Faxes window, using the instructions on the previous page.

Once you remove a printer from the Printers and Faxes window, then it won't be available to print your work, until you reinstall it again.

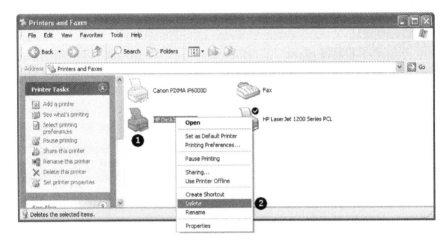

These are the steps, as you can see on this screen capture, to remove a printer from the Printers and Faxes dialog box:

1. Right click on the name of the printer you want to delete.
2. Now click on delete. If you are asked, on this step, if you also want to delete the software that was installed for the printer to function, then click on "Yes", if you are sure you won't be using this particular printer anymore. Otherwise click on No, so that the next time you connect this printer to your computer, you won't be asked to produce its software.

Bear in mind that if your user account doesn't have enough rights, if for example you have a limited account, you might not be able to remove a printer from this list.

If you delete the default printer, that designation will be given to another printer on the Printers and Faxes list. The system might designate a printer you don't use frequently, but you can always change the designation by following the instructions of the previous pages to select another printer as your default.

Tips you should follow to avoid some problems while printing your computer work

Most of the time printing the documents you are working on will be uneventful, off course this will depend if you've followed some good practices to avoid experiencing problems while printing, at other times you will end up with less ink on your printer and a stack of half printed paper.

Here are some tips to avoid some common printing problems:

- Make sure, if you have more than one printer, to select the right printer for the job. For example, if you want to print a 20-page letter and you have a black-and-white laser printer and a color inkjet printer, make sure you choose the laser printer.
- Never power off a printer, while is in the process of finishing a job, by pulling on its power cord or by turning off the power strip where is plugged in.
- Make sure the printer has enough paper to complete the job you sent to it. If you have not used the printer in a few months, remove the paper in the printer and fan it order to remove the static cling. If the paper looks wrinkled, remove it and replace it with new paper.
- Make sure the printer has no error lights blinking. If it does, follow your user guide to troubleshoot the problem before printing. A warning light will usually be amber in color, and might indicate a paper jam or lack of ink.
- Never leave a printer in a place where it will catch direct sunlight or near a radiator, because this might cause the ink in it to dry prematurely.
- Decide beforehand what part of the document you want printed, and take care to specify, using the print-dialog box, the appropriate page range.

Most programs show you what page you are currently working on. For example, in the above screen capture from Microsoft Word, you see that you are on page 3 of a 12-page document. This feature may be useful in determining the range of pages you wish to print.

Now a word of advise; if you find yourself printing a lot of documents in which you only need to print in plain text (with no color), and you currently own a inkjet printer, then it is worth it to consider getting a printer of the laser type, because they can print thousands of pages, with very low cost per page.

Part V
The Internet & the Electronic mail or e-mail

Chapter 13

Guide to Using the Internet with the Internet Explorer Web Browser

What is the internet?, and what do you need to use it

The Internet is a worldwide system of computer networks physically located on every continent that seamlessly exchange information amongst themselves, with very few errors. This is largely possible due to the use of a common data protocol, called TCP/IP or Transmission Control Protocol, which is used by all of the networks (big and small), who connect to the Internet.

To use the Internet you must have the following:

- A personal computer or a PDA with either a direct connection to the Internet (i.e., a connection via cable, DSL, or a dial-up modem and phone line) or an indirect connection to the Internet (i.e., a connection that links your computer to another computer that is used solely to connect to the Internet, such as in an office LAN environment);
- A web browser, which is a program that allows you to see, hear, and interact in a Windows-like environment with the web sites you visit.

The implementation of different ideas to transmit information over the Internet is also called the World Wide Web. The explosive growth of the World Wide Web has been made possible by the Hypertext or HTML language. This language is used to build web pages containing links; a link is an area, button, or graphic on a web page that, when clicked on will load a different web page or document on your browser. The inner workings of the Internet happen automatically, in the background, and the average computer user will never have to worry about building a webpage.

These are some of things you can do with a connection to the Internet and a web browser:

- Use your bank's online web-site to pay your credit-card bills online
- Rent cars and pay for airline tickets
- Buy prescription drugs
- Get information to finish your school homework
- File your taxes online
- Access your company's e-mail from anywhere in the world.
- Check for traffic delays by accessing web cams placed over intersections and bridges

Because the Internet is very young in relative terms (about 24 years old), its usefulness and impact at all levels of society has increased and will continue to increase each day.

What are the definitions for; a web site, a web page and its URL

There are three web-related terms you might hear or read about with some frequency: "web site", "web page", or "URL", that is important you know about it:

- The term "web site", refers to the entire group of pages under a domain name such as (for example) Coke.com. When you hear someone talking about the Coke.com web site, he or she is referring to the whole site, which might comprise many computers (also called web servers) spread out over various locations, sometimes even in cities or even states apart from each other.
- When people talk about a "web page", they are referring to a single page within a particular web site. (Although it's technically possible for a web site to have only a single page, this is very rare.) A web site might comprise thousands of web pages, each with its own URL.
- One of the most important concepts to keep in mind while using the World Wide Web is that every web page has a unique virtual address called the "URL" (which is an anachronism for Uniform Resource Locator), which you can think of as the virtual address of a web page. The URL of a web page is unique, for this reason if its wording is dictated to you, and if you mistype it (even by a single letter), then the web page that you are looking for won't load on the work area of the browser.

For example, the following URL refers to the Science and Technology web page of the Smithsonian Museum web site:

http://www.si.edu/science_and_technology/

If you told a friend about this web page and he sent an e-mail asking you to send him its URL (so that he too can visit it), he would be referring to the letters above. They appear in the **address bar on your browser** when you visit the page.

For instance if you have AOL, and want to send your friend the URL of an interesting web page you could simply highlight it, by clicking once in front of the address bar in your web browser. Now press and hold the CTRL key and then the C one to copy the URL, change to the AOL window (to start composing your e-mail message). Now click on Write, and then click once on the main window of the message that opens, and then press and hold the CTRL key and then the V one to paste this URL into the message. If you have cable or DSL Internet service and use the Outlook 2003 or Outlook Express e-mail client, you can click on the Envelope button (on the Internet Explorer Program **toolbar)** to see some options available to send the URL of web pages you are visiting.

Intro to the Microsoft Internet Explorer web browser

Microsoft Internet Explorer belongs to the family of programs called web browsers, which are the type of program needed to navigate the web. The information in this chapter (such as the sample screenshots) is based on Microsoft Internet Explorer 6, but most of the instructions you find here will work with previous releases of Internet Explorer, or even with browsers not made by Microsoft, such as Mozilla Firefox and Netscape Navigator.

If you are connected to the Internet, open your Internet Explorer browser. To do so, go to the windows desktop and double click on the blue icon with an "**e**" or look in the Start menu, then click on it.

This is a typical view of the Internet Explorer browser window; notice that the URL following the word "Address" reads: *http://www2.jpl.nasa.gov/galileo/*

On the main screen—the working area of the browser—you can see the content of the web page whose URL you see in front of Address. In this main area, you can interact with the web site you are currently visiting; here, for example, you can learn more about the Galileo journey to Jupiter by following the various links.

Parts of the Internet Explorer window

The Internet Explorer's program window is very similar to other program windows found in other Windows applications, but some of its parts are unique. Please take the time to read through the following explanation of those parts so that you can learn to use Internet Explorer.

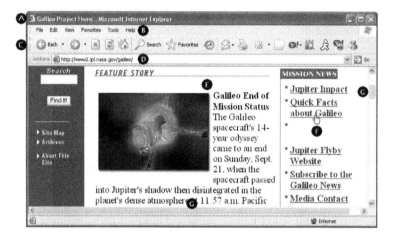

These are the main parts of the Internet Explorer window:

A. The title of the web page you are visiting.
B. The menu items. For example; to print, click on File and then select Print.
C. The standard toolbar, explained in more detail on the next page.
D. The address toolbar. This is where you type the URL of the page you want to visit. Additionally when you are browsing the web by navigating through various links, the URL or virtual address of the page you are presently visiting will appear here.
E. This is the work area of the browser; where you interact with the web page you are visiting.
F. When you move the mouse indicator around the page, it will sometimes turn into a little hand. This indicates that you have found a link (you will learn more on this later in this chapter); if you click on it, you will be directed to another web page on the same site, or to a web page on a different web site.
G. Use the vertical scroll bar to advance or return to a previous section of a very long web page, which can also be achieved by pressing the Page Down/ and Page Up keys, and the horizontal scroll bar to shift the contents of a page into view.

The Internet Explorer standard toolbar

The standard toolbar is the main navigation toolbar available that you can use in Internet Explorer. As you have learned elsewhere in this book, a toolbar is a group of buttons that act as shortcuts to different commands, you can also complete by clicking on the file menu. Clicking on the buttons on this toolbar, will allow you to navigate through the web pages you visit with relative ease.

These are the main buttons on the Internet Explorer standard toolbar, and the tasks they complete when clicked on:

A. The navigation arrows are useful to return or advance to web pages **you've already visited** since opening the browser. Click on the left arrow to return one page and the right arrow to advance one page. The arrows are available to perform these functions only when they are green.

B. Click on the X to stop the loading of a web page.

C. The refresh button will begin again the process of loading a web page. For instance click on the X, when a web page is taking a long time to load, to stop loading the page, and then click on the refresh button to reload it.

D. Click on the Home button to return to the default page (appropriately called the Home Page) you see every time you open your browser.

E. Click on "Favorites" button to open a panel on the left side of your browser that contains all the web sites you have saved for easy access. To return to a web site, whose name you see on this list, just click on it.

F. If you use cable or DSL Internet, and use Outlook or Outlook Express to Send/Receive e-mail messages, and click on the envelope button, then you will see a few options (click on them), such as sending the URL or web address of the web page you are visiting (if you click on Send Link).

G. Click on the print button to print the web page you are looking at. If the web page you are visiting is many pages long, then is better to follow the instructions of chapter 12 and only print a range of pages that interest you.

The fastest way to learn how to use these buttons is to try using them. And on a web page there is no harm, with the exception of the print button (which may waste ink and paper if you click on it), on trying all of them.

The different ways to Navigate the web in search of information

One would think that because the web is a vast array of computers, located all around the world, it would be difficult to find information in it, but in fact the opposite is true: Despite the web's vastness, you can sit at your home computer, visit different web sites, and find information with great ease.

There are three common ways of navigating the web to find information:

1. Typing the exact URL or virtual address of the page you want to visit in the address toolbar of your browser.

For example, if someone suggests that you visit the virtual home of Tai Shan or "Butterstick"at the Smithsonian National Zoological Park's website at the URL; *http://nationalzoo.si.edu/Animals/GiantPandas/*, do the following:

1. Open your web browser and click on the space in front of Address (this is called the Address Toolbar).
2. Notice that now the URL or virtual address shown is highlighted (bluish). If you press on any key this will delete the URL address currently there. To remove just a part of it, press the right arrow key. Now you can reduce segments of the address there by tapping the Backspace key to remove everything that follows "http://" or "http://www."), and then type the new address. For instance to visit the URL shown above; remove the last parts of the URL shown on your own browser up until it just reads "http://" and then complete it to read; "http://nationalzoo.si.edu/Animals/GiantPandas' Alternatively if the URL you need to visit starts with "http://www." then remove everything before the "http://www." and then type the new URL of the web site you need to visit.

Finally, press the Enter key, or click on the Go button (on the right hand side of the Address bar) to load the web page whose URL you've typed in the address bar.

Bear in mind that at times the URL you type here (even if you type it right) will fail to open a web page after you have pressed the Enter key.

On the next example you can see some content around the error message "404: Document not Found.", meaning that this is real working web site even though the particular web page can't be found. If this were to happen to you don't despair, because you might still be able to find the information that might have been moved. To do so reduce the URL, one segment at a time:

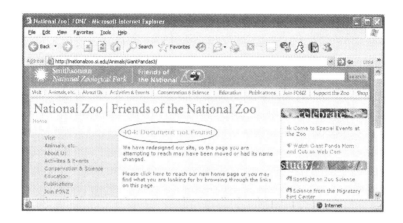

A. Notice the URL (which I purposely mistyped)—in this case,

http://nationalzoo.si.edu/Animals/GiantPandas3

To remove the last section of an URL, slowly click once on the last letter of the URL shown (If the address is bluish, then press the right arrow key). Now slowly tap the Backspace key to remove (letter by letter) the last part of the URL, for this example I removed "GiantPandas3".

B. Always shorten the URL by working backwards from the last section, until you reach the previous forward slash "/" sign.

http://nationalzoo.si.edu/Animals/

Please notice the new address on this example. To load the new shorten URL press Enter, or the F5 key.

If this doesn't work, remove another segment. Continue doing so until you find a working page. Alternatively, you can click on the home label of the web page you are visiting in order to return to the main page of the web site.

2. You can also navigate the web by clicking on links, which contain references to other web pages. You will often find links in web pages, word-processing documents, e-mail messages, and other programs for Windows.

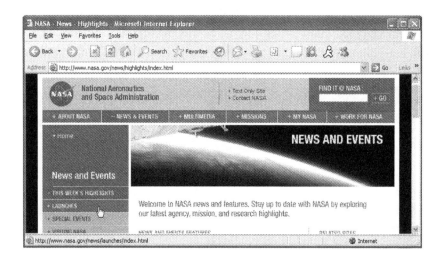

When you move the mouse pointer across a web page or any other program that supports links, the mouse pointer turns into a little hand. On the screen capture above, for example, notice that there is a little hand over the word "Launches."

When you click on a link, three things can happen:

- You are directed to another page within the same web site, and the new page loads in the same window as the link that you clicked on.
- You are directed to an external page belonging to another web site, but the page loads in the same window as the link that you clicked on.
- You are directed to a local or an external page, but this time the page opens in a new Internet Explorer window that overlaps the window containing the link you clicked on.

By following various links, you might start out reading an online newspaper at a web site based in your hometown but end up on the Science and Technology page of a University in Australia. This sense of travel has given rise to the metaphor "surfing the web."

From time to time, you might also get e-mail messages with links you can click on to open commercial offers, or just to visit web pages suggested by family or friends. The pages that follow describe how I dealt with a particular e-mail that came into my AOL inbox.

After reviewing the incoming messages, in the Inbox, I saw one that had been sent from the following e-mail address; *HLD@email.chase.com*. This e-mail address is associated with a known bank, Chase, so I know is a safe e-mail address. When I double clicked on this particular e-mail message, the AOL program immediately asked whether I wished to open the e-mail. I clicked on Yes because I knew it had come from a legitimate address.

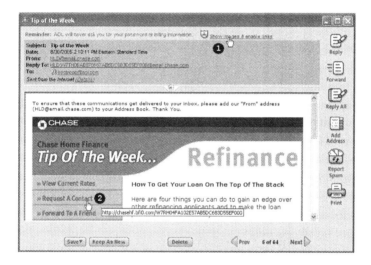

To work with the contents of an e-mail message using the AOL software, follow these easy steps:

1. Click on "Show images and enable links." These words disappear once you click on them.
2. To respond to an offering, place the mouse pointer over the labels that interest you. When you are over a link on the e-mail message, the pointer will change into a little hand, and you can open the link by clicking on it. On this example I clicked on Request a Contact.

Before you open an e-mail message, try to ascertain who sent it to you, by reading the e-mail address of front of From:, and be particularly cautious about opening e-mail messages from unknown senders.

Once you have clicked on a link embedded on an e-mail message, your default browser launches, and its program window will show the offering to which the e-mail message referred.

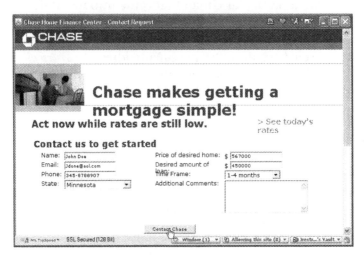

After filling in the requested information, you can submit it by clicking on a button on the web page. (In this case, the button reads, "Contact Chase.")

If you click on a link in an e-mail whose sender you don't recognize and a lot of windows start opening up, you should close these windows right away (click on the X on the upper right corner of each window).

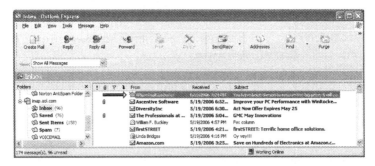

Please bear in mind that you can delete an e-mail message you receive in your e-mail client program Inbox—if you suspect is Spam, even before you open it, by carefully selecting it (click on it only once) and then pressing the Delete key.

3. You can also begin navigating the web by using a search engine to find the information you are looking for. This is perhaps the best way to start navigating the web if you don't know the exact URL of the web page you are looking for.

    For example, if you want to look for information on Abraham Lincoln's birthplace but don't know where to start, use a web search engine such as Yahoo.com or Google.com

    To start your search using Google, open your web browser and then change the URL on the address toolbar to: *http://www.Google.com,* and then press the Enter key or click on the Go button (on the right of the Address Toolbar) to load the page of this excellent search engine.

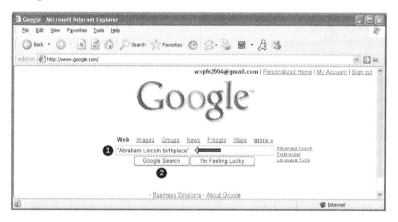

You can follow the steps below to conduct your search for information on the web.

1. To begin, click on the white cell in the middle of the page (if you see a blinking cursor then there is no need to do that), then type "Abraham Lincoln birthplace" in parenthesis (or any other words that describe the subject you are looking for).
2. Now click on "Google Search."

Please bear in mind that at times, after summiting information you typed on a form or on a search engine, that the browser will warn you (in a little window) that the information you are sending can be viewed by others, to continue you must click on Yes or OK.

Most of the time the search engine should return a list of the web sites that match your request, but if the word or word combination you asked to get information on is too uncommon, then the search engine will say that it could not find the information you are looking for.

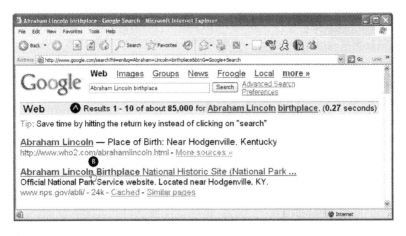

On the above screen capture, you can see the search results for "Abraham Lincoln birthplace." Notice the following:

A. On this line you can see the total number of results for your query. At times this number can be very high—in this case, 85,000 web pages have turned up—but the good news is that you'll usually find the information you're looking for on the first result page.

B. The second result reads, "Abraham Lincoln Birthplace National Historic Site." This looks like an excellent match—both because of its title, and because it is hosted on a government web site (note the .gov in the URL). To go to the information on this site, just click on the link.

If the information you are looking for doesn't turn up on the first page of results, then press on the Page Down key and look to see if the search engine found enough matches for the information you are looking for, and now is offering it to you across a few pages. If that is the case click on page two, and then to page three, and so on, until you find what you are looking for. If, after several pages, you haven't found what you need, it might be necessary to change the wording of your query. To do that just click on the Google name on the top left corner of the page and start your search again.

Working with the "Favorites" feature of Internet Explorer

The easiest way to return to a web site or a web page, you have already visited, is to save it in your Internet Explorer "Favorites" list (which saves its URL or web address), so that you can return to visit it by just looking for their saved name.

To save a URL address as a favorite:

1. Visit the web page whose URL you want to save (for example, *www. dell.com*) by typing its address in front of *Address*. (You can also save pages you've just happened to find while surfing the web). The rule is simply that you must have the page open in order to save it.

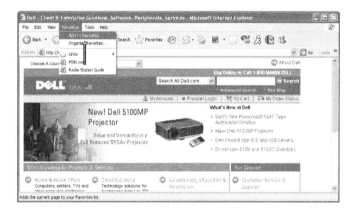

2. Now click on the Favorites menu item; then click on "Add to Favorites" and choose "OK" on the little window that opens, to save this URL. Once you have clicked on OK, the web page has been saved to your Favorites list. If you have the Mozilla Firefox web browser you can follow these steps to save the URL's of web pages, albeit in Mozilla they are called "Bookmarks."

To return to the web site you have saved, click on Favorites, and then click on the name of the web site whose URL you saved on this list and now want to visit again.

To delete the saved URL of a web site or a web page, return to the Favorites list and just right click on the saved name, select Delete, and press the Enter key.

What are cookies?

The term "cookie" refers to the name given to a file left in your computer by a specific web site you've visited. This type of file can save information about you, such as; the user ID you used to get into the site, and even some shopping cart information, etc.

When you return to visit a web site, from which your web browser has already accepted a cookie, your browser will send a copy of the cookie to the web site, which in most cases will use the information stored in it to present you with a customized web page.

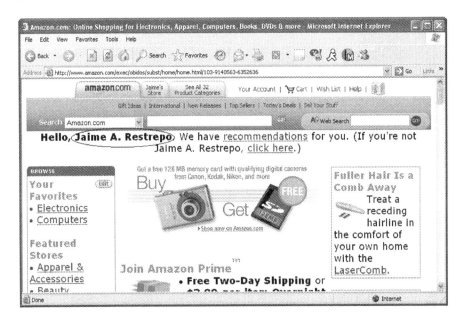

On this screen capture of the Amazon.com web site, you can see an example of how cookies are used. I've given my name to this web site previously, when I made an online purchase, and the next time I went there, the welcome page greeted me by name. Cookies also help web sites remember what you bought in the past in order to offer you similar products on your next visit.

Note

Banks also use these "cookies", while doing online banking, to monitor and keep your login information so that the next time you visit their web site, you won't have to provide it again.

Changing the way Internet Explorer handles cookies

There are several types of cookies, and using the Internet Explorer privacy setting you can choose to allow some, none, or all of them to be saved on your computer. Keep in mind that if you choose not to allow cookies at all, you may not be able to view some web sites or take advantage of the customization features in them.

Follow these steps to change how Internet Explorer handles cookies:

1. First open Internet Explorer.
2. Now click on Tools, then on Internet Options.
3. Next click on the Privacy tab.

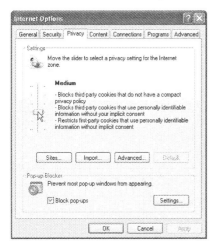

4. Now place the mouse pointer over the slider, press and hold down the left mouse button, and move the slider higher to forbid certain types of cookies or lower to allow them.
5. Click on Apply when you're done making changes. To close the dialog box, just press the ESC key.

To delete the cookies left by the web sites you've visited, click on the General tab, on the same Internet Options dialog box window. Now click on "Delete cookies." But bear in mind that the information they've saved, such passwords to automatically let you in into some web sites will be lost. And the next time you visit the save web site, it will prompt you to type a password. I also recommend that from time to time you click on "Delete files", on this same page, in order to free space on the hard drive.

Using the new pop-up blocker in Internet Explorer

This is a new Internet Explorer feature, and is only available in Windows XP computers if they've been upgraded to the service pack 2. If you've recently bought your computer system, chances are it came with the pop-up blocker already on it.

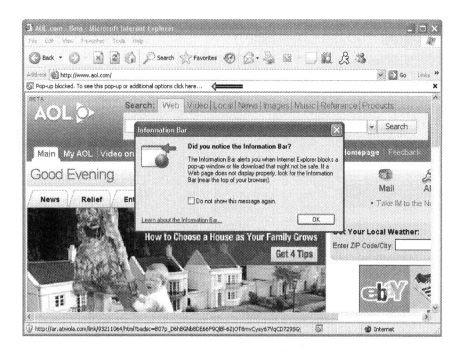

You can see on the screen capture above that some of the content on this web page (the opening page of AOL.com) has been blocked. Next to the arrow, you can see a message that reads, "Pop-up blocked." A dialog box has also opened on top of the main window to advise you that a pop-up has been blocked.

If you don't want to see the extra content on the web page you are visiting, just click on OK to close this dialog box. But if you want to see the blocked content, press the Enter key (to close this little window) and click on the line that reads; "Pop-up blocked . . ." and then on "Temporarily . . ." to load the missing content on this web page. To avoid seeing this message, while visiting some web pages, press and hold down the CTRL key while the page you are visiting is still loading. If the page is already loaded, then you can also hold down the CTRL key, press F5 to refresh/reload the web page, or click on the refresh button on the Internet Explorer toolbar.

How to allow or prevent pop-ups while using Internet Explorer

If Internet Explorer seems to be stopping you from experiencing content on some web sites—or, alternatively, it is allowing all kinds of pop-ups to open—then you should adjust the pop-up blocker settings.

To do so, open Internet Explorer, and then click on the Tools menu item. Next, click on "Pop-up Blocker," and, finally, "Pop-up Blocker Settings."

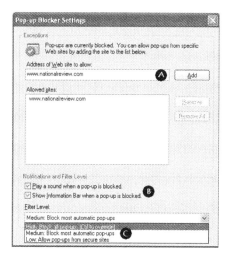

Once the Pop-up Blocker dialog box has opened, finesse its settings as follows:

A. In this line, you can type the URLs of web sites you visit often (click on it and type them). Once you have typed the name of the web site whose extra content you don't want blocked, click on "Add." This will keep this site' pop-ups from being blocked.

B. Here you can choose how to be notified when a pop-up is blocked—either with a sound, an information bar, or both. If you click on both of these options (to unselect them), then you won't be notified at all.

C. On this menu, select the filter level most appropriate for your needs. Pick the high setting if you work with sensitive data and are concerned that a child that is using the computer might visit a web site, and that this web site might present him/her a pop-up, that when click on might try to install malicious software on your computer. Choose the low setting only if you don't have any important work to lose.

Finding and using a wireless hot spot to connect to the Internet

You may have noticed that more and more cafes, airports, and hotels are offering wireless Internet access trough the use of "Wi-Fi HotSpots." These hot spots may be useful to you if you frequently work away from your home or office and have a laptop computer with a Wi-Fi or wireless network card.

If wireless access at a HotSpot is open and free, you need only turn on your laptop and open your browser before you are ready to surf the web.

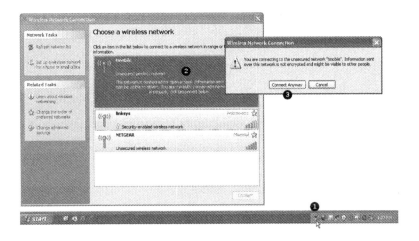

If you are not able to surf the web right away, you need to check whether you are actually connected to a HotSpot. To do so:

1. Double click on the wireless connection icon (this icon might have an X on it).
2. On the list shown here, click on the name of the HotSpot you are trying to connect to. (For example, at Starbucks the wireless service is provided by T-mobile.) If this list is long and you don't know the Hot Spot's name, ask someone that works at the place you are visiting.
3. Now click on connect. (If the connection is secure, you will need to type the network key before connecting.)

These instructions only apply to you if you are letting Windows XP manage your wireless setting. If your wireless card has its own client software, and you've chosen to use it, then simply follow its instructions to connect to the HotSpot.

Now you can open your web browser and see what steps are needed to start using the Internet. For instance if you get a message asking, "Do you want to display the non-secure items?" Click on OK to continue.

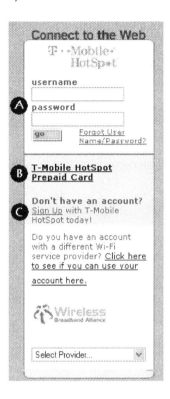

The screen capture above was taken at a local Starbucks while I was trying to connect to the hot spot there. In this particular case, using the Internet requires that you first perform a few steps:

A. If you are a returning customer, enter your username and password on these lines.

B. Click here to add the information from a prepaid T-Mobile hot-spot card. These are cards that are akin to a phone card but for Internet service that most Starbucks can sell you.

C. If you have never used T-Mobile's wireless service, click here to open an account.

If you will be traveling and need to find a local hot spot, you can do so at *http://cnet.jiwire.com/* You can simply enter a zip code at the site, and it will give you a list of nearby hot spots you can find on most big cities across the USA.

Chapter 14

Guide to using e-mail or Electronic mail in Windows

Using e-mail of the POP3/IMAP kind in Microsoft Windows

If your Windows based personal computer is connected to the Internet, then you can use it to send and receive electronic mail or e-mail—that might have embedded text, sound, video, or a combination of the three—anywhere in the world.

To use e-mail you need three things: a computer with Internet access, an unique e-mail address account assigned to you, such as *Jdoe3432@yourwebsite.com*, and a computer program called an e-mail client (such as Microsoft Outlook Express).

Reading this chapter you will learn to use e-mail accounts of the POP3 type (which is the kind given to you by your Cable or DSL ISP or Internet service provider) or even e-mail accounts of the IMAP type (provided by your company), using either one of these e-mail client programs; Outlook 2000/2003 or Outlook Express.

These are the general steps to Send and Receive e-mail messages:

- To create and send an e-mail message:

  1. If you are using Outlook Express, open it and click on *Create new Message*. If you are using Outlook 2003, open it and click on *New*.
  2. At this time, if more than one e-mail account has been added to Outlook 2003 or Outlook Express, select the account you want to use to send the message.
  3. Now you must add the e-mail address(es) of the person/companies to whom you want to send your e-mail message.
  4. Next click on the main space and compose the message itself.
  5. If you want to add any attachments, do so now.
  6. Finally, click on *Send* to send the e-mail message.

- To receive an e-mail message;

  1. To begin click on the *Send/Receive* button on the toolbar.
  2. Now click on your Inbox, which is the incoming mail folder.
  3. Double-click on the message you want to read, to open it.
  4. If you've received a file attached to and e-mail message, open it or save it to your hard drive.

In this chapter you will also learn the steps to add your AOL IMAP e-mail account to either the Outlook 2003 or Outlook Express, so that if you have an AOL e-mail account you too can take advantage of the instructions in this chapter.

Opening the Outlook 2003 or Outlook Express e-mail client programs

Please note that the instructions in this chapter can be followed if you use either Outlook 2003 or the Microsoft Outlook Express e-mail client programs. To begin using e-mail or electronic mail, open the one you'd like to use.

These are the steps to open/launch the Outlook 2003 or the Outlook Express e-mail client program, to start sending and receiving e-mail messages:

Microsoft
Office Outlook
2003

Outlook
Express

A. From the Windows Desktop:

- Find the proper icon, depicted above, and then double click on it to open your e-mail client. If you can't find the correct icon on the Windows Desktop, then you can learn how to add it to the desktop by reading chapter 6 (Using Computer Programs in Windows).

B. From the Windows Start menu:

- First click on the *Start* menu button, now over *All Programs* menu. Now find the Outlook 2003 icon (in the Microsoft Office group of programs) or the Outlook Express icon, and click on it to open it.

C. From the *Run* command box:

- First click on the Start menu button, and then click on the Run command to open its dialog box window.
  - To open Outlook Express, type: "*msimn.exe*" (in front of Open) and then click on OK, or just press the Enter key, to launch this program.
  - To open Outlook 2003, type: "*C:\Program Files\Microsoft Office2003\OFFICE11\outlook.exe*" (in front of Open) and then press the *Enter* key.

Bear in mind that, if you alternate between using the Outlook 2003 and Outlook Express, every time you open the one not defined as the "default e-mail program", a little window will pop up asking you if you want to make the one you've opened the default e-mail client. If this is the e-mail client program you want to use as your default e-mail client, then click on *Yes*. Otherwise click on *No*.

The Microsoft Outlook 2003 and Outlook Express e-mail clients

Once the e-mail client of your choice opens, and you are connected to the Internet, then you will be able to start sending and receiving e-mail messages right away.

These are the main working areas on the Microsoft Outlook 2003 e-mail client:

A. On the left side panel you can see your *Personal Folders*, which contain the e-mail messages you've sent, received, deleted, etc. These messages are filed in different folders (such as the *Inbox*). On the top part of the left panel you can see the list of the folders you've used recently, under "Favorite folders." To work with a particular folder just click on it.

B. In the middle you will see the e-mail messages contained on the folder selected on the left panel.

C. This is the preview panel, which displays part of the message selected in the middle panel. To change how the preview panel is displayed, click on *View*, and then on *Reading Panel*. To close this panel, click on Off. To see previews of e-mail messages at the bottom of the screen, click on *Bottom*.

If you've used previous versions of Outlook (such as Outlook 2000), you will find that the user interface of Outlook 2003 has changed slightly. However, basic tasks are achieved in essentially the same fashion as before.

Why use one e-mail client program instead of another? The Outlook Express e-mail client, which is included as part of the Windows operating system, is free, while the Outlook 2003 is more expensive and more robust (with more features). Additionally, the price of Outlook 2003 depends on whether you buy it as part of a package—such as the Microsoft Office Suite—or as a standalone program.

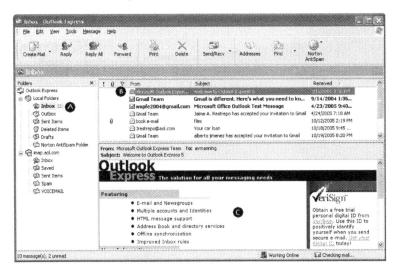

These are the main working areas on the Microsoft Outlook Express e-mail client:

A. On the left side panel you can see your *Personal Folders*, which contain the e-mail messages you've sent, received, deleted, etc. These messages are filed in different folders (such as the *Inbox* or the *Sent Items* folder). Note also that there is an IMAP account here, which I have added to send/receive messages using my own AOL e-mail account. You will also learn to do this later in this chapter. To work with a particular folder just click on it.

B. In the right panel you will see the messages contained on the folder you've selected in the left panel.

C. This is the preview panel, which displays part of the message selected in the middle panel. To change your preview options, click on *View*, then *Layout*.

For security reasons, it is not recommended that you enable the preview panel feature for Outlook Express or Outlook 2003, because some e-mail messages might carry a pernicious attachment that can be triggered just by previewing a message without actually opening it.

Working with folders in Outlook Express and Outlook 2003

E-mail programs such as Outlook Express and Outlook 2003 automatically file your sent and received e-mails in various folders, for organizational purposes.

As you can see below, in Outlook Express the root of the folders is called Local Folders (left graphic). In Outlook 2003 (or earlier), it is called Personal Folders.

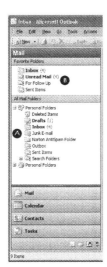

There are some important folders you will work with in either e-mail client program:

A. In both Outlook 2003 and Outlook Express, the:

- *Inbox*, where all your received messages arrive and are stored.
- *Outbox*, where copies of your outgoing messages are temporarily stored, until they are finally sent.
- *Sent Items*, where copies of the messages you've sent are kept.
- *Deleted Items*, where you will find the messages you've deleted.

B. In Outlook 2003, just above the regular folder list, you will see a list of shortcuts to the folders you've used most often, called *Favorite Folders*.

To work with an e-mail folder just click on it. In the *Drafts* folder, you will see the messages you've worked on and saved, but which you have not yet sent. To work with a message you've saved, click on the *Drafts* folder. To open a message saved there, double click on it. When the message is ready, click on the *Send* button.

Creating new folders to better organize your e-mail messages

You can even create new additional folders in your e-mail program to better organize, your e-mails messages. Once the new folder is created it, select the messages you want to move there, and then drag them to the new folder.

To create a new folder, to the folder list, open your e-mail client program and then press/ hold the keys combination CTRL + SHIFT, and then press the E one.

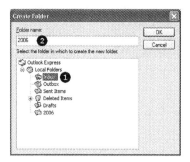

These are the steps to create a new folder using the *Create Folder* dialog box:

1. To begin select the folder under which you want to create the new folder. Do this by clicking on the name of an existing folder (such as Inbox).
2. Now click under *Folder name,* and type its name (such as 2007), and then click on OK to create the new folder under the existing folder.

In the example below, I selected to create the new *2006* folder under the *Inbox.* In order to reach this new folder I clicked on the *Inbox* first, and then the 2006 folder.

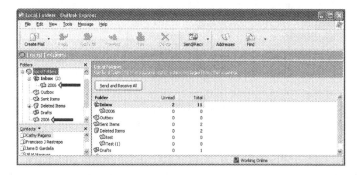

Now you can use the new folder you've created, to store messages you've received or sent. Later on this chapter you will learn how to select and move the e-mail messages you want to file on this new folder.

Using your AOL e-mail account with Outlook 2002, 2003 or Outlook Express

If you have an America Online e-mail account, that you access using the AOL 9.0 Software, you can benefit from the instructions in this chapter by adding it to either; Outlook 2003 or Outlook Express. And you will still be able to keep using your AOL e-mail account (with the AOL 9.0), as long as you don't remove it.

These are the steps to add your AOL e-mail account to your Outlook Express e-mail client program:

1. First open your Outlook Express e-mail program. Now click on the *Tools* menu, and then select *Accounts*.
2. When the *Internet Accounts* dialog box opens, click on the *Mail* tab, and then click on *Add*, and then select *Mail*.
3. Now on the *Display name* field, enter your name as you would like it to appear on your outgoing email messages. For instance, "Jane Doe"
4. Now click on *Next*.
5. In the *Email address* field, enter your full email address, which is usually *yourscreenname@aol.com*.
6. Now click on *Next*.
7. On the *Email Server Names* screen, click in front of "My incoming mail server is a . . ." (POP3), and select *IMAP* from the drop-down menu.
8. In the *Incoming mail server* field, enter: imap.aol.com
9. In the *Outgoing mail server* field, enter: smtp.aol.com.
10. Now click on *Next*.
11. On the "*Internet Mail . . .*" window, enter your AOL screen name in front of the *Account name* field, which is the same screen name you use to login to AOL.
12. Now enter the same password you use for your AOL account, in front of the *Password* field. Don't click on the *Remember password* check box, unless you don't mind that other people with access to this computer will be able to send/receive e-mail messages using your AOL account.
13. Now click on *Next*.
14. To complete adding your AOL account to Outlook Express, click on *Finish*.

Please don't close Outlook Express yet, because we must return to the *Accounts* menu and open the AOL e-mail account you've just added. This is necessary to make some additional configuration changes, to the new account.

Now if you need to add your own ISP (for instance Pacific Bell) e-mail account (only follow steps 1-14) to Outlook Express, and instead of IMAP select POP3 (step 7), then add your own Pacific Bell e-mail account and the name of their servers.

These are the additional steps needed to complete configuring your Outlook Express email client, so that you can use it with your AOL e-mail account:

1. First click on the *Tools* menu item again, and then select *Accounts*.
2. When the *Internet Accounts* dialog box opens, click on the *Mail* tab, and then double click on the *AOL IMAP* account you've just created, to open it.
3. When the *Properties* dialog box opens, click on the *Servers* tab.
4. Now, on the Outgoing Mail Server section (on the lower part of this dialog box), click on the *My server requires authentication*, then click on *Apply*.
5. Next click on the *Advanced* tab.
6. In the *Outgoing mail (SMTP)*, click on the number displayed there, and change it to *587*. In the *Incoming Mail (IMAP)*, change the number there to 143.
7. Now click on *Apply*.
8. Now click on the *IMAP* tab and on the *Special Folders* section. If the *Store special folders on IMAP server* is checked, then click on it to uncheck it.
9. Now click on *Apply*, then on *OK*, then on *Close* on the *Internet Accounts* dialog box. Finally, if you receive a message prompting you to download folders from the America Online mail server, then click on the *Yes* button to download them now.

These are the steps to add your AOL e-mail account to your Microsoft Outlook 2000/2003 e-mail client program:

1. Open your Outlook 2002 or Outlook 2003 e-mail program
2. Now click on the *Tools* menu item, and then click on *E-mail Accounts*.
3. On the *E-mail Accounts* window, click on *Add a new email account* and then click on the *Next* button.
4. On the *Server Type* window, click on *IMAP* and then click on the *Next* button.
5. On the Internet Email Settings (IMAP) window, you must enter the following information (by clicking on each field first):

   ✓ *Your Name*. Enter the name you wish your recipients to see when the get an e-mail message from you.
   ✓ *Email Address*. Enter your AOL email address, e.g., John12xd@aol.com.
   ✓ *User Name*. Enter your AOL screen name, e.g., JaneSue.
   ✓ *Password*. Enter your AOL password, unless you want the extra security of having to enter the password every time you use this email account.

✓ On the *Incoming mail server* field, enter: imap.aol.com
✓ On the *Outgoing mail server* field, enter: smtp.aol.com Now continue on the next page (step 6), to finish adding your AOL account.

Now if you need to add your own ISP (for instance Pacific Bell) e-mail account to Outlook 2000/2003 (only follow steps 1-5), and instead of IMAP select POP3 (step 4), then add your own Pacific Bell e-mail account and the name of their servers.

6. On the highlighted field, enter in the name by which you'd like to refer to this account, e.g., JanetSue@aol.com or My AOL E-Mail.
7. Now click on the *Outgoing Server* tab, then click on the *My outgoing server requires authentication* check box, if it is not already selected.
8. Now make sure that the radio button next to *"Use same settings as my incoming mail server"* is selected. If it is not, click to select the button.
9. Now click on the *Advanced* tab.
10. In the *Outgoing mail (SMTP)*, click on the number displayed there, and change it to *587*. In the *Incoming Mail (IMAP)*, change the number there to 143.
11. Now click on the *OK* button, then on the *Next* button, then on *Finish.*

Later on you can return to check the settings for your AOL account, this way:

- In Outlook 2003/2002; click on *Tools*, then *E-mail accounts*, then select *View or change . . .* , then click on *Next*, and finally double click on *imap.aol.com*.
- In Outlook Express, click on *Tools*, then on *Accounts*, then double click on the *imap.aol.com* e-mail account.

These AOL Mail features are not available in Outlook Express or Outlook 2000/2003:

- The e-mail addresses you saved to your AOL 9.0 address book are not available in either Outlook 2000/2003 or Outlook Express.
- You will not be able to check the status of a sent message.
- You will not be able to create or delete e-mail folders.
- And the main drawback is that the IMAP Inbox doesn't seem to keep very old messages. If you must save a message, drag it to the AOL Saved folder.

Finally, to begin using your AOL mail account, click on the plus sign next to the *imap.aol.com* or on the name you chose for it (for instance AOL mail). Now click on the Inbox or on the folder you want to work with.

Composing and sending e-mail messages using Outlook Express or Outlook 2003

The process of writing an e-mail message is similar to writing a letter using a word-processing program, but instead of printing or saving your document, you add the e-mail address(es) of the recipient(s) and then click on *Send* to send it.

To begin composing a new e-mail message, open your e-mail program and click on your *Inbox,* now click on *Create Mail* (Outlook Express) or *Write* (Outlook 2003).

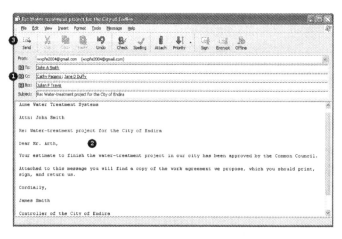

These are the general steps, to prepare and send an e-mail message:

1. First add the recipient information by typing the email address(es) of each one of your recipient(s). For example click in front of, and write:

   - *To:* the e-mail addresses of the primary recipients for this e-mail.
   - *CC (carbon copy):* the e-mail addresses of the people who should also receive copies of this e-mail.
   - *BCC (blind carbon copy):* the e-mail addresses of recipients who for privacy reasons should not see or be seen by the other recipients.
   Press the comma "," key after each one, to separate them.
   - *Subject:* the purpose of the e-mail message, as a reference.

2. Now click on the message area and type the text of your message.
3. Finally, click on the *Send* button. If you are not connected to the Internet, the message will stay in the *Outbox* folder until you connect to the Internet.

If you don't see the *BCC* field right away while using Outlook 2003, then click on the *View* menu on the e-mail message you are working on and select the *Bcc* field. In Outlook Express, click on *View* and then on *All Headers* to see the *Bcc* field.

Bear in mind that if you've added two different e-mail accounts to your Outlook Express or Outlook 2003 program (for instance your office e-mail account and your Optimun Online ISP one) then you should choose the account from which you wish to send each e-mail message. Otherwise, your e-mail will always be sent from the e-mail account defined as the "Default" one.

These are the steps to temporally send an e-mail message from a different account, other than the default one:

- In Outlook Express, after clicking on *Create Mail,* click in front of *From:* and then select the e-mail address you want to send the message from.
- In Outlook 2003, after clicking on *New,* click in front of *Accounts:,* and then select the e-mail address you want to send the message from.

If you want, you can open the *E-mail Accounts* dialog box to change the default e-mail account. To do this in Outlook Express, click on the *Tools* menu, then on *Accounts.* In Outlook 2003, click on the *Tools* menu, then on *E-mail Accounts,* then on *Next.*

These are the steps to change the default-account designation:

1. First click on the name of the e-mail account you want to designate as the default one.
2. Now click on *Set as Default.* Change this designation as often as you need to.

You might also consider (for security reasons) not saving the account passwords by un-checking the *Remember Password* option. In this case, you will have more security for your accounts because you will need to type your password every time you want to use the account whose password is not saved.

If you are traveling, and are having trouble sending e-mail messages (they stay in your Outbox folder), then find out (from your host) if port 25 is being blocked, and the settings you need to change to send-email messages.

Opening e-mail messages you've received

To receive new e-mail messages addressed to your e-mail account, you have to:

✓ Be connected to the Internet.
✓ Open your e-mail client program, which will automatically look for new e-mail messages addressed to you. Most e-mail client programs are also set to send/and receive new messages automatically, at a set time interval
✓ To receive new messages right away, after your e-mail client program has been open/idle for some time, click on the Send/Receive button (on the Toolbar).

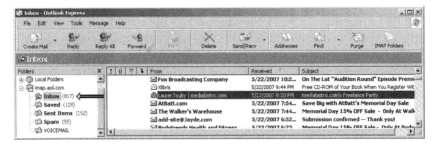

To begin click on the Inbox folder, to work with the new (they appear in bold letters) and even the e-mail messages you've opened. To open a message you want to read, double click on it or press the Enter key (once is highlighted).

When you receive and open an e-mail message addressed to you, you can:

• Read it, Reply to, Forward or Print it, and it will stay in your *Inbox* folder, until you move it to another folder or delete it.
• Delete it right away by **single** clicking on the message (to highlight it), if you suspect is Spam. Now click on the *X* on the Toolbar or press the *Delete* key. You can also, after opening the message, click on the *X* button to delete it (on the message Toolbar).

You can use the *Up/Down* arrow keys, the *Page Up/Down* keys, the arrow keys or the Scroll Bars on the side to navigate through the messages in any folder. Remember to occasionally click on the Spam folder, to see if any of your e-mail messages have been mistakenly moved there by your e-mail program.

Working with e-mail messages you've opened

Once you open an e-mail message, it will appear in its own window and you can start working with it right away.

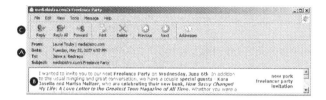

Please notice the following details, illustrated on the above example:

A. This is the delivery information;

- *From:* shows you the name of the person who sent you the message.
- *Date:* shows you the date and the time the message was sent.
- *To:* shows you the e-mail address of the **intended recipient**, important point if more than one POP3 e-mail account was added to your Outlook 2003 or Outlook Express e-mail client, because the e-mail messages for all the accounts are delivered to the same Inbox.
- *Subject:* will show you the subject of the e-mail.

B. This is the message itself. If the message is very long, use the *Up/Down* arrow keys, the *Page Up/Down* keys, or the scroll bars to see the rest of it.

C. On the message toolbar, you can click on:

- *Reply,* to reply to the sender.
- *Reply all,* to reply to all the people shown in the delivery field.
- *Forward,* to send a copy of the message to whomever you chose.
- *Print,* to print the message on your default printer.
- *X,* to delete the message and send it to the Deleted Items folder.

To close a message, click on *File* and then on *Close,* or just click on the X, located on the upper-right corner of the screen. To read the next or previous e-mail message in the folder you are working in, click on the Previous or Next buttons on the toolbar.

Forwarding or Replying to an e-mail message

When you choose to reply to an e-mail message by clicking on one of the reply buttons (*Reply* or *Reply All*), the e-mail message window you were working with will resemble the "Create a new e-mail message" window, and the addresses of the person (or persons if you clicked on *Replay All*) found in the original message are automatically added in to the *To* field.

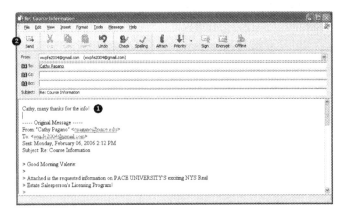

These are the steps, to finish replying to an e-mail message you've received:

1. First click above the original message, and then write your reply to it.
2. At this point you can also add additional people (in front of *To*, *Cc*, or *Bcc*) to whom you also which to send a copy of your reply to this message. To delete a recipient click on its name, and tap the Backspace key.
3. When you are finished, click on the *Send* button to send it.

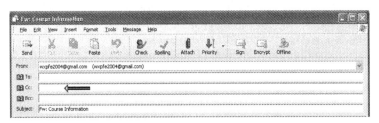

The steps to complete forwarding an e-mail message (after clicking on the *Forward* button on the original message) are the same as the ones required to reply to an e-mail message, although you must provide the e-mail address of any recipients to whom you want to forward a copy of the original message.

Working with e-mail messages saved in your Local folders

After you've been using your e-mail account for some time, you might notice that some of your folders will have accumulated a great many e-mail messages. To begin click on the folder whose messages you want to work with (such as the Inbox).

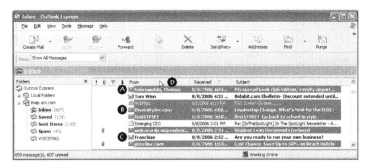

These are the steps to select e-mail messages you want to delete or move:

A. To select a single message, just single click on it once.
B. To select a group of contiguous messages, press and hold the *Shift* key. Now click on the first email of the block you want to select, and on the last one, while holding the *Shift* key the entire time. To finish, lift your finger from the keyboard. If the messages you are trying to select are spanned across many pages, then click on the down arrow on the scroll bar (on the right side of the window) *while still holding the Shift key*, and click on the last message you want to select. Alternatively press and hold the CTRL key and the A one, to select all of the messages.
C. To select non-contiguous messages, press and hold the CTRL key and then click on each one of the messages you want to select. (You can also; select a block of contiguous messages, release the shift key. hold down the CTRL key and click on a few more non-contiguous messages.)
D. You can sort your messages by clicking on any of the column labels. For instance when you click on the *From* label, all the messages are alphabetized.

To delete them, once they are selected, press the *Delete* key (or on the X on the toolbar), then right mouse click on the *Deleted Items* folder, and then click on *Empty Deleted Items folder* to permanently delete them. Or to move them to another folder, click and hold the left mouse button on your selection of e-mails, and then drag them over to another folder (such as the AOL Saved), or over one you've created. In this example I dragged a group of e-mail messages to the 2006 folder.

Using the Address Book feature in Outlook Express or Outlook 2003

The Address Book or Personal Address book feature allows you to store people's or company's contact information, such as their e-mail address, which you can then use to complete the addressee information on an e-mail message.

On the pages that follow you will see examples of how to add new contacts to the Address Book, and to create new groups using the contacts you've added in both Outlook Express and Outlook 2003. To begin, return to your e-mail client program and then click on the Inbox folder.

Now click on the Address Book button, to begin adding new contacts.

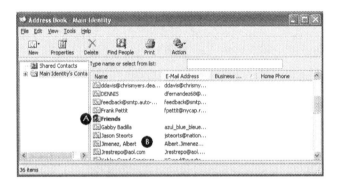

There are the two important types of objects you will see in the Address Book:

A. The individual contacts you've saved. In Outlook Express these contacts can be sorted alphabetically. For instance click on the Name label (top), to sort your saved contacts by their name.
B. The groups of contacts. Notice that their icon, on this example the group "Friends", is similar to a double face.

The look of the Address Book feature in Outlook 2003, is slightly different than the Outlook Express one, because of that I will indicate when the steps to complete a task are different for each one of these Address Books.

Adding a new contact to your Address Book

Once the Address Book is open you can begin creating new contacts along with their information. This will save you time later when you need to send someone an e-mail message: Rather than typing in their e-mail address, you will be able to simply select it from their saved contact information in your Address Book.

There are two ways to add a new contact to your Address Book:

1. By taking a person's or company e-mail address from a message you've received and opened, this way; click on the sender's name or e-mail address (in Front of From:), then right click on it.

- In Outlook Express, click on *Add to Address Book*, and on *OK*.
- In Outlook 2003 select *Add to Outlook Contacts*, and then click on *Save and Close*.

   If you've previously added this contact to your Address Book, then you will see a message that this contact is already saved in your Address Book.

2. By manually typing their e-mail address after opening the Address Book and creating a new contact entry. To add a new contact entry:

- In Outlook 2003 or earlier version. Open the Address Book (as shown before).

   1. First click on *File*, then on *New Entry* (alternatively click on the left most button, *New Entry*, on the toolbar)
   2. Now double click on New Contact. (Please bear in mind that in some editions of Outlook it might read "*Other Address*")

Now the *New Contact* properties dialog box window opens up, and on the next page you will learn the steps to add the information of the person or company you want to save on this New contact entry.

If you only want to save the e-mail address of a person or company, to this *New Contact* entry, then you don't need to add any other information (such as their Phone Number or their home or business address).

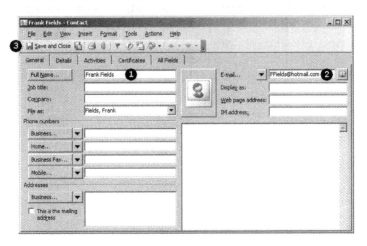

These are the steps, to fill in the information for the new contact:

1. To begin write the name of your contact. This will be the name that you will use to find the contact; at the time you are adding it to the recipient field (To:, Cc: or Bc:) of an e-mail message you are creating.
2. Now write the E-mail address of the contact.
3. Finally click on Save and Close.

To later remove a saved contact entry, return to the Address book, click on the name of the contact entry you want to remove (to select it), and then press the *Delete* key (or click on the X on the Toolbar). Now click on *OK* to confirm that you want to delete the contact entry. To change the saved e-mail address, double click on the name of the contact entry, and then change the e-mail address, or any other info that has changed.

- In Outlook Express. Open the Address Book (as shown before).

  ➢ Click on *File*, then on *New Contact*, and then select *New Contact* (alternatively click on the *New* button on the left side of the toolbar, and select *New Contact*).

Now the new contact *Properties* dialog box window opens up, and on the next page you will learn how to finish adding their personal information in it.

In Outlook Express you can also add the e-mail address of a person or company (while reading the e-mail message they've sent), to a contact entry in your address book, this way; first click on the *Tools* menu item, now click over Add to *Address Book*, then over Sender. Finally click on Ok to save it on your Address Book.

These are the steps, to fill the new contact information in Outlook Express:

1. To begin click on each one of these 5 cells, and then write in as much information in each cell about your contact. For instance click in front of First:, and write the name of your contact (for instance Doris).
2. E-mail address: Write the complete e-mail address of the person or company, and then click on *Add* to add it to this contact entry. If you've added more than one e-mail address here, click on the main one. Now click on *Set as Default*, and finally click on OK to save it.

Outlook Express can also be configured to automatically save, to your Address Book, the e-mail addresses of people, when you reply to their e-mail messages. To see if this setting is enabled, click over *Tools*, then *Options*, and then on the *Send* tab. Now make sure that the *Automatically Put People I Reply To In My Address Book* option is checked. If it is not, click on it to enable this feature.

To remove a saved contact entry at a later time, return to the Address Book, click on the name of the contact you want to remove, and press the *Delete* key. To change the saved e-mail address of a contact, double click on the name of the contact entry. Next click on the *Name* tab, then click on the e-mail address there (under *E-Mail addresses*), and then click on *Edit*. Finally, type the new e-mail address for this contact, and when you are done making change click on OK.

Creating a new group of contacts in your Address Book

If you often find yourself sending the same e-mail message to a group of people, then you can create a group of contacts with these people's information, that later on you can use it to complete the recipient part (using their saved e-mail address) on an e-mail message.

The main advantage of creating a group of contacts is that, when you are composing a new e-mail message you want to send to a group of people, you won't have to manually add (one by one) each one of these saved contacts to the recipient part (To:, Cc: and Bcc:) of the e-mail message you want to send them.

To begin creating a new group of contacts, open the respective Address Book:

> In Outlook 2003 or earlier version. Open the Address Book (as shown before).

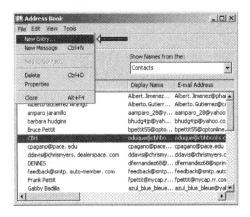

1. To begin click on *File*, then on *New Entry*
2. Now double click on New Distribution list or *Personal distribution list*, but before make sure that under the label *Show Names from the*, that it reads *Contacts* or *Personal Address book*, if not click on the name shown there (which might be *Active directory*) and select *Contacts* or *Personal Address book*.

Now, if you work for a company, and the computer you use is part of a Windows 2003 server LAN, then under *Show names from the*, it might need to read; Active directory (if not, click on the name shown there to change it), otherwise you might not see any of your saved contacts you want to add to the new group you are creating.

Please keep in mind that some ISP's have enacted a limit on the number of addressees you can add to a **single e-mail message**. For instance if the limit is 50, and you add 52 contacts to a single group, then when you add the name of this group to the recipient part (such as CC:) of an e-mail message, the end result will be that this e-mail message won't be delivered, and instead will sit on your Outbox.

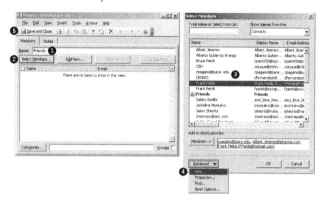

These are the steps, to create a new group in Outlook 2003:

1. To begin click in front of the *Name* field, and type the name for this new group of contacts, such as Family or Friends.
2. Next click on *Select Members* or over *Add New* to create a new contact.
3. Now double click on each one of the contacts you want to add to your new group. To add everyone press CTRL + A. To finish click on Ok.
4. At this point, if you haven't clicked on Ok, you can also create a new contact to this group, by clicking over *Advanced* and then *New*, and then type their information. When you finish, click on OK.
5. Finally click over Save and Close to create your group of contacts. Later on you can: add/remove/delete members to the group.

To make changes to a group, first open the address book and then double click on the name of the group; a) to add a new member follow the instruction on this page, b) to remove a member in the group, click on its contact name, and then click on Remove or c) click on the name of the group and then press the Delete key.

> ➤ In Outlook Express. Open the Address Book (as shown before).

First click on *File*, then on *New Group*.

A new properties window should open; now you must add all the individual contacts you want to include in this group.

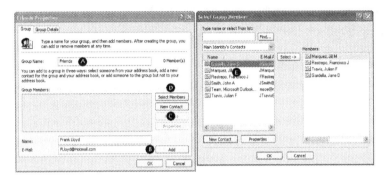

Here's how to add individual contacts to a new group in *Outlook Express*:

A. First, type a descriptive name in the *Group Name* box, such as Friends.
B. At this point, you can add people you know are not already in your address book directly to the group—without also adding their contact information to your Address Book. Type the person's name and e-mail address in the lower half of the *Properties* window, and then click on *Add*.
C. To add a person to both the group and the Address Book, click *New Contact* and fill in the appropriate information (as explained on previous pages, under *Add new contact*). When you are finished click *Ok* to save the contacts in your address book; this will also add them to the group.
D. To add a contact to the group that's already in your address book, click on *Select Members*.
E. Now double-click on each one of the contacts you want to add to the new group. At this point you can also add someone else to the address book and the Group by clicking over *New Contact*. To finish click on *Ok* to close the *Select Group Members* window, then click on *OK*.

To make changes to a group, first open the address book and then double click on the name of the group; a) to add a new member follow the instruction on this page, b) to remove a member in the group, click on its contact name, and then click on Remove or c) click on the name of the group and then press the Delete key.

Using the saved contacts or groups of contacts, in your Address Book, to fill in the recipient field of an e-mail message

After you've added new contacts or created groups of contacts in the Address Book then you can use them to fill in the recipient field of an e-mail you are; creating/replying or forwarding to. But first click in front of the field you want to add a recipient e-mail address, for instance click in front of "To:" to add a recipient e-mail addresses there.

To add a contact e-mail address to an e-mail message, follow these instructions:

- On the Outlook Express Message window:

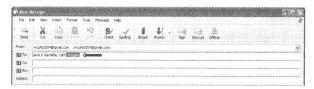

   Begin by typing the name/nickname (for instance "mother") of the saved contact you want to add to the recipient list. Notice that, *as you type* a word or even a letter the program might suggests a match you can use. When the saved name is shown, then press the right arrow key to use it.

   On the Outlook 2003 Message window:

   Type the name/nickname of the person you want to add to the recipient list. Notice that, *as you type* a word or even a letter the program might suggests you use a saved match. Just click on the right match, to use it.

You can keep on adding as many recipient e-mail address as your ISP allows to a single e-mail message (some only allow fifty). For instance if you've added the e-mail address of someone, to the To: field, then press the right arrow key, the comma key and repeat the same steps to add additional names of saved contacts to this field, or click on a different field (for instance the "Cc:") to add the saved e-mail address of the person who you want to send a copy of this e-mail.

Bear in mind that when, while composing a new e-mail message using Outlook 2003, and you type a single letter (for example a "D") in one of the recipient fields (such as the To:), and there is only one saved contact that begins with that letter (for instance David), and you click on Send, that Outlook 2003 will automatically assume that David is the intended recipient. Now if you have more than one contact that starts with a letter, then you will be prompted to choose the right one.

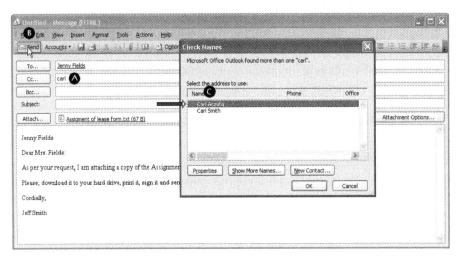

The above screenshot shows the window (Check Names) you'll see in Outlook 2003 and Outlook Express, to help you find a match for an incomplete address.

A. You can tell "carl" is an incomplete address because it isn't underlined. Note that *Jenny Fields* is underlined.
B. Now click on the *Send* button if you are ready to send your e-mail. If there is any ambiguity, as with "Carl," then the *Check Names* window opens. As you can see on this screen capture, in which more than one e-mail address start with the letter "C".
C. If you see the right contact name, just double-click it. Since you already clicked on *Send,* the e-mail will be send immediately.

Please know that there is really no particular set order you must follow to compose a new e-mail message, and the order I've show you in this chapter is merely a suggestion, because as long as you don't click on the *Send* button, you can still work on either adding additional people who you want to send a copy of the message, changing the message itself, or finding a file you need to send included as an attachment.

You can also add recipients by selecting them directly from those saved in your Address Book.

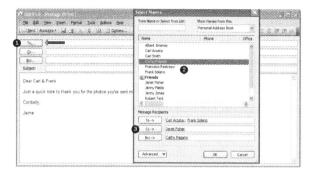

This is the way to easily add saved contact names to an e-mail message:

1. First click on the field button you want to add recipient addresses such as: "To:","Cc:", or "Bcc:", to open the *Select Names* window in Outlook 2003 or *Select Recipients* window in Outlook Express.
2. These are your individual contacts. Just double-click on each contact or group name you want to add to whichever field you clicked on.
3. You can even, for instance if you opened the Select Names window by clicking first on To:, CC:, or BCC, add recipients to the TO:,CC:, or BCC:, this way; a) Single-click on a contact or group name, b) Now click on the "To:" "Cc:" or "Bcc:" to add that contact to the appropriate field.

Please note that in the *Select Recipients* window in Outlook Express the *To: Cc:* and *Bcc:* fields are located on the right side, rather than on the lower panel. If you don't see any saved contacts in Outlook 2003, and you are a home user, then make sure that under *Show Names from The,* that the Contacts or *Personal Address book* is selected. If it's not, click on the name there and select *Personal Address book* or *Contacts.*

After you've added the contact to your message press the Enter key or click on *Ok to* close the *Select Names* window. All the e-mail addresses you chose are now copied to the appropriate fields. Just complete the e-mail, and then click on *Send* to send it.

Sending and receiving computer files as e-mail attachments

Sending and receiving files via e-mail is often though of to be one of the more contentions tasks for a computer novice to complete—because there are numerous types of files and numerous types of e-mail client programs.

These are the general steps to attach a file or files to an e-mail message:

1. First you should ascertain where on your computer, if you don't already know, the file or files that you wish to send are saved. For instance if the files you wish to send are saved under the main My Documents folder, then you should keep that in mind.
2. Now open your e-mail client program, and start composing a new e-mail message as shown on the previous pages.

3. Once the new e-mail window opens, click on the **paper clip** button (on the new message toolbar).
4. Now you must use the window that opens to find and select the files you want to send. Once you do, click *Insert File* (Outlook 2003) or *Attach* (Outlook Express).
5. Finish composing your e-mail, including the recipients, and click *Send.*

These are the general steps to receive a file (s) attached to an e-mail message:

1. To receive e-mail messages open your e-mail client program (if is not already open). Now double click on the e-mail message that contains a file or files. (On the left side of these messages you will see a little paper clip.)

2. When the new e-mail opens, you will see the names of the file or files attached to it (in front of "Attach"). Now you can; open or save them.
3. When you are finished with the e-mail, click on File and then on Close.

If you choose to save a file you've received, to a storage resource on your computer (such as the C:\Drive), then make sure to save it to a folder that you can find easily (preferable one located under the My Documents folder).

Tips to successfully attach files to e-mail messages

On the previous page you learned the general steps to send and receive files via e-mail. On the following pages we'll go into more detail, step by step, so that you can understand better the whole process.

But first let me offer some guidelines that will hopefully make this process, of sending and receive attachments, less stressful:

- Make sure that the file or files you want to send a copy of are saved and closed. If a file is still open, close it, before you attempt to send it.
- Do not attach a single large file or too many small files to a single e-mail message. Because, depending on their aggregate size, when you attach then to an e-mail message, your ISP might reject the message. To avoid this, if you must send a group of files, it is preferable to send them in 2 or 3 different e-mail messages with a few files in each one rather than to attach too many files (for instance 15) to a single e-mail message.

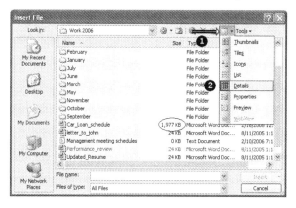

This is the way to ascertain, before you attach a file, if it is larger than the limit your ISP allows per single e-mail message:

1. To begin click on the View button (next to Tools), on the window that opens when you select to attach a file (by clicking on the paper clip button on the new Message window).
2. Now click on Details, to see more information on the file.

For instance, as you can see on the screen capture shown above, the selected file (Car_loan.) has a size of 1,977 kb, which is 1.9 Megabytes. That's not very large. But if you attach 13 files of this size, then you might go over the limit allowed by your ISP. If the file is very large (over 20 megabytes), you might need to put it on a CD and send it via regular mail.

- Please also be mindful of the type of Internet connection the person who you are sending these files uses. For example if you are sending then to a relative and they use a slow Dial-up connection, then send them only one or two files (for instance vacation photos), per e-mail message.
- If a friend is having trouble opening a file (for instance a Word file) you've sent him/her, then try the following steps:

  ✓ To begin, ask the person who you need to send a file to, or vice versa (tell the person sending you files) what version of Word he or she has, if that is the program you/they are using to create the document you need to send (to find out the version of a program; open the program and them click on *Help*, then click on *About . . .*) or ask if they have at all the program you are using to create the file to be sent.
  ✓ If for instance you both use MS Word, but the intended recipient uses an older version of Word, then; a) Name and save your file the regular way, b) Click on File and then on Save As, to create a new file.

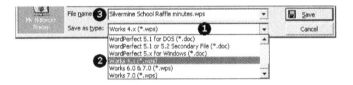

1. Now click in front of *Save as type*, to see the menu shown above.
2. Next click on the program version compatible with the previous release of word or even with a different program (such as WordPerfect) your **friend uses**. Navigate this list using the arrow Down/Up keys, when you find it click on it to select it.
3. To change the given file name, click on it. Now press the right arrow key. If you see the 3-letter file extension, then press the left arrow key four times to position the blinking cursor before the dot ".". Adding a single letter at the end of a file name, by typing a "1" or an "A". will suffice to change it. To save the file click on the Save button. This is the file you should send to your friend.

Now you should have two files; one compatible with the Word you use and the other compatible with the older version your friend uses. Otherwise when you choose to save a document you've just created, *without changing its name*, with a different format as the Word you normally use (to help your friend open it), then when you click on Open, you **MIGHT** need to click in front *Files of Type*, an select *All files* every time you wish to open it. Additionally, if later you get this file back, save it using Save As, then click in front of *Files of Type, and* select Word Document to use it.

Steps to attach a computer file to an e-mail message in Outlook 2003 or Outlook Express

The steps to attach one or more of your computer files in either Outlook 2003 or earlier versions of this program or Outlook Express are fairly similar, and the only difference is the dialog box window that you will use to complete this process.

These are the steps to attach a file or files to an e-mail message in either Outlook 2003 or Outlook Express:

1. Begin this process by ascertaining where in your hard drive (using the Windows Explorer) the files you want to send reside.

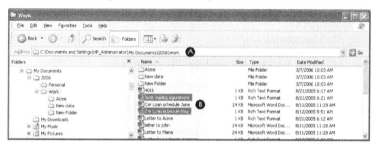

Please note, on this screen capture, the following details:

A. This is the path or virtual address of the folder where the files I've chosen to send reside. And they are located on the work folder, which is under the 2006 folder, and which in turn is under the main My Documents folder.

B. These are the two sample files I want to send.

2. Now open your Outlook 2003 or Outlook Express, and then click on your *Inbox* folder, and on *Create Mail* (Outlook Express) or *Write* (Outlook 2003).

To begin attaching files, using the Insert File (Outlook 2003) or Insert Attachment (Outlook Express) dialog boxes, click on the *Paper clip* button on the window of the new message toolbar. Remember also that you are only sending a copy of the file, whose original will remain saved in your computer.

Please note that there is no set order to attach the files you need to send. Attaching files can be done before you send an e-mail message that you've already finished composing or right after you've just opened a new message window.

3. Now you have to use the aforementioned dialog boxes windows (Insert Attachment) to find the files you want to send attached to your e-mail messages.

This is the way to attach computer files, using the Insert attachment (on this example I used the Outlook Express Dialog box window):

A. Please notice the name of the folder (My Documents), whose contents you see in the working area of this little Window, in front of *Look In*. You can click in front of *Look In* to find and select a different folder.

B. Now *double click* on the folder that contains the files you need to send (if the files are visible right away then select them). For this example I double clicked on the 2003 folder, to began looking there.

C. Additionally I double clicked on the Work sub-folder: because I know the files I am looking for, are located under it.

D. Finally select the files you want to send. On this example Word documents, which is easy to do; press and hold the CTRL key, and then single click on each one. Press and hold CTRL and A to select them all.

E. You can click on this green button with an arrow, if you must return to work with a folder you've previously opened.

F. To go back one level, click on the Yellow folder button.

4. Finally click on *Attach* to add the files you've chosen to your e-mail message.

Please note, as you can see on the next screen capture, that the *Insert file* dialog box window that opens up when you select to attach files to an e-mail message using Outlook 2003, has a few buttons on its left side that when clicked on act as shortcuts that make it easier to find the files you need to attach to your e-mail messages.

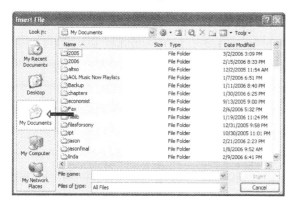

For instance, if there is a file you need to send which you know resides under the *My Documents* folder, click on the *My Documents* button, to see its contents. When you find it double click on it, or single click on it and then click on *Insert* to attach it to your e-mail message. Or double click on the name of the sub-folder under which the particular file you are looking for resides. If you have more files you need to attach, click on the Paper clip button again, to re-open the Insert File dialog box window.

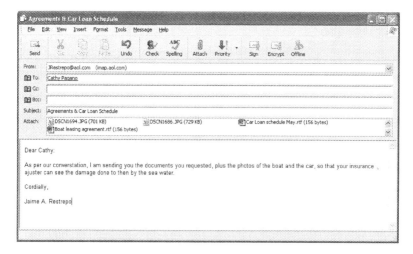

Now you can see that the file or files you chose are attached to the e-mail message, and now you can complete it, if it is not already finished. When the e-mail message is ready then send it, by clicking on the *Send* button.

How to use the *Send To* menu to attach files to an e-mail message

If you use Outlook 2003 or Outlook Express and are having trouble finding the files you want to attach to an e-mail message—using the dialog box window's shown on the previous pages, then open the Windows Explorer (explained on chapter 8), to find those files, and once you find them use the *Send To* menu, to easily attach them to your e-mail messages.

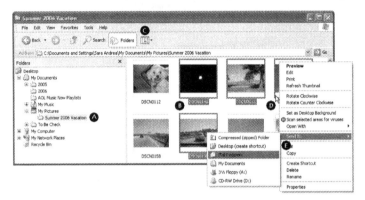

This is the way to attach files to e-mail messages, using the *Send To* menu, after opening the Windows Explorer or the My Documents folder:

A. In Windows Explorer click on the folder where the files you want to send reside, to see them on the right panel.
B. Now select the files you want to send, for this example I picked some photos, I found under the My Pictures folder, this way.
  ▪ To select a group of contiguous files you want to attach, first click once on the right hand panel (next to a file you want to send), now press and hold the Shift key, then click on the first one you want to select, and then click on the last one. Now lift your finger from the keyboard. If the files you need to select are hidden behind the window, then click on the guides on the vertical scroll bar (on the side), while still holding the Shift key, until you find the last one you want to select and then click on it to highlight the entire selection. To select a single file just click once on it.
  ▪ To select additional files that are non-contiguous, press and hold the CTRL key and then click on each one of the ones you need to select.
  ▪ To select all of the items saved in a folder: press and hold the CTRL key and then the A one.
C. If you want to see more details about your files (right now they are shown as Thumbnails), such as the date they were created or their size, click on the View menu, and then select Details.

D. Now right mouse click on **any** of the files you've selected, and then take the mouse pointer over to the *Send To* menu item

E. Next bring the mouse pointer over *Mail Recipient* and then click on it. Finally you must decide if you want to Make all the Pictures Smaller (if sending photo files), or click on Keep the original file (which is not recommended, unless you were specifically ask not to reduce them), and then press Enter. This process also works to send document files, such as Microsoft Word files.

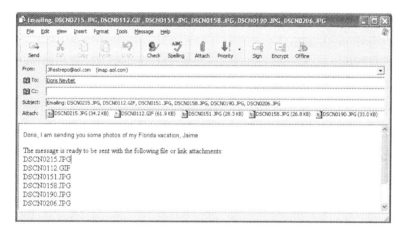

Now, once the new e-mail message opens up, you should be able to see the names of the files you choose to attach. Now click on the space above; "The message is ready to . . . ", type your message, add the recipient e-mail addresses, and then click on the *Send* button to send it.

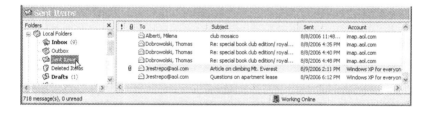

Bear in mind that if there is a problem sending an e-mail message, it will remain on the *Outbox* folder. To see the last message you've successfully sent, click on the *Sent Items* folder; now look for it on the right panel. On the message line, you can even read the time and the day each message you've sent left your computer.

Please read this info before opening e-mail messaged with files attached to them

Before we jump into the section on opening e-mail messages, which contain files attached to them or "attachments", I will like to go over some of the things that can happen when you try to open the files attached to an e-mail message.

These are examples of four things that can happen; when you open an e-mail message that contains a file attached to it (these are the messages on your Inbox folder with a paper clip next to them). When you open a message:

- You are able to see, because of the security settings defined on your e-mail client, the files attached to the message right away in the main message window (for instance some photos a relative sent you).
- You open the message but you are only able to see a list of file names, in front of a section called *Attach*.
- After you double click on the name of the file (attached to the e-mail message), it asks you to choose a program to open it, but after selecting a program you think is compatible with, you are still not able to see it.
- You are warned that the e-mail client blocked ("Some pictures . . ."), some of the content embedded on the e-mail message. In most cases, once you ascertain who sent it to you (looking at the From:), all you need to do is click on "Click here to download . . ." to see the hidden content of the message.

If you are usually not able to see the content embedded on e-mail messages (as on the last example) or receive *the files* attached to them, try making the following change:

- In Outlook Express; Open it, now click on Tools, then Options, now click on the Security tab, uncheck the "Do Not Allow Attachments . . . " settings, and then click on Apply, and then on Ok to close this window.
- In Outlook 2003; Open it, now click on Tools, then Options, and now click on the Security tab. Now click on "Change Automatic Download Settings", and uncheck as many setting on this dialog box, as deemed necessary by your current needs, then click on Ok to close this dialog box window, and then on Ok again to close the Options dialog box window.

For example if you only get files attached to e-mails from your sister or friend, and is always pictures of the family, then is very safe to uncheck the *Don't download pictures and other content automatically in HTML.* Although you should, if you don't have one already, buy a good Antivirus before you change this setting to a more permissible level. I also recommend that you always protect your computer, using a good Firewall program.

How to open and save the files attached to an incoming e-mail message

The general process to start receiving computer files, attached to your e-mail messages, is fairly simple in the surface; if you see a paper clip, next to an e-mail message you've received, then there is a file attach to it.

On the next screen capture you can see the main working area of the Outlook Express e-mail client. Now notice that on the left panel, the Inbox is selected, and on the right panel you will see the e-mail messages that were sent to you.

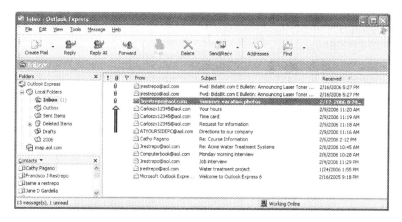

When a new e-mail arrives on the Inbox, as you can see on this screen capture, you will be able to gather some information about it right away, such as; the sender (on the From column), the subject and the time it was sent, and if it has an attachment you will see a paper clip next to it. Once the message is in your Inbox you can:

- Highlight it, by *single clicking on the e-mail message itself,* and then select to delete it (by clicking on the X on the Toolbar or by pressing the delete key), if somehow you think it might be a harmful e-mail message, or if you don't know who sent it to you.
- Open it, by double clicking on it.

If you choose to delete it will be sent to the Deleted Items folder, and later you should right mouse click on that folder, and then select *Empty Deleted Items folder.* On the pages that follow you will see a few examples of how to work with e-mail messages, which contain a file or files, after you've chosen to open then.

Steps to open/view or save the files attached to an e-mail message

Because, as I explained earlier, the process of working with the file (s) attached to an e-mail message, can be a little contentious for the novice to the computer world, I've written four examples of the steps needed to open/view or save those files.

But before we jump onto the examples you might want to consider creating two new folders; naming the first one, *My Downloads*, under the *My Documents* one, and the second one, *My Downloaded Pictures* under the *My Pictures* folder (which is also under the *My Documents* folder), which you can then use to save the files you've received. This process is explained in chapter 7 (Using computer Files and Folders in Windows),

To open/view or save the file or files attached to an e-mail message:

1. In Outlook 2000/2003

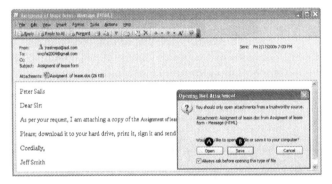

Once you open an e-mail message with a single file attached, double click on the name shown in front of "Attachments:" :

A. Now, if you want to open this file, click on Open. If you uncheck the "Always ask.", then this type of file will always open right away after you double click on it. Some graphic files will open right away.
B. If you want to save it, click on Save and now the *Save As* dialog box window opens. Alternatively if you don't want to do anything with this file, just click on *Cancel*, and close the e-mail message, by clicking on the *X* on its corner.

If right after you click in front of attachments, another message window opens up, showing you the names of more files, then double click on them (to see if they open), if not follow steps A and B on them.

2. In Outlook Express

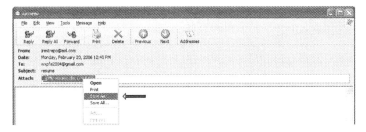

Once you open an e-mail message with a single file attached, right click on the name of the file (shown in front of *Attachments*):

A. Now if you want to open this file click on Open. Alternatively double click on the name of the file to open it. If you uncheck the "Always ask . . . ", then this type of file will always open right away after you double click on it.

B. If you want to save it click on *Save As*. Now the *Save As* dialog box window opens. If you don't want to do anything with this file, just click on *Cancel*, and close the e-mail message, by clicking on the *X* on its corner.

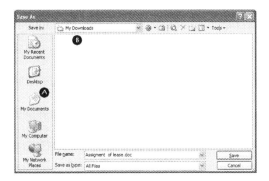

Now use the Save As dialog box, to save it to your hard drive this way:

A. First click on the My Documents button (if that is the folder you want to save it to). If in front of *Save in* doesn't already read *My documents*.

B. To save to a different folder, click in front of *Save in*. When you find it double click on its name, to open it. For this example I used the My Downloads folder I've created earlier, but you can save the file anywhere you want.

Finally click on *Save*, to permanently save this file to your hard drive. As you become more proficient, you will be able to save it to any other folder on your hard drive.

3. In Outlook Express

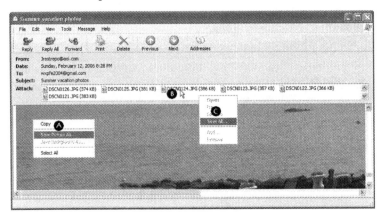

This is the way to work with the digital photo files that you've received, attached to an e-mail message:

A. If you are able to see the photos, on the main body of this e-mail message, use the Page Down/Up keys to scroll among them. If you find/see the one you want to save, then right mouse click on it, and then select Copy or *Save Picture As*. You can also double click on the name of any of the files you've received (in front of Attach:), then on Open, to open it. If you uncheck the "Always ask . . . ", then this type of file will always open right away after you double click on it.

B. To save them all, right mouse click in front of *Attach:,* over the names of the files.

C. Now you should select *Save All* on the menu that opens, to start the process of saving all the photos you got attached to this e-mail message.

On this sample screen capture of an e-mail message I've received using Outlook Express, you can see a group of graphic files attached to it, which are digital photos in the JPG format (this is easy to ascertain because of the 3 letter file extension at the end of the name of the file). Please know that you should have no trouble opening this type of file, because many different graphic programs, such as the included Windows Paintbrush, can open them.

Bear in mind that if you download photos, of a mature nature, to a computer that a child can access, that he or she might be able to see them, unless you've secured your account with a password, which is explained on chapter 5 (Working with Windows XP Local User Accounts).

4. In Outlook 2000/2003

Please note on the next screen capture, of an e-mail message I did received/ and opened in Outlook 2003, that because of the preview settings (see page 350), in the working area of the e-mail message, the photo files attached to it are not readily visible.

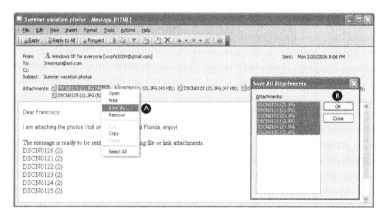

This is the way to work with these files, in Outlook 2000/2003, attached to this e-mail message, to open or save them:

A. Double click on the individual file and select to open it, to preview it, as opposed to saving it first to your hard drive. If you decide you want to save this single particular file, then double click on it again and select *Save* or right mouse click on the name of the file and then select *Save As.*

B. To save them all (if more than one file was attached to the message), click on File (located at the top of the message window), and then select *Save Attachments,* and then when you see the *Save All Attachments* dialog box window, click on Ok

Also bear in mind that if the e-mail message you've received included digital photo files mixed with document files (such as Microsoft Word document file), that you can also saved them to the same folder as the digital photo files, and what is important is that you remember the name of the folder where you've saved them to. Later on you can move them, to the My Document folder, or to a particular folder you've created.

On the next page you will learn how to finish saving these files, to a folder in your hard drive, where they will reside until you move them or delete them.

Now you can complete the process of saving the files you received attached to an e-mail message (on this example a group of photos), the following way:

In Outlook Express:

- If you chose—see page 354—to begin saving a *single picture file* that you were able to see embedded on the body of a message, by right mouse clicking over the photo and selecting *Save Picture As, then:*

  1. First click on the *My Documents* button, on the left side of the *Save Picture* dialog box window.
  2. Now double click on the *My Pictures* folder, to be at that level. Or on any other folder or drive you want to save these files to.
  3. Next double click on the *My Downloaded Pictures* folder you've created earlier, or any other folder of your choice.
  4. Finally click on Save, to save the photo to your hard drive.

- Now of you choose to save all of the files, after right mouse clicking in front of attachments and selecting Save All, then:

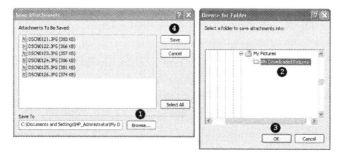

  1. First click on *Browse*, to open the *Browse for Folder* dialog box window.
  2. Now select the folder where you want to save these files to. For this example I clicked on a folder I previously created, under the *My Pictures* folder, called my *Downloaded Pictures* folder.
  3. Now click on Ok, to select this folder.
  4. Finally click on Save, to save these files to the folder you've selected.

You can also, inside the *Save Attachments* dialog box window, click to unselect a file you don't want to download to your hard drive. This process will work just as well to save document files (for instance Microsoft PowerPoint files).

In Outlook 2000/2003:

- If you choose to save all the digital photos files, by clicking on *File* and selecting *Save Attachments, then:*

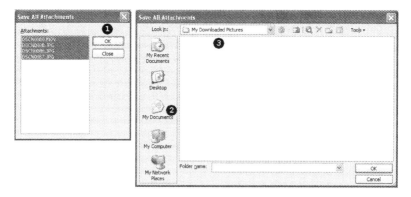

1. First click on Ok, to confirm that you want to save these files.
2. On the next Dialog box window that opens, click on the *My Documents* button (if you want to save them there), to be at the level of this folder.
3. Next double click on the name of the folder where you want to save the photos. For this example, I picked the *My Pictures* folder, and then the *My Downloaded Picture* folder. Finally click on Ok to save the files.

Bear in mind that if while using any of these two e-mail client programs, Outlook 2003 or Outlook Express, to save files to any folder that currently contains files with the same name and extension (which is akin to a last name) then the program might ask you if you want to keep the older files currently on that folder.

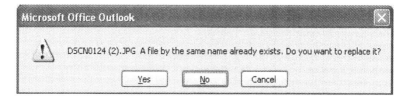

To replace a file currently on this folder, click on Yes. Click on No to avoid replacing a file currently there. If you are saving a group of files, you might be asked once for every file whose name matches one already in the folder you are copying them too. The workaround is to save them to a different folder, and then use the Windows Explorer to see which files are which.

How to see and work with the pictures or documents you've saved to your hard drive

Once you've saved the file (s) you got—attached to an e-mail message, then you will able to work with them, as long as you have the a program that was used to create them, or at least a compatible one. For instance, if you've received a Word file, and you don't have Microsoft Word, then you will still be able to open it using the included Microsoft Windows WordPad. The best way to find out if you have a compatible program, to open a file you've received, is to double click on its name. If the file doesn't open right away, then try finding a program to open it with.

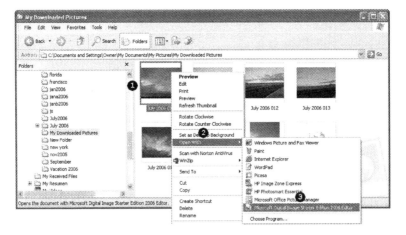

For instance, this is the way to select a program installed on your computer, after finding the folder in which the files you want to work with are located (using the Windows Explorer), to work with your digital photo files:

1. Double click on the file you want to work with—to see if it opens up in a good photo editor, or right mouse click on it to select one.
2. Now bring the mouse indicator down to *Open with.*
3. Finally bring it to the right and down and click on a program you think it might be compatible with. For this example, I clicked on the *Microsoft Digital Image Starter Edition 2006 Editor* to open this photo file.

If you can't find a graphic editor on your computer (which comes included with the digital camera or a scanner you bought), to work with your digital photo files, then you can consider buying one of the *Microsoft Digital Image* families of programs.

Part VI
Using Hardware Devices in Windows XP

Chapter 15

Working with Hardware Devices in Windows

Intro to using hardware devices in Windows XP

In Microsoft Windows XP it is much easier than in previous versions of Windows (such as Windows 98) to install new hardware devices (such as a new video card or a scanner). Because in most cases, after you connect a new hardware device to your computer, Windows XP will automatically recognize it, a feature that is known as "Plug and Play." This is possible because Windows XP includes a very large database of the software called *Device Drivers*, which are required to operate the various hardware devices connected to your computer.

To see at a glance, in all the different editions of Windows (such as in Windows 98), the list of all the hardware devices installed on your computer, you can use a software tool called the *Device Manager*. To open it right-click on the My Computer icon, which is located on the Windows Desktop. Then click on the *Properties* item, and select the *Hardware* tab, finally clicking on the *Device Manager* tab to open it.

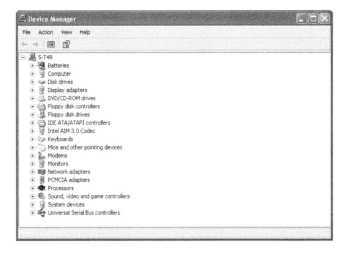

On the Device Manager window, you will see the hardware devices installed on your computer, grouped by type (such as the group of Network adapters group). When you click on the plus sign next to the name of a group, a list of all the devices under this particular group will be displayed. If there is a problem with a particular device, you will see a yellow exclamation mark next to its name.

Bear in mind, that most of hardware devices, that you see listed in the Device Manager window, were automatically configured at the time the operating system was installed on the computer at the factory or by you.

What is a Device Driver and how to use it?

A device driver is the software that tells the Windows operating system how to interact with a particular hardware device (such as a printer) that is connected to your computer. Further in most cases the company that manufactured a particular hardware device also wrote the device driver software for it. For instance if you buy a video card made by a company called ATI, it will be included with the ATI provided device driver software you need to install it. I must clarify that the only time you have to think about device driver software, is; a) when some hardware device attached to your computer is malfunctioning or b) when you want to add additional hardware devices to your computer. If this is not the case then you can skip this chapter and jump to the next one.

These are the two most common ways to use device-driver software:

- By using the installation CD that was included in the package with your printer, scanner, or other hardware device that you have purchased. To use this installation CD, just put it into a your CD-Rom drive, now wait for the software to load and then click on *Yes* or *Next* to agree to the installation, which will then add the device-driver files to your computer in the appropriate way. At the end of the software installation you might also be asked if you want to restart the computer, to which you should answer *Yes* (after saving any documents you have open). When the computer reboots, the hardware device you've just installed should work.
- Alternatively, you can also obtain newer device drivers by visiting the tech support area of the website of the company that manufactured the hardware device you need to attach to your computer. Once you find the correct one, you can: a) Apply it right away to your system or b) Save it to your hard drive (Later on; find it and double click on the driver file to begin installing it). The advantage of obtaining a software driver this way, as opposed to using the software that was included with the hardware device and might have been packed many months ago, is that you will get the latest software. And if you had problems using the hardware device, then the newer device driver software will most likely have the fixes to solve those problems.

On the pages that follow, we will go over two examples of finding device drivers on the web by visiting the tech support websites of; Hewlett Packard and Dell Computer Corporation. And after following these examples, you should be able to gather enough insight into the process so that you too can repeat this process to visit the particular website of the company that manufactured the hardware device you need to add to your computer.

How to obtain a newer Device Driver for a hardware device

The first steps to begin looking for software drivers are; 1) Establish a connection to the Internet (which is always open if you have a cable or DSL type of connection), and 2) Double click on your web browser icon, such as Internet Explorer, to open it.

The first example highlights the search for a new device driver for a Hewlett Packard printer:

To begin, once your Internet web browser opens up, click on the address bar and type the following URL or web address: http://www. hp.com/country/us/en/support.html. Now press the Enter key.

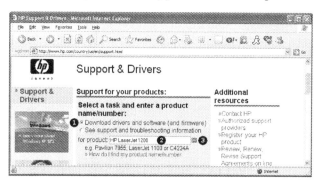

To look for drivers for all HP-manufactured hardware devices, once the web page (shown on this screen-capture) finishes loading, follow these steps:

1. Click to select what action you want to perform: "*Download drivers . . .*" or "*See support . . .*" To look for drivers, click on "*Download drivers . . .*"
2. Now you must type (first click on the text field, in front of *product*) the exact model number of the HP hardware device you need drivers for. For this example I typed *LaserJet 1200.*
3. Now click on the continue symbol ">>". You can also click on *Start Detection,* if you don't know the model of the hardware device you are looking for, to have the HP website help you find it.

Bear in mind that the wording of a company (for instance the company that made the scanner you were given) URL or web address, unless you were given a specific alternative, is almost always: *www.nameofthecompany. com,* and that you should look for the device-drivers you need under the technical support section of their website.

Now your web browser will load a different page, called the *Product search results* web page, showing you the name of one or more hardware devices that match your search criteria.

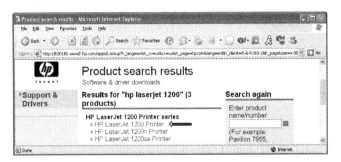

If the HP product-search-result page displays more than one result, then choose the *exact model* of the hardware device you need software drivers for. Notice that some of the product names are different by just a single letter, such as the "n", found on the second printer listed. For this example, I clicked on the HP LaserJet 1200 printer.

On the next web page that opens, click on the version of the operating system that you have installed on your computer, on the *Select Operating System list* (press the PageDown key to see the complete list). For this example I clicked on Windows XP.

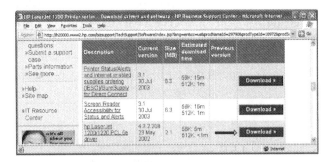

Finally, you will see another web page that presents you with the appropriate device drivers for your printer and operating system. For this example I clicked on the name of the driver (*hp LaserJet 1200/1220 PCL 5e driver*) that seemed to be the best fit for my hardware. To return to the previous page, click on the left Arrow on the Toolbar.

Bear in mind that some companies might require you to first register with their website, before you are allowed to download the device driver software you need.

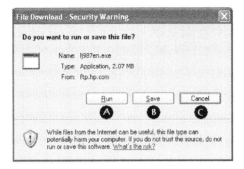

These are the steps to answer the question that this *File Download* dialog box window poses: *Do you want to run or save this file?*:

A. Click on *Run* to copy the device driver software into temporary memory. Once the files have been copied to your computer, your browser will show you a different dialog box, prompting you to select if you really want to run the installation files. Click on *Run* to continue installing the device-driver software. If you are not sure click on *Don't Run*. When the next window opens, asking you if it is okay to install the device software to a particular location on the hard drive, click on *Next*. When the installation program is finished copying the necessary software to the hard drive, another window will open saying that "The InstallShield Wizard is complete." From here, click on *Finish* and then turn off the computer by clicking on the Start menu and then selecting *Turn off computer.*

B. Alternatively, you can click on *Save* to download the package software to your hard drive for later use. This choice doesn't make sense, unless: a) You don't have high-speed Internet access at home, and are now downloading the driver software using someone else's high-speed internet connection, to be burn into a CD you can take with you (to be used later), or b) You have a very slow dial-up connection and are downloading the software overnight.

C. Or if you prefect, click on *Cancel* to abort this task.

If you chose to *Run* the software, and it successfully installed, then connect your hardware device, using the appropriate cable, and then turn the computer back on. In the case of internal expansion cards, you don't need to remove them while this process is ongoing, unless the card instructions tell you to do so.

If you chose the *Save* option, to save the driver software to your local hard drive for later use, then the *Save As* dialog box will have opened up, prompting you to select a folder on your hard drive where you want to save this particular device-software file.

These are the things you should keep in mind, when the *Save As* dialog box opens up to help you save the driver file you found on the web:

A. First note the name of the folder where you are saving this file. If the name of the folder shown is not the one where you want to save it, then click in front of *Save in* or on the buttons on the left side of this dialog box to navigate to the correct folder.
B. This is the name of the driver-software file.
C. Once you find the correct folder, then click on *Save* to copy the software to your hard drive. Later on, when you are looking for this particular device-driver file you will need to remember the name of the folder you've saved it to, and its file name.

When you are ready to install the device driver software; 1) Open the Windows Explorer or the My computer program, and 2) Return to the folder where you've saved the device-driver file software, and then double-click on it to begin install it.

Tip

If you don't remember how to work with the different buttons on the *Save As* dialog box, then please return to chapter nine of this book, to re-familiarize yourself with the process.

The second example highlights the search for newer device drivers for original hardware devices found on computers made by Dell Computer Corporation.

For instance if your computer screen looks faded, then this is due to a corrupted video device driver. Now, before you begin the search for the new video driver, find the complete make and model number of the computer you own. Or, in the case of Dell computers, find the service-tag number or the Express-service code, which are almost always located on the side of the computer or underneath it (if you own a laptop).

To begin searching for Dell device drivers, open your Internet web browser and type the Dell support web page URL; *http://support.dell.com/support/downloads/,* on the address bar. Now press Enter, to load this web page, and then click on "Choose by Service Tag".

This is the way to begin searching for drivers for Dell hardware devices:

A. To begin click inside the cell in front of *Service Tag,* and then type your service tag.
B. On the Drivers & Downloads website, you can also look for software drivers by selecting the drop-down menu beside *Product model* and then using the second pull-down menu to select the appropriate model.
C. Now click on *Go,* to tell this website to look for all the device-driver software that pertains to your particular hardware device.

Now your web browser will open the *Drivers & Downloads* web page (for the product you have chosen), from which you can complete your search for software drivers.

Tip After making a selection on a drop-down menu, your browser might ask you if is Ok to send information that might be viewed by others to the Internet. Click on Ok, to send the information.

Although the steps needed to download the device drivers for your particular hardware device will be different, if you own a computer system not manufactured by Dell, the idea is more or less the same; visit the website of the company who manufactured the hardware device you own, to find the device drivers you need.

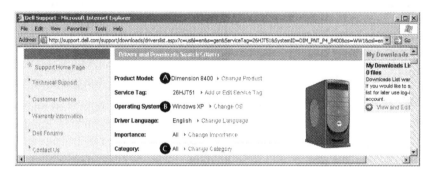

Follow this screenshot-of the new web page that opens up, to learn how to find the exact device driver you need:

A. Notice the model shown here (it should match the exact model of your computer).
B. This is the operating system for which you are presented downloads on this page.
C. Click on "Change . . . " in front of any field you need to make changes, or to narrow the scope of the information shown. For instance to see only the Video drivers click on "Change . . . ", in front of Category, and on the Drop-down menu scroll down to the Video Adapters item and click on it. Finally click outside to refresh this list.

Bear in mind that if you are not comfortable following the process of downloading and installing a new device driver, then you should consider hiring a recommended professional computer consultant to help you with this task. This is due to the fact that if you were to install the wrong one, then the operating system might not load correctly and instead might show you a blue screen. Additionally if this were to happen, then you won't be able to get back to use your computer until someone undoes the changes you've made to it, or worse reinstalls the Windows operating system with potential loss to some or all the work you've saved on your computer.

Note Computer support Web sites are updated from time to time, because of that when you visit this webpage, it might look a little different that the one on this screenshot.

Now, Page Down or click on the down arrow on the Scroll Bars (on the side of this window) to see (if you haven't changed the setting in front of Category) a categorized list that reads; *Applications, Audio drivers, Chipset . . .* , from which you must click on the correct type of hardware device you need device drivers for.

To finish selecting a Device driver, on the Dell support website:

A. Click on the name of the device driver that matches the hardware device you need software drivers for, to see more information about it. Bear in mind that if you see more than one device-driver file name on this page on the category you are looking for (for instance if you see a few names under Video Adapter), then you **must** ascertain which one is the right one for your system, by: a) Reading your Dell packing slip or b) By calling the Dell support phone number at 1-800-418-8590

B. However if you are sure of the name of the device driver you need drivers for, then click on Download.

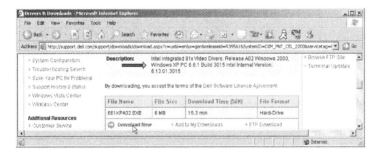

If you clicked on the name of the device driver (step A), then please read (in front of Description) the name of the device driver you have selected and the name of the operating system it is compatible with. If this is the right combination for your system, then click on Download Now. If that is not the case (for instance, if you have XP and it reads 98), then this is the wrong device driver for your system, and now you must return to the previous page to look for the right one.

On the next dialog box that opens, you must decide what to do with the software you've asked for, and that is now ready to be executed right away (to unpack the device drivers).

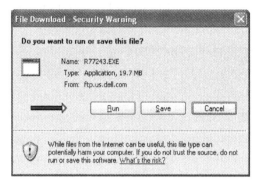

Please return to the example shown previously (pages # 367 & 368), if you need guidance on answering the question that this File Download window poses to you. Which is: "Do you want to run or save this file?"

Bear in mind that if you have an older computer system and cannot find the right device-driver software you need, to complete adding a particular hardware device you want to use, that there is a third-party web site called Driver Guide (http://www.driverguide.com/), that you could use—with the help of a computer professional—to find thousands of different device drivers. Using this website is free of charge, but you will have to register with them.

If the device driver you downloaded from a company website doesn't properly configure a hardware device, then you will need to return and download a different one.

Adding new hardware devices in Windows XP or Windows 2000

Adding any additional hardware device to a Windows base computer used to be a very tricky undertaking, but in Windows XP this process has become a lot easier. First, you must ascertain that the particular hardware device you want to install is compatible with the operating system (such as Windows 2000) your computer uses.

The most common types of ports to which you can add hardware devices in a Windows based computer system are:

- PCI, AGP, and PCI Express internal expansion ports.
- USB or FireWire (IEEE 1394) ports. These types of ports are available on the outside of the computer.

For instance, if you are planning to buy a new video card, make sure it is of the right type (newer computer systems might have a PCI Express port available for video cards) for your computer. To ascertain this information read the outside of the box (if you haven't purchased it yet), or if you already bought it or it was given to you, the documentation that accompanied the hardware device you need software drivers for.

Once you have the hardware device you want to add to your personal computer system, follow the instructions that came with it to install it.

If you are not able to find the instructions to install a hardware device you want to add, because for instance someone gave you a used printer with the software on a CD but without the user manual, then you can install it the following way:

1. If you are adding an internal expansion card, such as a video card, first physically install it in your system.
2. Now install the software that came with the hardware device. If you don't have this software, then follow the instructions of the previous pages to find a device driver for it on the Internet. When you find the software, download it and click on *Run* to install it.
3. If you are adding an external device such as a USB device, plug it in now (unless otherwise instructed by the driver-installation software.)
4. Restart the computer, if advised by the installation software.

Your device should now work. If it doesn't, then you most likely need to obtain a different or a newer version of the device-driver software.

Step by step instructions on how to install a new hardware device using the *Found New Hardware Wizard*

Every once in a while, when you add a new hardware device and after following the steps of the previous page, Windows XP won't automatically install the driver software for this device. In this case, a dialog box called the *Found New Hardware Wizard* will open.

For instance consider the following sequence that illustrates the process to install an Epson Scanner, for which I had the installation CD, but not the installation instructions.

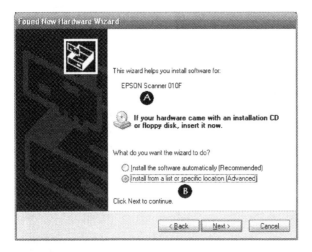

This is the way, if you have the CD-Rom that came with your hardware device, to add a new hardware device once the *Found New Hardware Wizard*, opens up:

A. This window will show you the name of the device you've connected to your computer. On this example it reads "Epson Scanner 010F".

B. Click on *Install from a list of specific location (Advanced)*, to use the device-driver software you have on the installation CD. Now open your CD-Rom drive and insert the CD that came with your hardware device.

Now click on *Next* to jump to the next step of installing the device driver for the hardware device you've connected to your computer.

Bear in mind that you should not personally add any hardware devices if you work in a company with an IT department, because this might be forbidden by the internal policies of your company.

Next another dialog box window opens, and now you must tell/show this Wizard the location where the device-driver software for your hardware device is located.

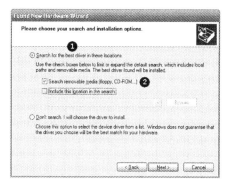

These are the steps to show the *Found New Hardware Wizard* where to look for the installation software for your new hardware device:

1. First click on *Search for best driver in these locations*.
2. Now click on *Search removable media (floppy, CD-ROM...)* If you've downloaded drivers to your computer from a website, and you know the location of these drivers, then you can pick *Include this location on the search*, and then click on *Browse* to specify the folder in which you've saved them.

Now click on *Next*, to have the *Found New Hardware Wizard* look for the installation software on the locations you picked.

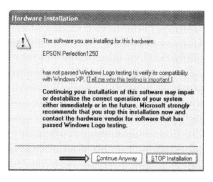

If you receive the message, "*The software you are installing* ...," then click over *Continue Anyway* to complete the installation. Now the *Found New Hardware Wizard* should have completed the installation of the new hardware you've added, and you should click on *Finish*. If you click on "Stop Installation", then this window will close, and the software won't be installed.

Safely removing USB hardware devices

USB devices such as digital cameras, printers, and USB removable-storage drives are the most common and easiest-to-use type of hardware devices you can connect to your Windows XP/2000 computer. For instance, most USB removable-storage drives are recognized immediately by Windows XP/2000 and assigned an available drive letter, so that you can work with them without delay.

Note that when you click on the My Computer icon or open the Windows Explorer after connecting a USB removable-storage device, a new drive letter is added under the Devices with Removable Storage. (In this example, the UDISK 20X I connected was automatically given the E: drive letter by Windows.)

It is recommended that, when you are done using one of these removable devices, that you use the *Safely Remove Hardware* dialog box before actually unplugging them.

These are the steps, to safely remove a USB storage device:

1. First click on this icon, on the System Tray.
2. When the *Safely Remove Hardware* dialog box window opens, double-click on the name of the particular USB storage device you want to disconnect.
3. On the *Stop a Hardware device* dialog box window, click on the name of the USB device you want to disconnect, and then click on OK. If the device is in use, then you will get a warning to try again later.

Bear in mind that you might see more than one entry in the *Stop a Hardware device* dialog box, depending on the number of USB drives you've attached to your computer. In this case, be careful to only disconnect the correct one.

List of some computer company's support URL's or web addresses

This is a list of some of the leading companies in the computer business and the corresponding web addresses for their support/driver websites, in case you need to visit their website to obtain new device drivers, or just to get technical support.

ATI Technologies, Inc.: *http://www.ati.com/support/driver.html*
Dell Computer Corporation: *http://support.dell.com*
Fujitsu: *http://www.fujitsu.com/us/support/*
Hewlett-Packard: *http://www.hp.com/country/us/en/support.html*
Lexmark: *http://support.lexmark.com/*
NEC Corporation: *http://www.nec.com/index.html*
Sony Corporation: *http://esupport.sony.com/perl/select-system.pl?DIRECTOR=DRIVER*
Toshiba: *http://www.toshiba.com/tai-new/Support.htm*

Please bear in mind that you can often solve some device-driver issues by visiting the Microsoft update website, at this URL: *http://update.microsoft.com/*

These are the steps, as you can see on the above screen capture, to download a device driver using the Microsoft Windows Update:

1. First click over *Hardware, Optional*, to see on the right panel the name of the driver you can update from this website.
2. Now click on this checkbox, to put a check mark there, to tell the Windows Update website to download the updated Device Driver.

Finally, click on *Review and install updates*, and then again on *Review Install Updates*. You will see a window that reads: *The updates are being downloaded and installed*. When this process completes, click on *Restart now* to finish updating the computer.

Chapter 16

Guide to using digital Cameras and Scanners in Windows XP

General information about using imaging devices in Microsoft Windows

People who have never used a personal computer often ask me; what will I gain by using a Windows PC?. One of the answers is that they can use it, alongside a digital camera, to work with the photos it takes. And once these photos are saved to your computer, then you can; edit, print or even send them to someone via e-mail.

For instance one of the advantages of using a digital camera, instead of a regular film one, is that you can choose the photos you want to keep or delete, in addition to deciding which ones you want to print. You can also make changes to the pictures themselves: such as changing their brightness and/or their contrast.

Take for instance this digital camera, a Nikon Coolpix 7900, which is an excellent choice for regular digital photography.

Bear in mind that if you are a professional photographer and want to consider replacing your current SLR camera for a digital one, that you should buy a digital SLR, such as the Nikon D2X Digital SLR.

A computer scanner (such as this Epson Perfection 4490 Photo), which (once connected to your computer) can function in a similar fashion to a copy machine, is also a good addition to a computer system, because it allows you to convert hard copies of anything that you can fit on its glass-plate surface, into computer files you can work with. For instance using this hardware device, you can bring old photos, or even copies of invoices (for instance to send a copy to a credit card company via e-mail) into your computer.

The basic process used to create an image file that your computer can use

The process used by digital cameras or scanners to bring images into your computer is called the Digitizing process. Once the image is digitized, and transferred/copied to your computer, as a computer file, then it can be used to complete your every day computer work.

These are the two most common devices used to digitize images:

- Scanners, which can digitize hard copies of anything that you can fit onto their glass-plate surface.
- Digital cameras, which take pictures and automatically store them as digital computer files, which can be transferred onto your computer.

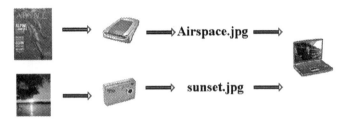

This is the general process to digitize an image, which is very similar when using a scanner or a digital camera, to bring it into a computer:

1. On a computer scanner, you scan a hard copy of a document, such as the page of a magazine. On a digital camera, you take a picture of anything you can see through the viewfinder, such as a sunset.
2. Now the picture is digitized, or translated into bits of electronic information that a computer can understand, and given a name. In this example, the scanner created the file "Airspace.jpg," of the cover of a magazine, and the camera created the file "Sunset.jpg," of a sunset.
3. Now the digitized image is brought into the computer as a computer file. Notice also on this example the three letter jpeg file extension, or "last name of the file". Now, most cameras/scanners automatically generate image files of the JPEG type, which is the most compatible (almost any program will be able to open it) type of graphic file format in use today.

Once the digital rendering of your image is saved on your computer, in the form of a computer file, it will remain there until you delete it. In the meantime, you can: use it on a school paper, send it as an e-mail attachment, or print it.

Intro to using digital cameras

A digital camera is basically a camera that doesn't use conventional film to store the photos it takes. Instead, it processes the photos internally, and stores them in memory cards (which can be reused thousands of times), where they are kept until the time you are ready to copy them to your computer.

If you are in the market for a digital camera, then you must know that they come in many different sizes and price ranges. And one of the most important considerations when buying one is its megapixel capability: Higher megapixel ratings, such as 8 or 9, translate into better-quality prints, because they produce higher resolution photos. The tradeoff is that higher-resolution photos (from high-megapixel cameras) take up more space on memory cards. However, most high-megapixel cameras have a feature that allows you to use a setting to take lower-resolution photos if you want to conserve space.

These are some tips you should keep in mind when using digital cameras:

- Hold the camera steady while taking a picture. This is the main drawback of digital photography, in almost all non-professional cameras: the lag time between the actual moment when you depress the shutter and the time your digital photo is actually taken. Because of this at times, if you don't have a steady grip on the camera, your photos might appear blurry.
- Learn to turn off the flash when using the camera indoors, because some times using the flash leads to the "red-eye" effect on people. Because is easier to adjust the brightness/contrast on a photo (using a photo editing program), that to remove the "red-eye" effect you see on some photos.
- Always carry an extra memory card with you, of smaller capacity (such as 64 MB), just in case you need to take 20 or 30 additional pictures and don't have the space in the camera or the time to go through the camera menu and delete the photos that you no longer want to keep.
- Learn to erase/format the internal memory of the camera, as soon as you are sure that you have transferred all of the old pictures to a folder on your computer's hard drive.
- Keep your batteries charged, or keep a spare set of batteries with you.

In this chapter we will review the use of a software tool, included with Windows XP), called the *Microsoft Scanner and Camera Wizard* that you can use to import digital photos into your computer, although bear in mind that most digital cameras also come packaged with computer software to help you select the photos (saved in your camera), you want to bring to your computer hard drive. Is your choice.

General steps to import the photos you've taken from your Digital Camera to your computer

Once you've taken photos with your digital camera, you can copy those photos to a personal computer hard drive or take the camera's memory card to a self-service photo place, such as a CVS pharmacy, to print them right away.

These are the general steps to import pictures, from your digital camera:

1. First plug your camera into your computer, using the provided cable.
2. Now turn the camera on. If your camera requires you to move a dial or to press a button to start downloading the photos, then do so now.
3. Now import your photos in one of these ways:
   - Using the software that shipped with your camera.
   - Using the Microsoft Windows XP *Scanner and Camera Wizard.*
   - Using the Windows Explorer or the My computer program to open the photos on its Internal memory card (for instance the E: drive), select and copy them, and finally paste them to a drive/folder on your computer.

Bear in mind that most digital cameras store the photos you take with very descriptive file names, followed by a picture number. For example, the files that my Nikon camera creates follow this pattern: DSCN0087, and so on. Now most of the times, if you use the software included with your particular camera, the photo files will retain those names once they are imported into your PC.

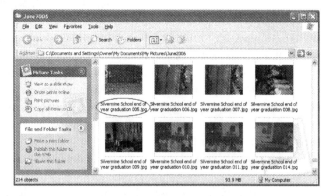

Now, if you choose to use the *Scanner and Camera Wizard,* to import them into the computer, they will be named according to a name you chose. In this example, the name I choose was *Silvermine School end of year graduation,* so this program gave the files the name *Silvermine School end of year graduation* 001, and so on.

How to download/copy photos from your digital camera to your computer using the *Microsoft Scanner and Camera Wizard*

One of the easiest ways to copy your digital photos into your computer is by using the *Scanner and Camera Wizard* software tool (Windows XP only), and this is because of its built-in software Wizard that will guide you step-by-step trough all the choices you need to make, such as: where (drive/folder), you want to copy them to.

These are the steps to use the Microsoft *Scanner and Camera Wizard*;

1. To begin, plug the digital camera cable into the appropriate port in your computer and then turn it on. Alternatively insert the camera memory card into your computer or printer memory card reader (if it has one).

This is the way to work on the Removable Disk dialog box window:

A. Now click on the appropriate name for the action you want to complete. For example, to import your photos, click on "Copy pictures to a folder in my computer using Microsoft Scanner . . ." Additionally if you click on "Always do the . . ." (To select it), then the next time you connect your camera you won't be asked again to chose an action, and instead the action you previously chose will be automatically selected.
B. Now click on OK or press the Enter key (click on Cancel to close this window), and if you've selected to "Copy pictures to a folder in my computer using Microsoft Scanner . . .", then the Scanner and Camera Wizard will open up. Click on Next to proceed to the next step.

Or click on " . . . advance users only . . . " (In blue letters), to work with the photos saved on the camera right away, although this is most contentious for the novice. Now if instead of the *Scanner and Camera Wizard* another window opens up, bearing the name of the company that manufactured the camera, then just follow its instructions.

Please consider the following points before we go on to step number two (next page), choosing the photos you want to copy using the *Choose Pictures to Copy* dialog box:

- Although a memory card (such as a 512 XD card) can hold hundreds of photos, before you know it might be full up to capacity.
- When a memory card is full up to capacity, then you won't be able to take any additional photos, until you remove/delete some photos.
- Please keep in mind that the photos you select, following the instructions on the next page (Step 2), will be applied the settings you chose on step 3 (using the *Picture Name and Destination* dialog box window). For instance if you clicked on Next on the *Choose Pictures to Copy* dialog box window, without **unselecting any photos**, and later on Step 3 select to "*Delete pictures from My device*", then: a) All of the photos will be copied to the folder you choose, and b) when the copy operation is over the photos will be removed/deleted from the camera memory
- For instance if you run out of space on your memory card (while on Vacation), find an Internet café-to save some of the photos, before you remove them from your camera's memory, the following way:

  ✓ Connect your camera to the Internet café computer.
  ✓ If the Microsoft Scanner and Camera Wizard opens up (otherwise use the Windows Explorer), then; a) Click on **Clear All** to unselect all the photos on the camera (on next step 2), and b) Select **only** as many additional photos you need to take. For instance if you think you need to take 30 additional photos, then only select to copy 30 photos.
  ✓ On the *Picture Name and Destination* dialog box window (step three) click to select "*Delete pictures from My device*", to delete them, otherwise the pictures you choose on the *Choose Pictures to Copy* dialog box window won't be removed from the camera memory.
  ✓ Once the *Scanner and Camera Wizard* process finishes your selected photos will on the Internet café computer hard drive. To retrieve them: a) E-mail them to yourself, or b) ask the people at the Internet café to help you put them on a CD or DVD disk. Otherwise you will lose them (if you clicked on "*Delete pictures from My device*"). Finally ask for help in **erasing the photos** from the Internet café hard drive.
- Do not turn off your camera or remove its memory card while using the *Microsoft Scanner and Camera Wizard* to copy pictures into your computer.

You should also consider (after removing a few photos) changing the resolution camera setting from High to medium, which will allow you to take twice as many photos as when you use the High-resolution setting.

2. Please note that, when the *Choose Pictures to Copy* dialog box opens up, all of the pictures currently saved on the camera memory will be selected (note the check-mark on the right upper corner of each photo) by default, to be copied.

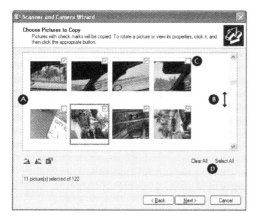

This is the way to work, on the *Choose Pictures to Copy* dialog box, to unselect/select the photos you want to import into your computer:

A. On the work area of this window you can see small renderings (called thumbnails) of the photos you took, and are now saved in your camera.

B. Please note that this preview window only shows you a few of the photos (eight at a time) saved in your camera. To see the rest of the photos saved on the camera (On this example 22, of which 11 are selected) use the Scroll bar (on the right) to move up or down the groups of pictures, or press the Page Down/UP keys to see a different page of photos.

C. Now you can; a) Do nothing here (to leave all the photos now in the camera selected to be copied) or b) Unselect each one of the photos you don't want to import into your computer, by clicking on the corresponding square box on the upper right corner of the photo.

D. To unselect all of the photos, click on *Clear all.* If you unselect a photo, then the *Select All* option will be available. Click on it to select them all again. To select a single photo click on the square box on the right corner of the photo.

To finish working on the selection part of this process and move to the next step, to see the *Picture Name and destination* dialog box Window, click on *Next.* Bear in mind that if you unselect a given photo—as long as you don't deleted it from the camera, that the next time you run this process it will show up ready to be copied/imported into your Computer.

3. Now use the Picture Name and Destination dialog box window to finish importing the selected photos from your camera, into your computer.

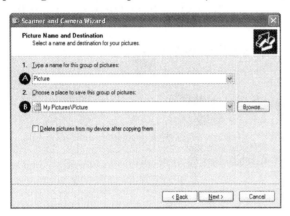

This is the way to name and select a place (drive/folder) to copy your photos to:

A. First you must decide what name you wish to give the series of photos you are about to import. To use the suggested name (shown under "Type a Name . . . "), which on this example is: Picture (the suggested name is either Picture or the name you used last), do nothing here. Now the file names of the photos on this series will be known as Picture 01, Picture 02, and so on (although, if you've used this name before to copy photos to the same folder, the series number will be higher). To use a different name, such as Summer vacation, click on the name shown; now tap on the backspace key to remove part or the entire name, and then type the new name.

B. Please note the path under "Choose a place . . . ", if the last part of the virtual address matches the name you choose on Step A (for instances if you finish typing the word Summer, and the wizard suggest you use the folder; *My Pictures\Summer*), then you are also selecting to use a folder using as a cue the name you've chosen for your photos. To use the folder name shown, do nothing here. To save your photos to a different folder, than the suggested one, click on the name shown to see: folders you've saved photos before, and even ones using as a cue the current date. Now click to select a different one.

To delete the photos from your camera's memory card click on "*Delete pictures from My device* . . . ", to select it. Finally click on *Next* to begin importing/copying your photos to your choose drive/folder. At the end of this chapter you will learn how to use more variations (for instance how to save your photos to an external USB flash drive) you can use on this dialog box window.

4. Now choose, when the *Other options* dialog box window opens up, what to do with the photos you copied to your computer. If you just want to see them, leave the "*Nothing I am finished . . .* "selected, and click on *Next*.

Finally, another dialog box will open, reporting how many pictures have been imported/copied (on this example, 27 pictures) to your computer. To see them, place the mouse pointer over their path and click on Finish. Now wait a few seconds and then click on the window that opens up, to unselect them.

This is the way, to work with the imported photos:

A. To open one just double click on it. If the "Windows picture and Fax . . . " opens up, use the arrow keys to see them. To edit one right click on it (return to their window), take the mouse pointer over *Open* with (to the right or left o the menu), and click on any graphic program on this list to open it. To select a group of them use the instructions on chapter eight.

B. On the left panel, click to select an action you want to apply to the photos you've selected. For instance, click on *Copy to CD*, to save them to a CD.

To return to work with the photos you copied, double click on the My Documents folder, on the My Pictures, and finally over the name of the folder you've saved them to. Using chapter 14 of this book, you will learn to use the *Send To* menu to select/ and send files you've copied to your computer to family and friends (using e-mail).

Intro to using flatbed computer Scanners

A computer scanner works by processing/digitizing anything placed on its glass platen using a scanning device that moves from one end of the image to the other. Once a scanned image is brought into the computer, you will be able to use your computer's image software to enhance or liven it up.

Epson Perfection 4490
PHOTO

The most commonly used type of scanners are the "flatbed" type, such as this Epson Perfection 4990 Photo, in which you place the document face down on the glass platen.

When shopping for a scanner, consider one with buttons on the outside (such as the ones shown on this graphic, that you will find on the Epson Perfection 4990 Photo and Pro) that will simplify some tasks, such as:

A. E-mail button, which when pressed will automatically attach a copy of the scanned image as a file in a new e-mail message. Bear in mind that this feature doesn't work with the AOL provided software (such as the AOL 9.0 software). Chapter seven of this book explains a work-around so that AOL users can easily find and attach files, to e-mail messages.
B. Copy button, which when pressed will send a copy of the document you placed on its glass platen to your printer.

Some scanners also include a software program (which you can also purchase separately) that allows it to extract text from scanned images using a process called OCR, or Optical Character Recognition. The extracted text can now be used in your own documents.

These are some of the things you should keep in mind when using a flatbed scanner

A computer scanner is an amazing piece of equipment that will work as advertised most of the time, but you must know that there are some things you can do to maintain your scanner's optimal functionality.

Here are some tips on how to prevent some problems while scanning documents:

- Always turn on the scanner before you turn on you computer, or else your computer might not recognize it properly.
- Keep the scanner's glass platen clean (but don't clean it with anything that can scratch it). A dirty glass platen will decrease the quality of your scans.
- Always remember to remove anything you've put on the glass platen, after you're done scanning (such as photos or magazines), so that they don't become attached to the glass.

- Place the hard copy you want to scan facedown on the glass platen (as you can see on this drawing I found on the instruction manual for the Epson Perfection 4990 Photo), and make sure that its top part is firmly against the front edge of the scanner and well centered on the arrow mark.

Finally, make sure that your document does not get jostled or skewed when you close your scanner cover. My advice is to close the scanner cover gently, to prevent the original document from moving.

There are two main ways to bring scanned images into your computer:

- Using the particular software that shipped with the scanner.
- Using the Microsoft *Scanner and Camera Wizard*, which you will learn to do in the following pages.

How to bring scanned images into the computer using the Scanner and Camera Wizard

On the following pages you will learn, step-by-step, how to use the *Scanner and Camera Wizard*, which is a program included with the Windows XP operating system to help you import scanned images into your computer hard drive.

Here's what you need to do:

1. To begin make sure that the Scanner is turned on, and that its interface cable is firmly connected to the computer.

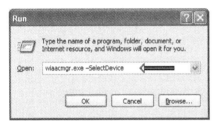

2. Now click on the Start Menu button, and move the mouse up and to the right until it is over the Run program—then click on its name to open it. Now use the *Backspace* key to remove any words that are already there, then type: **wiaacmgr.exe—SelectDevice** Now click on *OK* or press the Enter key.

3. Now the first dialog box of the *Scanner and Camera Wizard* opens up. To continue to the following step, just click on *Next.*

You can also open the *Scanner and Camera Wizard* by clicking on the *Start* menu button, then moving the mouse pointer over *All Programs,* then over to the *Accessories* group, now to the right and down, and them click on the *Scanner and Camera Wizard* name to open this program. If the *Scanner and Camera Wizard* refuses to open—if you get an error—then double-check to make sure the scanner is turned on. If it isn't, turn off the computer, turn on the scanner, and then turn the computer back on.

If the *Scanner and Camera Wizard* dialog box window still doesn't open, then the scanner might not be compatible with it, and you must use the software program that shipped with the scanner, to bring your scanned images into your computer.

4. Now you must select the type of image you want to bring into your computer.

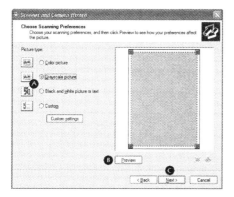

A. To begin click on the name (under Picture type), that matches the type of document you've placed on the Scanner glass or platen. The choices are;
- *Color picture* (this is the default setting)
- *Grayscale picture*
- *Black and white picture or text.*
- *Custom*, to define what is it that you need to bring into the computer.

B. You can even click on *Preview* to see a preview of the image you want to scan.

If you clicked on *Preview*, the image will be previewed. On the preview window you can also take the mouse pointer over one of its corners, right on the dotted line, press and hold the left mouse button, and drag it until you have selected as little or as much of the document you want to scan.

C. To continue, on to the next step, click on *Next*.

5. Now the *Picture Name and Destination* dialog box window opens up.

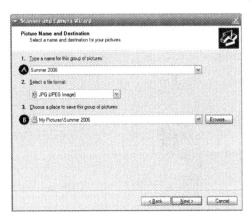

This is the way, to finish importing your scanned image:

A. First you must decide what name you wish to give to the scanned image you are about to import. To use the suggested name (shown under "Type a Name . . . "), which on this example is: Summer 2006 (the suggested name is either Picture or the name you used last), do nothing here. Now the file name of the scanned image will be known as Summer 2006 01 (although, if you've used this name before, then the wizard will automatically assign it a higher number, such as Summer 2006 02). To use a different name, such as Summer vacation, click on the name shown; now tap on the backspace key to remove part or the entire name, and then type the new name.

B. Please note the path under "Choose a place . . . ", if the last part of the virtual address matches the name you choose on Step A (for instances if you finish typing the word Summer, and the wizard automatically suggest the folder name; *My Pictures\Summer*), then you are selecting to use a folder using as a "cue" the name you've chosen for your scanned image. To accept to use it, do nothing here. To save your scanned image to a different folder, click on the name shown to see: folders you've saved your scanned images before, and even ones using as a cue the current date. Click to select a different one. Now click on Next, to go onto the next step.

Do not change the setting under *Select a file format* (right now it reads JPEG image), which is one of the most compatible graphic file formats, unless you know or were instructed to use a different file format one (such as BMP), by someone you are corresponding with. On the last pages of this chapter you will learn more about different combinations you can use here, to name and save your image files.

6. Now you need to decide, when the *Other options* dialog box window opens up, what to do with the scanned image. If you just want to see it, leave the *Nothing I am finished working with these pictures* selected, and click on *Next.*

Finally another dialog window opens, letting you know that 1 picture was downloaded/copied to your computer. To see it, click on the link, or on *Finish.*

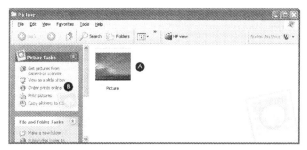

Now you have some options for working with the image you just imported.

A. Finally the image you've just scanned should be visible here. Please note that, if there is more than one image saved in this folder (which begin with the same name), the one you've just scanned will be the one with the higher number. To open it, just double click on it. To edit the scanned image, right click on it, take the mouse pointer over Open with (to the right or left on the menu that opens up), and click on any graphic program on this list to open it.

B. On the left panel, you can click to select the action you want to apply to the photos you've selected. For instance, click on Copy to CD, if you want to save them to a CD.

To return to this folder at some other time, double-click on the *My* Documents folder (if that is where you copied the scanned imaged to) on the Windows desktop, and then double-click on the *My Pictures* folder. Then double-click the on the name of the folder—in this example it was *Picture*—you copied the images to earlier. You can also use the instructions in chapter 14 to send the files in this folder—be they photos or scanned images—to your family and friends via e-mail.

Extra help using the Picture name and Destination dialog box window

To fully take advantage of the *Scanner and Camera Wizard* program to copy/save photos from a digital camera (see step 3), and to complete the process to copy/save scanned images (see step 5), then you should become familiar with the different choices available on the *Picture name and Destination* dialog box window. For instance:

- Keep this in mind when naming your photos/scanned images (see the name shown under "*Type a name for these group of pictures*");

    ➢ To use the suggested name shown on this line, do nothing here.
    ➢ To use a different name (for instance one you used before); click on the name shown, tap on the Down/Up arrow keys, until you find it. To change it, click on it, press the Right arrow key and remove all/ or part of it (using the *Backspace* key). Now type the new name for your photos/scanned images. Adding as little as a single number at the end of the name shown, for instance typing a 1 at the end of the "London vacation", would qualify as a new name.

- Keep this in mind when selecting a destination folder to save your photos/scanned images (see the name shown under "*Choose a place . . .*");

    ➢ To use the suggested folder name shown on this line, do nothing here.
    ➢ If you want, you can save your photos to a folder whose name matches the current date (for instance 2006-11-20) this way; click on the name shown (for instance *My Pictures)*, and when the drop-down menu opens up, click on My Pictures\2006-11-20 to select it. You can even select to use a folder name that uses as a "cue" a combination of the current date/ and the name you've given the photos or the scanned images. For instance if you've named the series of photos: My Wedding, then you can even pick to use the suggested: *My Pictures\2006-11-20,My Wedding* folder. Now when you click on Next the button of the Picture name and Destination dialog box Window, to go onto the next step, the images you chose to copy will be saved to the *My Pictures\2006-07-20,My Wedding* folder.

Bear in mind that all the references to the *My Documents* folder, or any other folder under it (such as the *My Pictures* one) are, unless preceded by a different drive letter (such as the E:\), meant to indicate that you are saving to the C:\ drive. Please read chapter nine to learn how to back up your work, saved in these folders, to CD's.

Now let's try three different scenarios of using different combinations of names and folders on the *Picture Name and Destination* dialog box window. For instance:

- Use the suggested name for your **photos/scanned** images, select one you've used before, or type a new one. Now, for the **destination folder**, use a name whose name matches the name you picked for your photos/scanned images, or use the one that shows the current date, or a combination of the current date plus the name you used for your photos/scanned images.

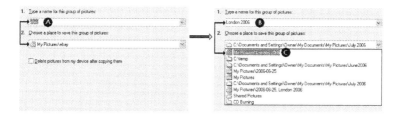

A. To use the suggested name shown (for instance eBay), do nothing here.

B. To use one you've used before click on the name shown and tap on the Down/Up arrow keys, until you find it. If you double click on the name shown here and press any key, it will be deleted. To use a new name: click on it and press the right arrow key. Now slowly tap the Backspace key to delete part/or all of it, then type the new name or just add a letter or a number to the name shown, to change it, for instance *London 2006A*.

C. To use a different destination folder, than the one shown (under "*Choose a place* . . . "), click on it. Now select the line that corresponds to the name you want to use for your photos or scanned image (for instance the automatically generated **My Pictures\London 2006**). If for instance you chose to saved your *London 2006* photos, to the: *Pictures\ London 2006* folder (by selecting it here), then to find them later: double click on the *My Pictures* folder (after double clicking on the *My Documents* folder), and on the *London 2006* folder to see and work with them.

Notice on the screenshot on the right, that when you click on the name of the folder shown under "Choose a place," that two of the choices read: *My Pictures\2006-06-26*, and one *My Pictures\2006-06-26, London 2006*. For instance if you selected the one that matches the current date (which will be created when you click on Next to go on to the next step), then to find these photos later: double click on the *My Pictures* folder (after double clicking on the *My Documents* folder), and then on the folder that matches the date you saved them (for instance 2006-06-26).

- Use the suggested name for your **photos/scanned** images, select one you've used before, or type a new one. Now, for the destination folder, pick a folder whose name doesn't matches the name you picked for your photos/scanned images.

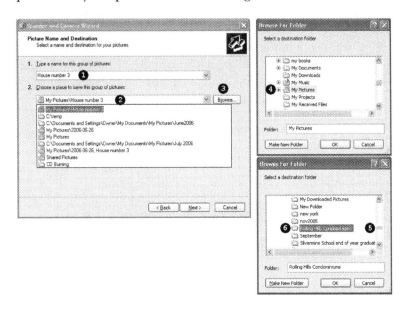

1. To use the suggested name shown (for instance eBay), do nothing here. To use one you've used before click on the name shown and tap on the Down/Up arrow keys, until you find it. If you double click on the name, and press any key, it will be deleted. To use a new name, click on it and press the right arrow key. Now tap the Backspace key to delete part/or all of it, then type the new name or just add a letter or a number to the name shown, to change it, for instance *House number 3*.
2. Now click on the name of the folder shown, under "*Choose a place . . .* ", to select a different one. If you find it, click on it.
3. If you can't find the folder name you are looking for, click on *Browse*.
4. Now look for *My Pictures* folder, and click on the Plus sign to see them.
5. If the list of available folders is too long, then use the scroll bar or press the Down/Up arrow to navigate thought it.
6. When you find the folder you want to save to, click on its name to select it, and press the Enter key to close the *Browse For Folder* window.

Click on "*Delete pictures from . . .*", *if you wish* to delete photos from the camera or the memory card after they are copied to your PC. Now click on *Next*, and on *Next* on the *Other Options* window, and finally click on Finish to see your photos.

- Use the suggested name for your photos/scanned images, select one you've used before, or type a new one. Now to save your photos/scanned images create a completely new folder name, under the local hard drive or even to an external storage resource (such as a USB flash drive).

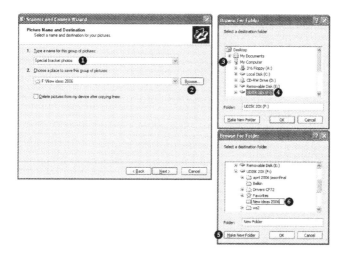

1. To use the suggested name shown, do nothing here. To use one you've used before click on the name shown and tap on the Down/Up arrow keys, until you find it. To use a new name, click on it and press the right arrow key. Now tap the Backspace key to delete part/or all of it, then type the new name or just add a letter or a number to the name shown, to change. For instance type *Special bracket photos*.

2. Now click on *Browse*, to open the *Browse for Folder* window.

3. When the *Browse for Folder* window opens, use the scroll bar to go to the top of its menu, which is *My Desktop*. Now click on the plus sign next to *My Computer*, to open the list of drives (such as C:, F:). If you wish you can also create a new folder (steps 5 and 6) under the *My Pictures* folder, which in turn is under the *My Documents* folder.

4. For instance click on the drive name assigned to a USB flash drive.

5. Now click on *Make New Folder*.

6. When you see the *New Folder* name (shown highlighted), type its new name right away, and now click outside of it to use it. Then press the Enter key to close the *Browse For Folder* window.

Click on "*Delete pictures from . . .*", *if you wish* to delete photos from the camera or the memory card after they are copied to your PC. Now click on *Next*, and on *Next* on the *Other Options* window, and finally click on Finish to see your photos.

Bear in mind, while importing/copying photos from your camera using the *Scanner and Camera Wizard*, that as long as you don't select (on step 3) to delete/remove the photos (you've previously selected on step 2) from you camera, that they will keep showing up on the *Choose Picture to Copy* dialog box window (step 2), ready to be imported into your computer.

Let's use this example; you are a building contractor, and are working on a big housing project called *Silvermine manor apartments*, and within this project there are a few different types of houses (one with two bedrooms, and another one with four), and you are in charge of documenting the use of raw materials and to photograph the progress of all the different building stages, to that effect you;

1. Begin by taking some photos (let's say 50) of the one-bedroom units, on a camera with no photos saved. Now, after you take the photos, these fifty photos are the only photos saved on the camera memory.

2. Now you follow the steps outlined earlier, and leave on the *Choose Picture to Copy* (step 2) window all the fifty photos selected to be copied.

3. When you reach step three of the instructions, you select to name these series of photos *House one*, and also elect to save them to a new folder called *Silvermine manor Apartments*, but neglect to click on **Delete pictures from My device** (step 3), before you clicked on *Next*, and then *Next* to copy your photos from the camera. So now, the first batch of photos (50) is still on the camera, and should remain there until you chose to delete them.

4. Later on, you take photos using the same camera (which still has the same memory card), of the house number two (which has four bedrooms). Now if; a) You chose to named them House two, and b) To save them to the same folder you saved the House One photos, and c) Forget to unselect the fifty House number one photos (on the *Choose Picture to Copy* window) you took earlier and which are still saved on the camera, then when you finish importing the new House number 2 photos, they will be brought alongside the first photos (for which you chose to use the name House one 01, House one 02 and so on) you took, and now some of the photos files you brought later, with the sequence; House two 01, House two 02, and so on, will have the **exact images** as the ones named House one's.

Now even though you haven't lost any of your photos, you've just copied the same files you needed twice (albeit with a different name). To avoid this; a) Use a different memory card for each project, b) Select, on the *Picture name and Destination, to* delete the photos once they are copied to your hard drive, or c:) Unselect the photos, on the *Choose Picture to Copy* window, you've copied before (so they are not copied a second time). Later on you can also copy the photos you chose not to copy this time, to a different folder on your computer or to another computer.

Finding the graphics files you've copied/imported to your computer hard drive

Taking digital pictures is very easy to do: Just point and shoot. And although copying them to your computer might take you a few tries to learn, in no time you will end up with hundreds of pictures saved on your computer.

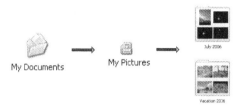

To find your photos, double-click on the *My Documents* folder (if you've saved them there), then double-click on the *My Pictures* folder, and finally double-click on the name of the folder into which you've saved the photos you are looking for. To return to the previous folder you opened, click on the green Up Arrow (under *Favorites*).

You can view your photos in a variety of ways:

1. First click on the views button, indicated by the arrow.
2. Now click on Thumbnails, or any other options on this menu, depending on how you like to view your images.

For instance. if you saved your image files to an external USB flash drive, then find them using the My Computer program (double click on it) or the Windows Explorer, as shown on chapter 8 (Guide to the Windows Explorer). Use the Windows Explorer to delete or move some of these saved photo files.

Learn to use a graphic-image file in a Microsoft Word document

In the pages that follow you will learn how to add the scanned images or photos you imported to your computer to a document you have created. Remember that practice makes perfect: Before you know it, combining images in documents will be like second nature for you.

Bear in mind that I used the word-processing program Microsoft Word in this example. But even if you don't have Word installed on your computer, you can still benefit from these instructions by downloading a free trial copy of Microsoft Office (which includes Microsoft Word) from the Microsoft website—or by following the instructions of the word processor you own.

To begin, open Word: If you can see its icon on the Windows Desktop, double-click to open it, or click on the *Start* button, take the mouse to *All Programs*, then to the right.

Now take the mouse pointer to *Microsoft Office*, and then up or down until you find the Microsoft Word icon. Click to open it.

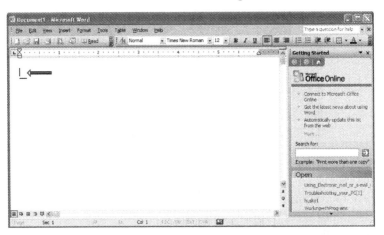

Notice the blinking cursor, which indicates the exact point in the document where text will appear if you begin typing—or where an image will be render if you bring/import it into your document. In the latest versions of Word you can change the position of the cursor by double-clicking anywhere in the work area.

Now write any text you want to have in the document. Afterward, you can insert an image, whether it is one you brought into your computer using a scanner, or a digital camera, or even one only present on a memory card you've just connected to your printer.

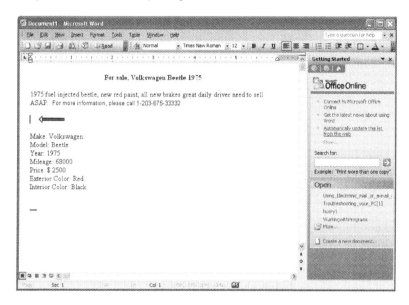

These are the steps to create your document:

1. First, write the text. This can be anything and everything—from flyers, like the above example, to wedding invitations.
2. Now select where on the page you want to insert an image. Double-click on that exact point, or press the *Return* key at the end of the proceeding line where you want to add the photo. The blinking cursor, indicated by the arrow in this screenshot, is where the photo will be placed.

Bear in mind that, when you are bringing scanned images or photos into a document, that you don't have to worry about making enough space on the document right away. In this screen capture there are only two lines between the blinking cursor. But once you import the image, your document will automatically make the space it needs to accommodate it.

Note

You can add your graphic first, before you write the text. But it is much easier to add the image later; because then you can figure out how much room you want it to take on the page.

Now you need to find the image on your hard drive that you'd like to insert, on this document. To begin, you need to remember what drive/folder you downloaded the digital photo/ or scanned image to.

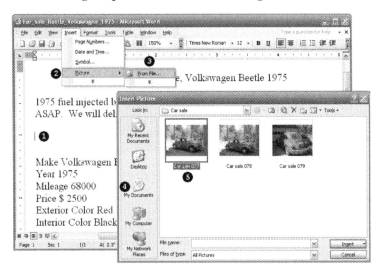

To add an image to your Word document, just follow these steps:

1. First double-click on the exact point in your document where you want to place the image. The cursor should be blinking at that spot.
2. Now click on the *Insert* menu item, and bring the mouse down to *Picture*. If the picture choice is not available right away, then place the mouse over the double arrows at the button of the menu to expand it.
3. Now bring the mouse over to the right, and click *From File*.
4. Now on the Insert Picture dialog box, look in front of *Look In*. If that is not the name of the folder where you've saved the image you're looking for, then use the buttons on the left or click in front of *Look In* to try to find the folder. In this example I clicked on *My Documents*, then I double-clicked on *My Pictures*, and finally I doubled-clicked on the name of the file I wanted to add to the document. Alternatively, I could have single clicked on it, and then on *Insert*.

If the picture you want to add to your document is on a Flash drive, and you've already plugged it into your computer's USB port, then: a) Click on the name (in front of *Look in*), and b) Click on the My Computer icon, and finally c) Click on the drive letter used by your Flash drive (for instance the E:\ letter). Now look for it there.

Now the picture you've chosen is added to the document, where it will automatically take up as much space on the page as it needs to.

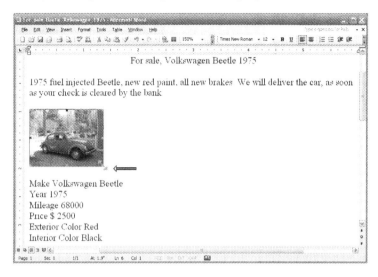

Resizing an image is very easy: Click anywhere inside it, and then take the mouse pointer over any of its corners, until it turns into a double arrow (as in the above screenshot). Now press and hold the left mouse button and start dragging it until the image is of the desired size.

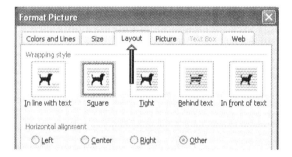

You can also have the text flow around the image. To do it, right-click over the image, then select *Format picture*. Now click on *Layout*, as in this screenshot, and then click on the option that best suits your needs. When you finish click on OK. To undo a change you've made here, click on *Edit* and then *Undo*—or press/and hold the CTRL key and then the Z one.

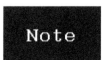

Once you have finished working with a document, you can save it, print it, attach it to e-mail message, or close it without saving it. Later on you can also delete it from your hard drive.

Part VII
Windows Technical Stuff

Chapter 17

How to keep your copy of Windows XP up to date

The importance of keeping Windows XP up to date

Windows XP, comprised of many thousand of individual software files, is one of the most complex operating systems ever released for use on a personal computer. For this reason, it might be necessary to update some of its software from time to time. These updates might involve only a few files or many dozens of them, and will either enhance a program's abilities or close a just found vulnerability within a program.

With those purposes in mind, Microsoft offers small software updates from time to time. They are free, and can be downloaded from the Internet. Microsoft also offers software packages called "service packs" for Windows XP. Service packs include the individual updates that have previously been released, and can affect many different parts of the operating system, such as the administration tools, drivers, and additional components. The Windows XP service packs are cumulative; each new pack contains all the fixes offered in previous packs, as well as any new changes.

Here are some reasons why you might consider updating your copy of Windows XP, to protect your important work:

- You are concerned about not having a firewall that protects you while surfing the web.
  - Updating to the Windows XP Sp2 easily solves this, because included in this service pack is free firewall software that you can enable to protect your system from hackers.
- Because you are concerned about pop-up windows while browsing the web.
  - Then you should know that the Windows Service pack 2 has a new Pop-up Manager feature, that if configured correctly will block most pop-up, which are more than a nuisance, and when clicked on can cause real harm to the computer work saved on your computer.

Bear in mind that these updates are completely free to people whose computers are running a legitimate copy of Windows XP. I know that the general though is that nothing is free in life, but Microsoft really does work hard to release software patches that address newly found vulnerabilities on the Windows XP operating system.

Additionally you can order the Windows Service Pack 2 (SP2) on CD, for instance because you have a slow dial-up Internet connection, by opening your Internet Explorer web browser and typing the following

URL: http://www.microsoft.com/windowsxp/downloads/updates/sp2/ cdorder/en_us/default.mspx on its address bar, then press Enter. Once the web site opens, provide them all the requested information, so that Microsoft can send you the Update CD.

How to check which version of Windows your computer has installed

If you buy a computer today it will most likely come preinstalled with one of the different editions of Vista or even Windows XP, but if your computer is a few years old, then you can ascertain exactly what version of the Windows (such as Windows 98) operating system it is running, as well as its version level (such as Windows 98 Second Edition).

To find this information, minimize all of the windows you've opened (or click on the desktop icon on the Quick launch Toolbar), to see the windows desktop. Then:

1. Right click on the My Computer icon
2. On the ensuing list, click on Properties.

Read the information under "System" to see the version of Windows you have, and at what level. If it reads; Windows XP Service Pack 2, then you can jump to the last pages of this chapter to learn how to work with the new Security Center. If it reads; Windows XP, but there is no mention of Service Pack 2, then your system lacks this important Windows XP service pack, and it is important that you manually update your computer using the instructions that follow.

If your computer is running Windows 98 or any version of windows (other than Windows XP), you can also manually update your operating system by following the instructions on the next page, but the information about the new Security Center doesn't pertain to your computer.

How to run Windows Update manually

The fist step in updating the Windows operating system in your computer is to establish a connection to the Internet. If you have a cable or DSL modem (as long is turned on), you should always be connected to the Internet. If you use dial-up software, you will need to connect to the Internet each time you wish to use it.

Once you are connected, follow these steps to update your computer:

1. To start this process, you have two choices:
   a. Click on the Start menu button, place the mouse indicator over "All Programs," now move the mouse pointer to the right and up, find the Windows Update icon and click on it to launch it.
   b. Alternatively, open your web browser and type the URL of the Windows Update website (on the Address bar), which is: *http://v5.windowsupdate.microsoft.com*, then press Enter.
2. If this is the first time you are running Windows Update, you might be asked whether it is OK to install a small program (called a plug-in) that allows the Microsoft website to determine what new software your computer needs. Click OK to install this plug-in.

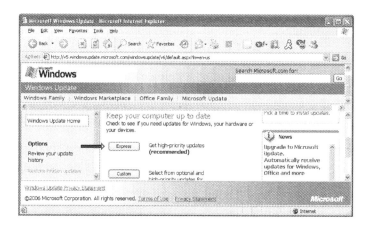

3. A new web page will open up, when the website is finished analyzing your computer. It will prompt you to select the way you prefer to download the upgrades your system needs (I recommend that you click on *Express*).

When your computer has been updated, then you will see the message; "You've successfully updated . . . ". Click on OK if you are asked to restart your computer.

What is new in the Windows XP Service Pack 2 (SP2)

On August 6, 2004, following a series of delays, Microsoft released the Windows XP Service Pack 2, which provides fixes to many of the security concerns of individuals and companies using the first release of Windows XP.

Windows XP SP2 includes enhancements in the following areas:

- Improved Automatic Updates allow your computer to automatically download the latest updates for Windows XP.
- Internet Explorer Pop-up Blocker helps your browser deal with annoying pop-up windows (usually ads) while surfing the web. (To tweak the settings for this feature of Internet Explorer, refer to chapter 13.)
- Internet Explorer Information Bar allows you to see information about downloads, blocked pop-up windows, and potential security risks.
- Outlook Express Privacy Update makes it harder for spammers to send you unwanted e-mail.
- Attachment Manager monitors and disables potentially unsafe attachments when you use Explorer, Outlook Express, and Windows Messenger.
- Windows Security Center allows you to easily view your security status and manage key security settings in one convenient place. (This is explained in more detail starting on the next page.)
- Better wireless support simplifies the process of discovering and connecting to wireless networks in your home or on the road.
- Windows Firewall, which is now part of Windows XP, helps protect your computer from viruses, worms, and other security threats that can spread over the Internet. If you wish, you will be allowed to use your own Firewall, like the one from the Norton Internet Security (Symantec).

Is recommended that, even after installing this very important service pack, that you return to visit the Windows Update web site from time to time, to check it your computer needs any new software update. In this chapter you will also learn how to change your systems settings (if you so wish), to allow your Windows XP computer to update itself, with very little user intervention.

 Note If you bought your personal computer recently (for example, anytime during 2006), chances are that is already up to the Windows XP Service pack 2 level.

Working with the new Windows XP SP2 Security Center

The new Windows Security Center, included with SP2, monitors the status of your security software—for example, your Internet firewall, the Automatic Updates service, and the anti-virus program on your Windows XP system. It also allows you to see at a glance whether these essential security capabilities are turned on.

To open the Security Center and see if a particular feature is turned on:

1. Begin by double clicking on the My Computer Icon on the Window Desktop.
2. Click on "Change a setting" below "System Tasks" on the left panel. If this option is not available, click on the double arrow pointing down (next to "System Tasks"), to see it.
3. Now double click on the Security Center icon. If you don't see this icon, click on "Switch to Category View" in the upper-left corner of this window.

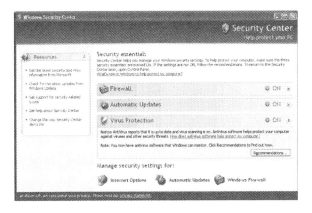

Using the Security Center, you can check if your system has:

- A current software firewall that is enabled.
- An up-to-date anti-virus program.
- The Automatic Updates featured enabled.

For example, on the screen capture above you can see that the Security Center is monitoring all of these options and right now they are all ON. If you see that one of these options is OFF, or if the operating system warns you about one of these options with a pop-up balloon message (on the System Tray), then you should investigate the problem by clicking on the arrow down shown next to the OFF button.

Working with messages in the Security Center

If, after your Security Center has updated SP2, you see that the firewall (a program that protects your computer while you are surfing the web) is OFF, you can do the following:

- If you currently have a firewall installed (other than the one offered by Windows)—for example, the Symantec Norton firewall—, then make sure that the program is enabled. If the Norton firewall is disabled it will show a red X, over its icon (on the System Tray).
- If you don't have a third-party firewall, you can enable the one included with the Windows XP Service Pack 2 as follows:

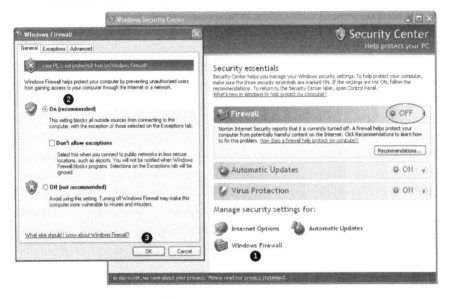

From the Security Center:

1. To begin click on the "Windows Firewall" icon, located at the bottom of the Security Center dialog-box window.
2. Now click on On (recommended), to enable the firewall.
3. Finally click on OK, to close this dialog box window.

If, later on, you decide to use a different firewall, you can follow the steps above and click on OFF in order to disable the Windows firewall included with Windows XP service pack 2. Microsoft recommends that you do not have two firewalls enabled at the same time.

If the Automatic Updates feature is OFF, then return to the Security Center (following the steps outlined earlier in this chapter) and do the following to enable it:

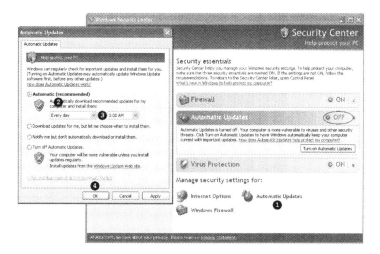

1. To begin click on "Automatic Updates".
2. Now select one of the following options:
   - Automatic; this is the best option for automatically downloading and installing recommended updates. Please read the cons and pros of choosing this setting at the bottom of this page
   - "Download updates for me, but let me choose when . . . ."
   - Notify me but don't automatically download or install them.
   - Turn off Automatic Updates.
3. Select the frequency with which updates are downloaded, as well as the time at which the software downloads will take place. (Think of a time at which your computer will be turned on and connected to the Internet.)
4. Click on OK to accept the changes and close the dialog box.

Bear in mind that there are pros and cons of setting your system to automatically download software updates. The pro is that if there is a newly found vulnerability (addressed by a just released update), then your computer will be protected right away after the update is downloaded, but the con is that if there is a not known incompatibility of an update with a software program you currently use, then your computer system might even crash after updating itself. Instead if you choose to update your computer manually a week or so after an update is issued, then this gives Microsoft extra time to find if there is a problem with it and issue a better fix.

If you chose to be notified when new updates for your computer are ready, then from time to time you will get a message that reads; "New Updates are ready to install." When you see this message, you have to manually approve the installation of updates that have been downloaded to your computer—or, if you chose only to be notified of available updates on the previous step, then you will need to manually approve both their downloading and their installation.

On the next screen capture, you can see a balloon message informing you that new updates are ready for your computer.

To download the updates, or to install updates that have already been downloaded, click on the balloon message. If the balloon message is closed, click on the yellow shield to finish installing the Windows updates.

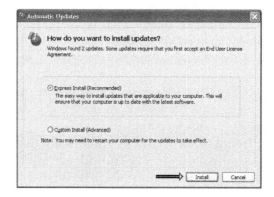

When a dialog box like the one above opens, leave Express Install selected and then click on Install to complete the installation or downloading of your updates. If another window opens and asks whether you want to proceed with the installation, click on "OK" or "I Accept." If you don't want the updates click on "Cancel." Alternative if you want to see what is the name of the update that is to be installed, click on "Custom . . . ", then Install, if you don't want this update click on the check box next to its name to decline it, and then click on "Close."

You will eventually see a message that your computer has been successfully updated. Click on Close to close this dialog box. Depending on the type of software update you have installed, the computer might restart itself.

The virus-protection feature might show you two different messages:

- o OFF
- o OUT OF DATE

If you see that the virus protection is OFF, you can turn it on as follows:
- Enable your anti-virus software.
- If you don't have anti-virus software, purchase and install an anti-virus software program.

Following the screen capture above, you can see how to enable the Norton Antivirus:

1. To begin click on the Norton utilities icon (on the System Tray). If you have an older version of Norton, this icon will look like a little computer.
2. Now click on Options, and on Norton Antivirus.
3. Finally click on Enable Auto-Protect, and then click on OK to close this dialog box window.

If you visit the Security Center again, the OFF message should now say ON. If you still get an OFF message, you might need to reinstall the anti-virus program.

If you get an OUT OF DATE message in the Security Center, you must update your anti-virus program. This involves visiting the Symantec website and buying a "yearly subscription" to the program with a credit card.

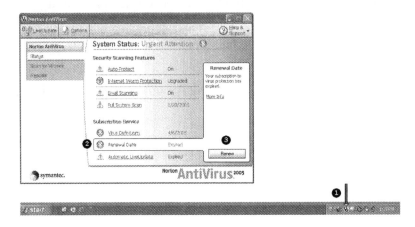

On the screen capture above, you can see how to renew your subscription to Norton Antivirus.

1. To begin click on the Norton utilities icon. If you have an older version of Norton this icon will look like a little computer.
2. Now click on Renewal Date.
3. Then click on Renew to commence this process.

Now you will be taken to the Symantec website, where you will have to provide a credit-card number so that you can be billed for your subscription. The length of the subscription is usually one year.

When you finish buying this update and return to the Security Center, the message under "Antivirus" should say ON. If it still reads OUT OF DATE, you may need to remove it and reinstall it again. If this doesn't work then you will need to contact Symantec.

Please note that if your computer is using an outdated version of the Norton Antivirus program (such as the Norton Antivirus 2003), and you update your Windows XP to the latest service pack 2, that this program might not work after the update and you will need to buy a newer version.

Chapter 18

Learn to troubleshoot your Windows-based personal computer

Steps you can take to prevent some computer problems while using a Windows based personal computer

Windows-based computers today are much more reliable than they have been in the past, owing to recent improvements in both software and hardware components. In former versions of Windows (such as Windows 98), a single program could cause the operating system to crash but in Windows XP is very rare for a single misbehaving program to bring down the whole system.

Nonetheless, the old saying holds true: An ounce of prevention is worth a pound of cure. So I will be remiss if I write that there is nothing you can do but to wait until your Windows based personal computer fails, because in fact there are some steps you can take to give yourself an extra insurance against some computer problems.

There are some simple steps that you can take to prevent against some malfunctions:

- Never use a personal computer (especially one that is connected to the Internet all the time) without installing and regularly updating a good Antivirus and Firewall program, such as Symantec Norton Internet Security.
- If you can avoid it, never place a computer close to a direct source of heat.
- If you must place your computer on the floor, make sure is not in a place where you can accidentally kick it when you sit to work on your desk.
- Try to avoid plugging your computer directly into a wall outlet, and always connect your computer to a power-surge protector or, better yet, a UPS or backup battery. A UPS will give you couple minutes to save your work and shut down properly, in case of a power outage.
- Do not connect too many devices that draw a lot of power (for instance an electrical heater or a laser printer) to the same power strip as your computer.
- Always properly shut down your computer, by clicking on the Start menu button and choosing the "Turn Off Computer", and then clicking on "Turn Off". And **only** power off the computer from the power button, by pressing and holding it for 10 seconds, when it stops responding to your commands (for instance 10 minutes have gone by since you were able to use the mouse or the keyboard).

If, after following this advice, your computer one day fails, don't panic. Simply write down everything you were doing at the time of the malfunction. This information will help the technical-support people to diagnose the problem and help you get the computer back into working order.

The types of problems that can affect a personal computer

Personal computers are the most sophisticated electronic devices ever to become available for mass-market use. They include many hundreds of components, and are prone to many types of malfunctions. But don't let this intimidate you: Most computer problems you will experience are not serious enough to warrant a call to technical support.

The two main types of problems that can affect any personal computer are:

- **Hardware problems**
  These are problems with any part you can touch, such as the monitor, the CPU (where all the internal parts reside), or the mouse. If, for example, you turn on your computer one day and hear an unusual grinding noise that won't go away, this is most likely due to a hardware failure.
- **Software problems**
  These are problems with the computer programs on your computer, such as the Windows XP operating system. If for example one day you turn on a personal computer, that has been working fine up until a day before, and it powers on fine, you are able to see the Windows opening screen, but as soon as you try to open a program, the screen turns blue and a whole set of numbers appears, then this is most likely due to a software problem. Because if the hard drive–a hardware device—had failed, it will have prevented you from even accessing the windows desktop.

It is also important to point that many problems can be caused by "user errors." Sometimes there is nothing wrong with your personal computer, but there might be something wrong with the way you are using it.

For instance, many people have problems working with pop-up windows when they are visiting websites. These pop-up windows can occupy the entire screen, causing some people to erroneously conclude that something is wrong with their computer. In such cases, however, all that is required is to minimize or close the pop-up windows.

Finally, I should emphasize that you *CANNOT* break your Windows based personal computer just by learning how to use it. And the worse that can happen is that from time to time you might accidentally delete an important file or two, but this is all a part of the learning process. Unless we are talking about your work computer, because if your company has an IT department, then they should be the ones to troubleshoot/fix any problems the computer you were assigned to use is having.

Basic hardware problems and the steps you can take to correct them

A hardware problem is one that affects a physical component of your computer, such as the monitor or the hard drive. Because of the possibility of hardware failure, it is *very important* to always keep backup copies of your important work files in removable media such as CDs or even on the new USB flash drives.

Here are some examples of hardware-related problems you might experience, along with some troubleshooting steps for you to follow:

- You press the power button on the computer but it doesn't power on, and there are no lights on the front of the unit.

Follow these steps to try to correct this problem:

1. Make sure that one end of the computer power cable is tightly connected to the computer and the other end to a wall outlet or to a power strip.
2. If the computer is connected to a power strip, make sure that the power strip is turned on.
3. Make sure that all the cables going from the computer to the keyboard, the mouse, and the monitor are connected tightly. A single loose cable might be all that is wrong with the computer.

Now try to turn the computer back on.

If the computer still fails to turn on, then you will need to call your technical support number (if the computer is still under warranty).

- You turn on the computer and you hear a high-pitched noise that you have never heard before. This might signal an impending hardware failure with your hard drive or one of the internal fans.

Please follow these steps to try to troubleshoot the problem:

1. Turn off the computer, using the "Shut Down" option on the Start Menu.
2. Wait a few minutes, and then turn the computer back on.

If the noise does not repeat when you turn the computer back on, then this was probably just a fluke. But if you still hear the unfamiliar noise after the computer restarts, then there could be a more serious problem, and you should have the computer checked by a computer professional.

- You turn on the computer, it powers on (you are able to see some lights on the front of the unit), but the screen doesn't shows you anything more than an amber light or after a few minutes the screen blanks out.

If the screen powers off, after a few minutes, then this might be due to something as simple as the fact that the computer has gone into a power-saving mode.

Please follow these steps to try to correct the problem:

1. Press any key on the keyboard to see if the computer wakes up. If it does, the energy-star feature in the computer might have caused the problem. To disable the energy-star feature; right-click on any part of the Windows desktop (not on an icon), and then click on *Properties*. Select the *Screensaver* tab, and then click on the *Power* setting. In the window that opens, you can increase the amount of time that will pass in the future before the monitor goes into power-saving mode.
2. If your monitor still doesn't show anything, then turn it off and follow the cable going from the back of the monitor to the Computer. Detach the cable and then connect it back again, and turn the monitor back on.

If you can, try attaching a different monitor to see if you are able to see anything. If this doesn't produce any image, and your computer is under a manufacturer's warranty, then call their 1-800 number for technical support. Depending on the type of warranty you have, your manufacturer may or may not provide assistance.

If you should ever need to call for technical support, you should have the following information on hand:

- A copy of your invoice
- The name of the store where you bought it
- The make and model of your computer
- Your computer serial number
- Your operating system and what software version level is at. (To find out this information, right-click over the My Computer icon, and then click on *Properties*.)
- What were you doing when the malfunction occurred?
- Did you see any error codes or messages displayed?

If your computer is not under a manufactured warranty, then try to find a local computer professional to help get your computer in working order.

Although it doesn't make sense to spend hundreds of dollar in computer repairs, as you can purchase a brand-new system, including the monitor, for under a thousand dollars.

Basic software problems and the steps you can take to correct them

Your Windows operating-system software is essential for your computer to function. From time to time this software will fail, in which case you might see a warning on the screen, or the computer might just stop functioning (freeze) without much warning at all.

Here are a few problems you might experience with your operating system, along with some troubleshooting steps for you to follow:

- You turn on the computer and it displays a message on the screen that reads "no boot device found."

The reason you see this message is that your computer has failed to find the necessary system software on any of your hard drives.

Please follow these steps to try to correct the problem:

1. Look in the floppy-disk drive, or on the CD drive to see if they contain any removable media. Remove any disks or CDs you find in the drives.
2. Turn off the PC by pressing and holding the power button for at least 10 seconds, and then press the power button again. If the computer begins operating normally, then this problem was probably only a temporary software failure or a hardware-related glitch due to a fluctuation in the power grid.
3. If the computer usually displays a list of choices during startup, under the "*Please select the operating system to start*" message, then make sure that you've selected the same option as usual (for instance Windows 2000). Use the arrow keys to highlight/choose a different option on the initial boot menu. Once the option you want to use is select (highlighted) then press the Enter key.

Bear in mind that this message might appear after you've finished adding/installing a new hard drive to upgrade and/or replace your old one, but which you have not properly prepared to be used by the Windows operating system (namely by installing a new copy of the Windows edition you use) to work on your computer system. If you are not able to make the computer load the operating system, after trying these steps, then you will definably need the help of a computer professional.

Tip

One of the best ways to seamlessly move all of the data, from an old hard drive to a new one, is by using a program called Symantec Ghost.

- After turning on the computer, it shows a dialog box that reads: *Windows is running in safe mode.*

The Windows operating system activates Safe Mode when it detects that a configuration change you've just made is likely to cause a problem with your computer. Safe Mode gives you a chance to disable the offending software or disconnect the hardware device that is causing the problem.

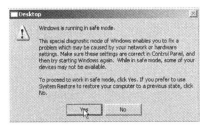

When you see the Safe Mode dialog box, click on *Yes* to see the Windows Desktop, which will look a little different (the icons will be bigger).

Now try the following steps to see if you can have Windows load the regular way:

1. Remove any software programs that you have added recently (see chapter six), and power down your computer the usual way.
2. Once the computer powers down, physically detach any hardware devices you have added recently, such as an internal modem or disk drive.

Now turn on the computer again. If the message clears, then the problem was related to the new hardware or software you had installed.

Bear in mind that sometimes when you call the technical support number of the company that manufactured your computer, for troubleshooting and diagnostic purposes, you might also be asked to start Windows in Safe Mode.

Sometimes a software problem might be due to an impending hardware failure, such as a hard drive that is beginning to fail, that is yet to manifest itself. For instance if you've frequently had to pay someone to reinstall your operating system, then barring an event (such as a virus affecting your computer) then you should; a) Backup often, and b) Also have the computer checked (namely the memory Ram and the hard drive.)

If, after restarting your computer, the error message still appears, there are two more steps you can try to fix the problem:

1. First, restart your computer system. If you are running more than one operating system on your computer, then, when you see the "Please select the operating system to start" message, use the arrow keys to select the operating system you want to troubleshoot. Press ENTER, and then press the F8 key immediately.

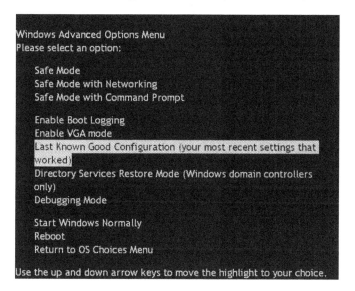

2. This should take you to the Windows Advanced Options menu, pictured above. From this screen, use the down Arrow key to select the menu entry *Last Known Good Configuration*, and then press ENTER.

If this causes your computer to start normally, then your problem might have been related to a recent change in its configuration. If the problem still doesn't go away, however, then you should seek the help of a computer professional.

If your computer starts failing sporadically, but still functions from time to time, it might not be too late to try to save your important data to a CD or another type of media, before it becomes irretrievable.

Tip Keep backup copies of your work files to removable media, because one day your computer will fail, damaging some or all the very important computer work you've saved to it.

- While the computer is booting up, or while you are using it, the screen turns blue and displays a detailed error message.

This is due to a fatal system error: Windows will stop functioning and automatically enter debug mode for troubleshooting purposes. The information on the screen (although meaningless to the layperson) will be informative to a computer professional.

This is an example of the screen you might see when your computer experiences a fatal system error. This screen is sometimes called the "blue screen of death."

These are the steps to troubleshoot a blue screen, in Windows XP or Windows 2000:

1. Turn off the computer by holding the power button until it shuts down.
2. Now turn it back on. If the computer works fine, you should take this opportunity to back up your important data.
3. If the blue-screen error message does not go away, then try to return to the previous *Last known good configuration*, following the steps outlined on the previous page.

If returning to the *Last known good configuration* doesn't allow you to use the computer normally, you should write down the numbers in front of *Stop*. Then try to search the Internet (using a friends computer) to see what the stop message refers to, or seek the help of a computer professional ASAP.

- While you are using a program it stops responding to your commands. Moving the mouse or typing on the keyboard doesn't seem to have any effect on the computer.

This might be due to a single program failure, or a situation where the computer is running at close to 100 % of its available resources, which makes it unstable to use.

Follow these steps to close the offending program or programs:

1. Click on the **X**, located on the upper-right corner of the program window, to close the offending program. Please bear in mind that if a program in which you've been working locks up, and you close it this way, then chances are you will lose the work you've done so far in it, or if you've previously saved the file you've been working on, then the changes up until the last time you chose the save command.

2. Now the *End program* dialog box might warn you that the program is not responding. To close the non-responding program, click on End Now. If the program doesn't close right away, keep on clicking on End Now until it does.

3. If the computer refuses to respond to your commands, you might need to force it to shut down by holding down the power button for 10 seconds, but only do this when nothing else works, because it will cause you to lose all your unsaved work.

Bear in mind that trying to open a single misbehaving program might cause your computer to work sluggishly/freeze. Once you identify such a program, refrain from using it until you are able to ascertain the cause of the problem (for instance the program needs to be updated). In most cases it be enough to remove and reinstall it, to fix it. If this doesn't work, then you should call a computer professional to help you with it.

How to close a program in Windows XP or Windows 2000 from the Windows Task Manager

In Windows XP or Windows 2000 you can use a program called the Windows Task Manager to close any program that is open at any time. To open the Windows Task Manager, use the key combination CTRL + ALT +DEL, or right click on any space (free of icons) on the Windows Taskbar and then select Task Manager.

Now the Windows Task Manager opens, and using it you will be able to close any program running at the time in your computer.

These are the steps to close a program from the Windows Task Manager:

1. First click on the name of the program you want to close, to select it. You can use this software tool to close a program that is not responding, as well as one that is running with no problems.
2. Now click on End Task. You might need to do this a few times, if the program doesn't close right away. If the End Program dialog box window, explained on the previous page, pops-up then just click on End Now.

The idea behind closing programs that are still responding is to quickly free up the computer resources that are being used by that particular program. This can be useful if your computer is running sluggishly, but keep in mind that closing a program in this fashion will cause you to lose any unsaved work you've been creating using it.

How to close a program in Windows 98 or Windows Me using the Close Program dialog box

In Windows 98 or Windows Me, you can also use the *Close Program* dialog box to close a program that is not responding. To open the Close Program dialog box, press the key combination CTRL + ALT +DEL **once**. If you press this key combination twice consecutively, the computer will restart with no additional warnings.

Once the "Close Program" dialog box opens, you could use it to close any open program running at the time in your computer.

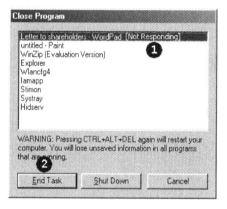

These are the steps to close a program from the *Close Program* Window:

1. First click on the name of the program you want to close. This could be a program that is running with no problems, or one that is not responding to your commands.
2. Now click on End Task; you might need to do this a few times, if the program doesn't close right away. If the End Program dialog box window, explained on previous pages, pops-up then just click on End Now.

In Windows 98, it is very common to have your computer freeze because of a single misbehaving program. If this happen to you frequently, then you should consider upgrading to Windows XP, which is one of the most stable operating system that Microsoft has released up to this date.

Today you can buy a new system, including the monitor, for around $600.00, which is less than what a 17" LCD monitor used to cost a few years ago.

How to adjust some visual effects to alleviate some performance problems in Windows XP

One of the easiest things you can do in Windows XP, to improve its performance, is to change some of your computer's visual-effects settings. Rendering the graphics of all the windows takes a significant amount of memory, so by working with these settings you can free up some of that memory.

To start making changes to the Windows XP visual effects, go to your Windows Desktop and right-click over the My Computer icon. Now click on the *Properties* tab to open the *System Properties* information program.

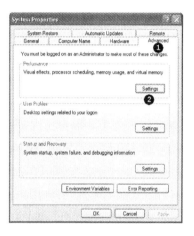 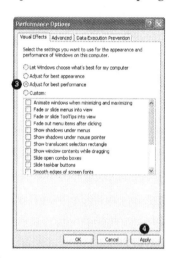

These are the steps to make the necessary changes, in the *Performance Options* dialog box, to increase the amount of memory available to other programs:

1. First click on the *Advanced* tab.
2. Now click on *Settings*.
3. When the *Performance Options* dialog box opens, click on *Adjust for best performance*.
4. Finally click *Apply*, and then click *OK* to accept this change and close this dialog box.

Now the edges of each window will now look a bit less fancy, but all of your programs will still work in the same fashion. If you wish, you can always go back into the *Performance Options* dialog box and change your windows graphics back to the way they were before.

Addendum

On November 2006 Microsoft added their new Internet Explorer 7 web browser, which is an integral part of the new Windows Vista operating system, to the list of items to be routinely updated by computers running Windows XP SP2, trough the Windows Update feature.

By the time of this writing millions of computers running Windows XP SP2 will have downloaded this new Internet web browser, which I had not planned to include in this book because some of its features will only work if you use it on a computer running the new Windows Vista operating system.

Because of this, as a courtesy to the people who bought this book, the pages that follow will show some of the new features that are different to the ones found on the Internet Explorer 6 web browser I used to write Chapter 13 of this book. For instance the way to work with Pop-up windows stays the same on this new Internet Web browser, albeit to temporarily allow a Pop-up window on this new browser you will need to press and hold the key combination CTRL +ALT, instead of just pressing the CTRL key. And most importantly: the changes to this web browser won't affect the instructions outlined on chapter 13, to find information on the Internet.

Please bear in mind that from time to time I might make available, on the Web, more information that might come out later, which you can obtain for free by visiting the book URL at:

www.windowsxpforeveryone.com

I am also hoping to have a Windows Vista book ready by the end of this year or the beginning of the next for those users who made the switch, or who bought a new computer preloaded with it.

NOTE: I just read in the news that Microsoft announced that consumers still using Windows XP after April 2009 will be entitled to five more years of "extended support." this assures you that Windows XP will be a good viable operating system, for some time to come. Albeit in the extended plan, while still being entitled to the free security fixes, Microsoft will charge you for providing you with the extra assistance you need.

The new Internet Explorer 7 window

Internet Explorer 7 is the first major upgrade to the Microsoft Internet Explorer web browser in about 5 years, and the main difference you will notice between this new version and its previous version (version 6), is the use of page Tabs.

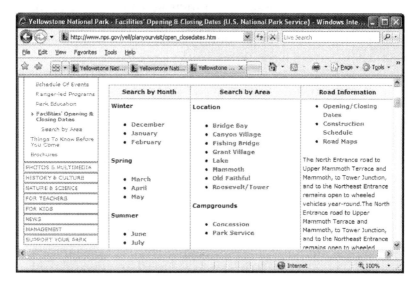

The page Tabs, as you can see on this screen capture, open above the main browser window (notice on this screen capture that there are four page Tabs open), to help you keep the web pages you've open readily available. Please notice that the Tab selected right now (see the arrow), is the one that reads; "Yellowstone..", which contents fill the main working area of the web browser. For instance if you are on the main opening page of an online newspaper, see a link that interest you, and will like to easily return to its main opening web page; press and hold the CTRL key and then click on the link that interest you.

Now, with very few exceptions (For instance when opening AOL web mail, which opens up on a completely new window), a new page Tab will be created. To see the information on this new page Tab, just click on it. If you click on a link, but don't press and hold the CTRL key, this new page should open normally under the same page Tab you've been working on.

Bear in mind that if you sub-sequentially select to open another completely new session of the Internet Explorer 7 web browser, by clicking on its icon again, that this new copy of this program will open on it's own separate window.

The new Internet Explorer 7 buttons

Most of the buttons on this Internet browser haven't changed that much from the previous version of this program (version 6), although some are now found on different locations on its program window.

These are some of the relevant buttons on this new Internet web browser:

A. The navigation arrows (Forward and Back), help you navigate between the web pages you've already visited (on the Tab you are working on). The arrows are available to perform these functions only when they are bluish. Click on the left one to return one page and the right one to advance a page.

B. This is the Menu bar. To enable it (if not shown), just right click on the space under the Address Bar and click on "Menu Bar", to select it.

C. Click on the "X" to stop the loading of a web page, and on the symbol next to it (Refresh) or press the F5 key to reload a page. For instance click on the "X", when a web page is taking a long time to load, to stop loading the page, and then click on the refresh button to reload it.

D. These are the new page Tabs. The foremost Tab (whose contents you see on the main browser window) will be bluer than the other Tabs you've opened.

E. Click on the Home button to return to the default page, appropriately called the Home Page (which is the page you see every time you open your browser), on the page Tab you are working on.

F. Click on the Star button or "Favorites" to open a panel on the left side of your browser that contains all the web sites you have saved for easy access. To return to a web site, whose name you see on this list, just click on it. To add a website to this list, click on the Star sign with a Plus sign next to it, and then on the menu that opens click on Add to Favorites and then click on Add. If you've added the Menu bar, then you can also click on the Favorites menu items, to work with the Favorites function the same way is done in IE 6.0.

If you use cable or DSL Internet, and use Outlook or Outlook Express to Send/Receive e-mail messages, and click on the Page button, then you will see a few options (click on them) available to you, such as Send page or Link by E-mail. Click on the print button to print the web page you are looking at.

How to work with the new page Tabs in Internet Explorer 7

To work with a new page Tab or one you've opened before, just click on it. If you are not sure what web page or the URL of the page it holds, then slowly take the mouse pointer over it, and this information will be displayed.

To close a single page Tab, click on the "X" next to its name.

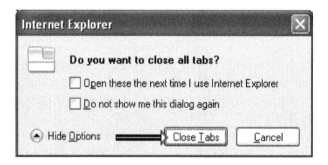

Additionally when you try to close this Internet web browser, by clicking on the red "X" on the upper right corner of the browser window, you are prompted to select; "Do you want to close all tabs?", if you do then click on "Close Tabs", otherwise click on "Show Options" and select "Open these the next.." and then click on "Close Tabs".

If you chose to keep the Tabs open, the next time you open the Internet Explorer browser, then they should be open the same way they were before you closed the browser and you can return to the web pages they contain by just clicking on the corresponding page Tab.

Press and hold the CTRL key and then the Q key or click on the four square symbol (next to the leftmost Tab), to see the different Tabs you've opened as small pages on a window. To return to work in one, just click on its rendering.

How to work with the online Phishing settings in Internet Explorer 7

Online Phishing is the action by which computer users are tricked into providing personal or financial information through a website or even when replying to an e-mail message. For instance, let's say you get an e-mail message that looks like a legit notice from a trusted source, such as a bank, a credit card company or even a reputable online merchant you've heard of. Once you double click on the e-mail message (to open it), you are directed to a fraudulent website. Now you are then asked to provide personal information, such as an account number or password. This information can then be used for identity theft.

This is the way to use the Online Phishing filter built in into the new Internet Explorer 7 web browser:

1. Begin by clicking on the Tools menu item.
2. Now click on Phishing Filter.
3. Finally click on Turn On Automatic Website checking.

Now, on the window that opens, click on Turn on Automatic Phishing Filter, to enable this feature. If you've just upgraded your Windows XP SP2 computer to this new browser, then you will also see this window the first time you open this Internet web browser, prompting you to select one of these options, and if you are not sure you can click on; Ask me later.

Once you make your choice click on Ok to close this window. If you've enabled this feature, when you attempt to visit a known Phishing site, you will be blocked from visiting the site and instead will see a red warning page. Additionally, for your protection, you will also be prevented from providing any information into that site. Later on you can return to this setting and disable this feature, by clicking on; Turn Off Automatic Phishing Filter.

Index